THIS LAND IS YOUR LAND

WOODY GUTHRIE AND THE JOURNEY OF AN AMERICAN FOLK SONG

ROBERT SANTELLI

FOREWORD BY
NORA GUTHRIE

Running Press
PHILADELPHIA • LONDON

Books published by Running Press are available at special discounts for bulk purchases in the United States by corporations, institutions, and other organizations. For more information, please contact the Special Markets Department at the Perseus Books Group, 2300 Chestnut Street, Suite 200, Philadelphia, PA 19103, or call (800) 810-4145, ext. 5000, or e-mail special.markets@perseusbooks.com.

ISBN 978-0-7624-4328-4
Library of Congress Control Number: 2011925147

E-book ISBN 978-0-7624-4508-0

9   8   7   6   5   4   3   2   1
Digit on the right indicates the number of this printing

Cover and interior design by Joshua McDonnell
Edited by Greg Jones
Typography: Akzidenz, Cambria, and Garth

Running Press Book Publishers
2300 Chestnut Street
Philadelphia, PA 19103-4371

Visit us on the web!
www.runningpress.com

Jacket, Front Cover: Woody Guthrie, ca. 1945. Courtesy of the Woody Guthrie Archives. Back Cover, Courtesy of the Woody Guthrie Archives.

p 18: Courtesy of the Woody Guthrie Archives. © Copyright 1956 (renewed), 1958 (renewed), 1970 and 1972 by Woody Guthrie Publications, Inc. & TRO-Ludlow Music, Inc. (BMI)

PP: 23, 30, 39, 95, 105, 118, 134, 139, 189, 197 (Dave Gahr): Courtesy of the Woody Guthrie Archives

pp. 39 & 134: Artwork by Woody Guthrie Courtesy of the Woody Guthrie Archives. © Copyright Woody Guthrie Publications, Inc.

p 51: CSU Archives/Everett Collection, p 78: Everett Collection, p 147: Elaine Thompson/AP Photo, pp 185 & 224: AP Photo, p 192: John Cohen/Hulton Archive/Getty Images, p 201: Michael Ochs/Getty Images, p 251: Alex Brandon/AP Photo

FOR JARON AND JAMES

"ALL YOU CAN WRITE IS
WHAT YOU SEE."

—WOODY GUTHRIE
FEBRUARY 23, 1940

CONTENTS

FOREWORD

What a long journey "This Land Is Your Land" has been on. Since it was first written down on paper on February 23rd, 1940 until today, we have heard Woody's words being sung, and occasionally altered, most of our lives. It's a song that seems to be open to all kinds of interpretations and manipulations.

We'll never really know for sure exactly what Woody's intentions were when he wrote down the words in a fleabag hotel on 43rd Street in New York City following a long journey "from California to the New York Island." The song was found in one of his many lyric notebooks, not separated out or highlighted in any special way. It was just another song among the thousands he wrote and placed in a three-hole school binder. The day after he wrote "This Land," he wrote one which he never recorded titled "Wimmen's Hats," and one that he did record, "Jesus Christ." That week, in the same hotel, he also wrote "The Government Road," "Dirty Overalls," "Will Rogers Highway," and "Hangknot Slipknot." It was a good week.

It wasn't until over a decade later that "This Land" became popularized. It was placed in a songbook for school music teachers in the 1950s who found that the chorus was easy for young children to sing. Pete Seeger also gets credit for the song's popularity, as he sang it throughout the 1950s and 1960s at all of his concerts. As a matter of fact, that's really how I first learned it. In the little elementary school in Brooklyn that I went to, we always sang the shorter version of "This Land" in music class and at the assembly programs in lieu of the national anthem. And Pete's concerts just hammered the words in as the rousing sing-along finale. It was also the song that, among all the others that my father wrote, everyone knew most of the words to, and could jam on together at all the hootenannies we went to as children.

One way of looking at the song is as an autobiographical journal written at the journey's end. Like many of his songs, I think he wrote "This Land" because, as he states on the bottom of the lyric, "all you can write is what you see." That seems to be the most honest thing anyone can infer regarding his intentions. It's just what he had seen—wheat fields waving, dust clouds rolling, people on food lines at churches, too many signs along the roads that said "private property."

And then there were the voices. The ones that he says he heard chanting "as the fog was lifting," riding on the winds swirling across the plains. Or was it the voices of people he met and talked to—"all around me a voice was sounding"—people on the road who were exhausted from the ravages of the Depression, the Great Dust Storm migration, the foreclosed homes and bankrupt farms? Could it have been one of these strangers on a train, a hobo around a campfire, a truck driver that he hitched a ride with, a homeless family in a jalopy, a migrant worker who wondered out loud in conversation something like, "Boy, and I always thought that this land was supposed to be *ours?*"

The idea that this land is your land, or that this land was made for you and me, is not one exclusive to Woody Guthrie. It is a longstanding idea that actually is no different from "of the people, by the people, and for the people." Everyone, in some way, learns this early on. After all, it is the premise of our democratic system.

Woody was in large part a journalist, working in the style of the old troubadours who told the story of what they had seen or heard, delivering the news, messages, and ideas from town to town and city to city. He reiterated what he heard, in verse. "I Ain't Got No Home," "Pretty Boy Floyd," "Hard Travelin'," "Ramblin' Around," "Dust Storm Disaster," "So Long, It's Been Good to Know You," and many others, all basically repeat what people were saying about all kinds of things, from tales of mythical outlaws to their own personal experiences. It's fascinating to look at many of Woody's songs through this lens. Talking about songwriting, he once wrote, "I'm just telling you something you already knew," and to be able to really hear what they're saying, "You've got to vaccinate yourself into the blood stream of the people." And that is exactly what many of his song lyrics do. His contribution to the national discussion about what this country actually is, was to put these ideas down in a form that would go beyond the individual experience. He could create a lyric that would *outlive* the individual experience and preserve the idea.

"This land is your land" is an idea that is still being discussed, debated, dissected, and sometimes, even destroyed. I have seen the lyric interpreted and manipulated by just about every faction or political ideology there is, from the KKK, to religious zealots, to fear-mongering groups and salesmen. Not unlike Bruce Springsteen's song "Born in the USA," everyone wants a piece of it. And, like "Born in the USA," they just want the piece that suits their agendas. Unfortunately, for these people, there will always be Woody's six original verses that ultimately ruin their efforts.

On the bright side, we've been fortunate that, for the most part, the song still remains in the public's mind, truthful to its original sentiment. Sometimes, it even hits the nail on the head. Most of us will always remember the moment when Pete Seeger and Bruce Springsteen led the nation in one of the largest sing-alongs in history at President Barack Obama's inaugural concert. In that moment, it wasn't being sung to inspire something to happen. It was being sung because something inspirational *had* happened. I remember thinking, "People all over the world are watching this and, right at this moment, this is a new impression of America." I also remember looking up and saying to my dad, "You did it. This is exactly where this song belongs, right now." For me, "This Land" had found yet another place in history where it was truly at home.

As you read through this book, I hope that you'll get a real feel for the actual cross-country journey that Woody made, that inspired him to write these lyrics. As you travel along with him, one road leading to the next road, you might also rethink "This Land," as one line leads to the next line. You might understand more deeply where he was coming from, literally and philosophically. This is where we are all coming from—these roads, these journeys, these people, these voices. And, though it may be at times a bit bumpy, we can choose to all travel together on Woody's road. By the time he had written "This Land," he had already made his choice: "Nobody living can make me turn back."

—Nora Guthrie

INTRODUCTION

I first came to Woody Guthrie the way I had come to the great bluesmen Robert Johnson and Sonny Boy Williamson: by looking and listening back. Like a lot of young people growing up in the late 1960s, I was a full-on rock fan and aspiring musician. I eagerly searched out new sounds, whether they came from London or Los Angeles or points in between, and took from the music and its culture so much that they became me.

I listened intently to Cream's version of "Cross Road Blues," which the group conveniently called "Crossroads," and not only marveled at Eric Clapton's guitar genius, but also wondered who Robert Johnson, the song's author, was. Not long thereafter I came upon *King of the Delta Blues Singers*, a monstrous early '60s collection of old Johnson sides from the 1930s, compiled by legendary Columbia Records talent scout and producer John Hammond. The music was deep and dark, mysterious and magical, and one day I realized that I was playing it more than I was playing the Cream album *Wheels of Fire*, where I had first heard "Crossroads."

A couple of years later, after picking up one of the greatest live rock albums of all time, *At Fillmore East* by the Allman Brothers Band, I wasted no time in searching out Sonny Boy Williamson, the bluesman responsible for the song "One Way Out," one of two of my favorite tracks on the set (the other being bluesman Blind Willie McTell's "Statesboro Blues"). Sonny Boy Williamson proved to be a harder research subject than Robert Johnson. I didn't find an easily accessible "greatest hits" album like Johnson's *King of the Delta Blues Singers*, and I soon found out that there had been not one, but two Sonny Boy Williamsons, each owning his small piece of blues history.

Further digging revealed that it was Aleck Miller, aka "Rice" Miller, aka Sonny Boy Williamson, aka Sonny Boy Williamson Number Two (John Lee "Sonny Boy" Williamson was the original) who recorded the version of "One Way Out" that inspired the Allmans. This Sonny Boy also happened to be the most amazing harmonica player I had ever heard, doubling the pleasure of my newest blues discovery.

Led Zeppelin and Lynyrd Skynyrd, Janis Joplin and the Doors, Jimi Hendrix and Johnny Winter, along with other great '60s and early '70s blues-rock bands and artists, encouraged similar searches with equally rich payloads. As a result, I fell in love with American roots music—blues, folk, and then early country, jazz, gospel, and every other kind of pre-rock sound that helped determine America's musical identity in the twentieth century. It was an exciting time for me. Every day seemed to bring a new revelation as I ventured back in time and in song, finding gems that broadened my understanding of American music and making me determined to somehow build a life in it.

Like so many kids back then, I had picked up a guitar, inspired by the arrival of the Beatles in America, had played in bands, and had imagined myself a musician and songwriter, though I wasn't really much of either. One day, a female friend of mine who had also played guitar and who had long, straight blonde hair like so many girls of the folk revival movement back then, had given me a copy of Bob Dylan's self-titled debut recording as a gift. Unlike later Dylan albums, it was comprised of folk and blues standards and only two Dylan originals.

By the time I heard Dylan's 1962 debut, he, of course, had already busted out of folk music and was blowing wide open the possibilities of rock with the seminal single "Like a Rolling Stone" and the critically acclaimed albums *Bringing It All Back Home* and *Highway 61 Revisited.* Somehow I had missed his first album and the other early folk albums he recorded. I'm sure the Beatles and the Rolling Stones had something to do with that.

If you know the album, you know where I'm going with this. Of the two original songs on *Bob Dylan*, the one I fell in love with was "Song to Woody." (The second Dylan original was called "Talkin' New York" and was pretty good, too.) Sung softly, like he was a bit embarrassed by the gratitude expressed in the lyrics, thus exposing just how much he had learned and borrowed from the legendary folksinger, Dylan, in effect, introduced me to Woody Guthrie. I listened to that album a lot the summer and fall of 1965, almost always starting and finishing with "Song to Woody."

Woody Guthrie became my new music interest. I hardly knew anything about him, other than what Dylan had taught me, but I was determined to learn more. It was clear that Guthrie had greatly impacted Dylan. I wanted to know why. As was my routine back then on weekends, I went over to Greenwich Village, taking the bus from my home in West New York, N.J., just across the Hudson River, and thumbed through the record bins in music stores there like Izzy Young's Folklore Center on MacDougal Street until I found what I was looking for. I came up with a couple of Guthrie's old Folkways albums, read the liner notes, and realized that I already knew one of his songs: "This Land Is Your Land." I didn't own it; rather, I had sung the song more than once with the rest of my classmates in Miss Chase's music class in elementary school. She never mentioned that Woody Guthrie wrote it, only that it was a "good sing-a-long-song" and "about America."

The fact that "This Land Is Your Land" was written by someone who so obviously influenced Dylan gave the song new meaning for me. I remember coming upon either a copy of *Sing Out!* or *Broadside*, the two top folk magazines of the day, and reading more about Guthrie. I found out that he had been sick for years and had spent some time in Greystone Hospital in Morris Plains, not far from where I lived in Jersey. Later I found out that Dylan visited him there and played versions of the many Woody songs he knew to the man who could barely acknowledge his happiness at hearing them. Guthrie was suffering from the final effects of Huntington's disease, a horrible neurological disease that causes cognitive and muscular disintegration and finally death, and for which there is no cure. Guthrie had been robbed not just of his speech, but also his ability to write, to sing, to laugh, to control his muscles and limbs, to swallow, even.

Just as I was learning more about Guthrie, I heard in October 1967 that he had died. A concert celebrating his life and legacy was produced at Carnegie Hall early the next year, but by that time my family and I had moved away from West New York, down to the Jersey Shore and soon-to-be Springsteen country. Back then, New York seemed a long way from Asbury Park and other shore towns, so the trek to Carnegie Hall didn't seem feasible, even though my parents permitted their fifteen-year-old son the freedom to do so. I didn't attend the concert, but later I experienced the next best thing: the records that resulted from it called *A Tribute to Woody Guthrie, Parts One and Two*, on which I heard the female folksinger Odetta, Woody's son Arlo Guthrie, and others sing "This Land Is Your Land" as a grand good-bye.

Over the years, the song stuck to me. I loved the lyrics and the way they described an America of boundless natural treasures and promise. It made me want to see it all: the mountains, the redwood forest, and the gulfstream waters. The melody, of course, was just what my music teacher had said it was: a great sing-a-long song, with words that were hard to get out of your head once they lodged there. And I especially admired how a single song could sum up so much. Though "This Land Is Your Land" was simple and direct, an entire book, I thought, could be written about the song. Funny thing is, back then, I hadn't even the most remote clue that it would be me who'd write it.

I played "This Land Is Your Land" in my folk-rock band and at the local coffee house. When I became a high school teacher fresh out of college, I played it for my social studies and English classes, skipping the "sing along" idea, but pointing out the incredible richness of the lyrics and the history of how the song came to be born.

When I became a father, I played it for my kids. As a cultural historian, I grew even more interested in "This Land Is Your Land," not just because it was one of the greatest of all American folk songs, but because of its social and political implications.

However, it wasn't until 1988, when my friend Dave Marsh took my interest in Guthrie and his famous song up a few more notches for me. Marsh, a *Rolling Stone* contributor and one of the most respected music critics at the time, was set to begin work on a book of never-before-published Guthrie writings with Pete Seeger manager and Woody Guthrie Archives head Harold Leventhal. The book was called *Pastures of Plenty: A Self Portrait (The Unpublished Writings of Woody Guthrie).*

Knowing of my fascination with Guthrie, Dave invited me to work with him and Harold on the project. My task was to go through Guthrie's unpublished writings in the New York–based Woody Guthrie Archives, retyping his words, making recommendations as to what pieces were interesting and important, organizing Guthrie's letters and lyrics, and finding handwritten gems that broadened our understanding of Guthrie's musical and literary brilliance.

For me, the project's highpoint came one day that summer when Harold unexpectedly called me into his office and showed me Guthrie's handwritten lyrics to "This Land Is Your Land," which was originally called "God Blessed America." He smiled and said, "I know how much this song means to you. Thought you might want to see it the way Woody wrote it." Harold sat back in his chair and clasped his hands over his protruding belly as he often did when awaiting reaction from the person across his desk.

Holding the lyrics in my hand, reading and rereading them, examining every nuance of Woody's handwriting, the side notes, the cross-outs, even the paper the words were written on instantly and forever deepened my connection to Guthrie and his song. I had never seen such an important document in American music history up close before, despite the fact that I was going through Guthrie's vast collection of writings, piece by piece. Harold told me to take it to the copy machine and make a duplicate for myself. "Put it in a frame," he said, smiling, which I did the next day, then hung it on my office wall back home where it stayed for years. I wish I still had it. I always thought that my career as a music museum curator unofficially began that day.

I had other personal experiences with "This Land Is Your Land" in the proceeding years. At the Rock and Roll Hall of Fame and Museum in Cleveland where I worked then, Woody's daughter Nora Guthrie, Harold and I created in 1996 the first-ever American Music Masters Series, which celebrated the life and legacy of Woody Guthrie. The concert featured Bruce Springsteen, Pete Seeger, Arlo Guthrie, Country Joe McDonald, Ramblin' Jack Elliott, and others interpreting Guthrie's greatest songs, including "This Land Is Your Land," one of the show's final numbers. I remember getting chills watching all these great artists up on the stage, singing the song, and getting everyone else at sold-out Severance Hall to sing it with them, including me.

A little more than a decade later, I moved to Los Angeles to create and run the newly opened Grammy Museum in downtown Los Angeles. One of our first public programs featured Tom Morello from Rage Against the Machine. It gave me great pleasure to listen and watch as he ended his set in our intimate, 200-seat theater with a punk version of "This Land Is Your Land," thus setting the standard by which all of the young museum's programming would then be judged.

And, like many other Americans, I was nearly brought to tears by the version of "This Land Is Your Land" sung by Seeger and Springsteen at President Barack Obama's inauguration. There could be few moments as important for Guthrie and "This Land Is Your Land" as the one that occurred on the mall in Washington, D.C. that cold January in 2009. For longtime Guthrie fans, it was an unforgettable performance, a triumph long overdue.

For me, this book is yet another personal "This Land" milestone. I planned to write it a while ago, but either the timing wasn't right or other book projects pushed it aside. But with 2012 being the centennial of Woody Guthrie's birth, I made sure I made time to get it finally done. It was one of the most satisfying books I have ever written. The song's unconventional history and Guthrie's remarkable story made it surprisingly easy for me to walk to my computer at 5:00 a.m. each day before going to work at the Grammy Museum in downtown Los Angeles, striving to get a few hundred words written before breakfast.

People who know of my interest in Guthrie often ask if I think "This Land Is Your Land" is his best song. Guthrie wrote so many songs and so many were great. It's hard to imagine a better song than say, "Pastures of Plenty," "Pretty Boy Floyd," "1913 Massacre," "Do Re Mi," or "Tom Joad." But yes, I think "This Land Is Your Land" is still his very best. No other Guthrie song possesses such poetic prowess and natural flow. It is about America, but it is about the promise of the American Dream, too. In the song, Guthrie transforms himself into something of a nineteenth century Hudson River School landscape artist, painting with words a vision of America that is rich and sacred. By writing "This Land Is Your Land," Guthrie carved himself a place next to Walt Whitman, Carl Sandburg, John Steinbeck and others who have so articulately and beautifully captured in words the physical and emotional essence of America.

And yet, none of this was Guthrie's original intention when he wrote the song. The version of "This Land Is Your Land" that most Americans claim familiarity with does not contain the lyrics that doubt America's integrity or questions the country's commitment to essential freedoms. Those lyrics in the fourth and sixth verses of the song often have been washed away or simply ignored, which is why "This Land Is Your Land" has been able to stand side by side with the other great patriotic paeans to America, including "America the Beautiful" and "God Bless America," which, you'll see, was the original inspiration for Guthrie's song.

Whether he did it on purpose is unknown, but Woody Guthrie's "This Land Is

God Blessed America
This Land Was made for you + me

This land is your land, this land is my land
From California to the New York Island,
From the Redwood Forest, to the Gulf stream waters,
    God blessed America for me.

As I went walking that ribbon of highway
And saw above me that endless skyway,
And saw below me the golden valley, I said:
    God blessed America for me.

I roamed and rambled, and followed my footsteps
To the sparkling sands of her diamond deserts,
And all around me, a voice was sounding:
    God blessed America for me.

✓   Was a big high wall there that tried to stop me
A sign was painted said: Private Property.
But on the back side it didn't say nothing —
    God blessed America for me.

When the sun come shining, then I was strolling
In wheat fields waving, and dust clouds rolling;
The voice was chanting as the fog was lifting:
    God blessed America for me.

One bright sunny morning in the shadow of the steeple
By the Relief office I saw my people —
As they stood hungry, I stood there wondering if
    God blessed America for me.

        *all you can write is
          what you see.

                    Woody G.
Original copy
of this song.
                    N.Y., N.Y., N.Y.
                    Feb. 23, 1940
                    43rd st + 6th Ave,
                    Hanover House

This Land Is Your Land by Woody Guthrie.

Your Land" is, essentially, a musical mixed message. No other classic song about America has the dual history or dual theme that it does, or the lyrical flexibility given that many songwriters, including Pete Seeger and Bruce Springsteen, have altered the lyrics, added to them, flipped them and slipped them into completely new political, social and/or cultural settings. Seeger once wrote that "the best thing that could happen to the song is that it would end up with hundreds of different versions being sung by millions of people who do understand the basic message." Consider that done.

And there's more. No other great musical tribute to our nation is burdened with such controversial baggage or contains such irony. No other American standard at the same time praises and dissents, celebrates and castigates, loves and warns as does "This Land Is Your Land." No other American song of similar stature has been so misunderstood or misinterpreted. Finally, no other American song has such an interesting and often tangled story.

If "This Land Is Your Land" isn't Guthrie's best song, it's certainly his most popular and most influential. "This Land Is Your Land" has been sung all over the world. It's synonymous with Guthrie and America. Years ago there was even a movement to replace "The Star Spangled Banner" with "This Land Is Your Land," making it America's new national anthem. Anyone, though, who knew *all* the lyrics to "This Land Is Your Land" also knew that having it become this country's representative song was never going to happen, given the contents of the verses most people never heard. (You'll find out all about them in Chapter Three.)

This Land Is Your Land: Woody Guthrie and the Journey of an American Folk Song isn't meant to be the definitive work on the song, or on Guthrie. The intent is to tell the story of both in a way that hasn't been done before. For more conventional and comprehensive biographies of Guthrie, I recommend Joe Klein's *Woody Guthrie: A Life*, and Ed Cray's *Ramblin' Man*. However, with *This Land Is Your Land* I hope I shed some new light on both the song and its author and inspire the reader to dig deeper into American folk music and the role Guthrie continues to play in it, a century after his birth in Okemah, Oklahoma.

———————•———————

Over the years, many people, from presidential hopefuls on down, have come to call "This Land Is Your Land" their theme song or have it symbolize their political convictions. Fact is, no one can claim "This Land Is Your Land," as his own, not even Woody anymore. That would be like claiming the Statue of Liberty or the Rocky Mountains as one's personal domain. "This Land Is Your Land" is embedded in all of us, thus making us all owners of the song and caretakers of it too.

If nothing else, I hope *This Land Is Your Land: Woody Guthrie and the Journey of an American Folk Song* is a connecting rod that brings you closer to the song and helps you remember that it is an undeniable representation of the American experience, one to be cherished and sung for as long as America is America.

—Robert Santelli

Los Angeles, June 2011

1

A cold, early winter wind swept across the Texas Panhandle just a few days before the Thanksgiving holiday in late November 1939. Signs swayed along Route 66, the interstate highway that had just recently been fully paved and that connected Chicago and the middle of America with Los Angeles and the rest of southern California. Dust from the dry fields that kicked up along the way and the tumbleweeds that blew across the blacktop made for a mostly sullen sight.

Despite being in the sturdy grip of the Great Depression as well as in the throes of a multi-year drought that turned so many once-fertile farms in America's heartland into a vast Dust Bowl, people in these parts still had a few things for which to be thankful on this uniquely American holiday. Most important, their country was not at war. Not yet anyway.

In September, Poland blazed with blitzkrieg. Radio, which had just begun programming news on a regular basis a couple of years ago, and the newsreels in movie theaters across the country attested to that, as did the daily headlines in American newspapers. The German army marched with determination and ferocity, while its Luftwaffe sent bombs spiraling downward on towns and cities, and its tanks roamed the countryside, destroying most everything in their path. In the North Atlantic, German U-boats preyed on ships, sinking many of them with impunity. Poland had fallen quickly. Belgium, France, and the Netherlands would be next.

The news from across the Atlantic that November made most Americans uneasy. Those old enough to remember The Great War shuddered at the prospect of their sons and grandsons going to fight the Germans again. What a horrible conflict World War I had been, and now with more ghastly weapons and the steely resolve of the Adolph Hitler-led Nazis, this war promised to be even more calamitous.

The black Chevrolet, a 1931 touring car as it was called, headed east on Route 66, its ultimate destination: the Texas town of Pampa. Inside the car, the young family fought off the cold by huddling together and sharing a blanket. The two children—four-year-old Gwendolyn, who her folks called "Teeny," and her two-year-old sister Carolyn, who everyone called Sue, her middle name—were practically chilled to the bone, as was their mother Mary, just twenty-two. In her arms she cradled a baby boy—Will Rogers Guthrie, born little more than a month earlier in Los Angeles. She held him close so that he could siphon off some of his mother's body heat.

Wrapped in his own blanket, gazing upward at his mother, young Bill (Mary preferred Bill to Will) had no idea that he had been named for the late Will Rogers, the Oklahoma cowboy and gum-chewing humorist who had been tragically killed in an Alaskan plane crash in 1935. Rogers was one of America's most popular personalities, a man whose homespun humor, wisdom, and general outlook on things had made him a folk hero to the common man and to baby Bill's father, Woody Guthrie, a fellow Oklahoman who strove to be just like him.

Woody, twenty-seven, was also named for a famous American: President Thomas Woodrow Wilson. Born July 14, 1912 in Okemah, Oklahoma, Woodrow Wilson Guthrie had come into this world the year Wilson, the former president of Princeton University, had been elected the 28th president of the United States. It was far too

Mary and Woody Guthrie. Pampa, Texas, 1933.

early to determine if Woody's son was aptly named, but it was all too clear that Woodrow Wilson Guthrie had not quite lived up to the standards that went with being named after an important American president.

Woodrow Wilson was stately, well educated, elegant in manners, and most proper on all accounts. Woodrow Wilson Guthrie was blue-collar common, mostly self-educated, sloppy, and often improper in many matters. Woodrow Wilson had been the leader of the free world, navigating America through the treacherous waters of World War I. Woodrow Wilson Guthrie had been barely able to support his young family and had been a questionable husband and father. Woodrow Wilson gave great speeches and articulated the merits of democracy. Woodrow Wilson Guthrie wrote and sang songs and articulated the misdeeds of capitalism. In short, except for their names, the two men were worlds apart.

Like his family in the car with him, Woody was cold too. Shivering, his crazy curly hair, chiseled face, and small wiry frame made for a funny portrait as he sat behind the steering wheel singing to his kids or creating little poems that made them laugh. Coming from Los Angeles, he and his family hardly had need for warm clothes, and their hasty departure left Mary little time to prepare her family for winter weather. Even if there was time, there was little money. The sad state of the old Chevy they were in was just one bit of proof of the family's gloomy financial situation.

Woody and Mary knew when they bought the car that it wasn't much of a bargain. Every time he gave it gas, gray fumes belched from the exhaust pipe. There was also a growing crack in the engine block and the rattling sounds under the hood grew louder the closer they got to Pampa. Still, it had puttered along, through the desert and over the mountains, past the filling stations and diners along Route 66 toward Amarillo, and then on the mostly unpaved road that led to Pampa, the dusty oil town Woody left more than two and a half years earlier, and the place where he and Mary met and married in October 1933.

When she was first introduced to Woody, Mary Jennings thought him cute and funny and certainly not like the rest of the Pampa boys she knew. The Great Depression had stomped the dreams of many a young person in Pampa, like it had in other places in both rural and urban America. Although the stock market crashed in New York four years earlier to the month and two thousand or so miles away, its effect on Pampa and similar towns on the Southern Plains was profound.

"It was a difficult time, there is no doubt about it," recalled Mary years later. "Sometimes I think back and I don't know how people got through it, how they survived in one piece. Pampa suffered just like the rest of America suffered. The poor people suffered the most."

Around America, many of those able to keep their jobs saw their incomes decrease; in some cases, breadwinners were earning half of what they made in the late 1920s before the crash. Blue-collar working people, in particular, felt the wrath of the Depression. Many had difficulty paying the mortgage or rent. Family members moved in with each other to share expenses. The divorce rate soared, despite the fact that many couples couldn't even afford the expense of separation. Birthrates fell. According to historian David Kyvig, while the population of America had grown by sixteen per cent in the 1920s, the years of the Great Depression in the '30s witnessed only a seven per cent population increase. Gradually, many of the unemployed lost confidence in their work skills, and their self-esteem withered. They began to doubt their ability to support their family and when they looked into the mirror, they often saw the face of defeat, and then, desperation.

In Pampa, good jobs were scarce and prospects of a return to good times were not bright when Woody and Mary began courting. Woody, however, seemed to take it all in stride. He didn't need many things to be content, and he really wasn't much interested in a steady job anyway, unless it had to do with music. He spent his days writing songs, drawing cartoons, reading books, and going to the picture show, often with Mary in tow. He did the occasional odd job to get by, be it sign painting or working behind the counter at Shorty Harris's drug store, but no one in Pampa would have ever called him ambitious or ripe with business acumen.

Mary Jennings was a pretty, Irish Catholic country girl. Blond and pleasantly shaped, she exuded a naïve, youthful innocence and had a warm, caring smile. Woody was lucky she took him for her husband, since he offered her little when she had said yes to become his wife. In order to pay for the ceremony at the Catholic rectory where they were married, Guthrie, a Christian, but of no particular denomination, painted a portrait of Christ and presented it to the priest in lieu of money, of which he had little. Mary was all of sixteen when she married Woody Guthrie. Her parents were not pleased with the decision, but after Harry Jennings, Mary's father, shared a bottle with Woody's father, Charley, Harry begrudgingly accepted the fact that his little girl was now a married woman.

Mary came from a decent Pampa family, and her brother Matt was Woody's best friend. It was through Matt that Woody had come to know and then court Mary. The two friends had gone to school together and had played in a local string band called the Corncob Trio, along with another Pampa musician, Winsor "Cluster" Baker. The trio performed at Pampa dances and socials, entertaining folks with standards and old-timey songs that everyone knew and loved.

Although in the mid-1930s the annual Pampa City Registry had listed Woodie [sic] Guthrie as a sign painter, he much preferred to be called a singer and musician, an entertainer. He played mandolin in the Corncob Trio (Matt Jennings played fiddle, and Baker, the guitar). But that didn't stop him from accepting other music jobs, like the one reported on in *The Pampa Daily News* on September 11, 1935. A Mrs. Virgil Camp was presented with a seventeenth birthday party, during which "Cake and ice cream were served while Woody Guthrie and Verdell Pate played string music."

Guthrie, Jennings, and Baker also played in a six-piece Pampa cowboy outfit called the Texas Centennial Band. A 1936 photo featured the band members in cowboy hats and garb, smiling at the camera. Guthrie, at five feet and a few inches, was the smallest member of the Centennial Band and thus had the privilege of being first in the line of musicians situated for the photo. He held a stand up acoustic bass that also supported the band's guitars and mandolin, making him look smaller than he actually was.

Despite the way he saw himself, Woody was hardly known in Pampa for his musical talent, except among friends and family. In 1929, when he was not quite seventeen, he had come to Pampa, joining Charley in hopes of capitalizing on the recent discovery of oil there. In Okemah, the small Oklahoma town east of Oklahoma City and south of Tulsa where he had been born and raised, Guthrie had learned to play the harmonica, but not properly. He had also listened intently to the radio, the Victrola, local musicians and string bands, and especially his mother, Nora, who sang to him the most beautiful of ballads. Still, he showed no particular signs of being musically inclined as a young boy.

It was in Pampa where he learned to play the guitar, along with the mandolin, the fiddle, and the basics of the banjo. His Uncle Jeff Guthrie, who also resided in Pampa and worked as a policeman there, showed him the rudiments of the guitar and how to tune it. But mostly Guthrie learned by experimenting with his fingers on the strings, eventually mastering enough chords to play some simple songs. Mary recalled much later on that during the evening Woody and brother Matt would play music in the house the Jennings had given the newly married Guthries to live in. "Oh, they'd play and sing and have a good time with it all. We didn't have no money to do much else, so we entertained ourselves. And over time, Woody and Matt got pretty good at playin' their songs."

Back then, Pampa had a radio station, KPDN, that played talk and music programs from 7 a.m. to 5:45 p.m. It wasn't anything special: such programs as "Women's Club of the Air," "Mid-Morning News," and "Know Your Public Schools" kept listeners aware of local goings-on. A few music programs like "Sweet or Swing" and "Rhythm and Romance" played the big band hits of the day. But if Guthrie sought out the music of the Carter Family, his favorite recording artists, or other samplings of the hillbilly music or gospel hymns he enjoyed most, he likely would have needed to tune into a station coming out of Dallas or Oklahoma City, or even farther away from Pampa than those two places.

Because of its local slant, KPDN, which was sponsored by the *Pampa Daily News,* occasionally featured during its noontime broadcasts the music of area bands and singers, including the Corncob Trio. Guthrie even performed on air with his Uncle Jeff and Aunt Allene, who played the accordion. Guthrie's appearances on KPDN marked the first time he had ever performed on radio, predating the more popular radio shows he would do in Los Angeles a couple of years later.

Guthrie recalled cutting his musical teeth in Pampa in a biographical sketch he wrote later on. "I . . . went off with a fiddling uncle of mine, Jeff Guthrie, (one of the best fiddlers in the West), who was also a deputy sheriff on the side, and a performing musician. His wife, Allene, played the guitar, accordion, chorded on the piano and organ, and I played the banjo and the mandolin, and learned a couple of tunes I could play on the fiddle while my uncle went outside to get a drink or something. We done this for five or six years."

Out in Los Angeles Guthrie had actually become a radio personality and a popular performer among the many migrants who had come to California looking for work. He arrived in the city in the spring of 1937—hopping freights and hitchhiking to get there—with the intent of finding work so he could support his family, which now included two young ones. He wasn't alone. Thousands more like him were already in California and still more were on their way. Oklahoma had lost nearly twenty per cent of its population in the 1930s. Some 440,000 people, according to historian Donald Worster, said good-bye to the Sooner state to search for new jobs and new hope.

"The people did not stop to shut the door—they just walked out, leaving behind them the wreckage of their labors: an ugly little shack with broken windows covered by cardboard, a sagging ridgepole, a barren, dusty yard, the windmill creaking in the wind," wrote Worster in his book *Dust Bowl*. "Ten thousand abandoned houses on the high plains; nine million acres of farmland turned back to nature."

Woody and his cousin, "Oklahoma" Leon Jack Guthrie, who lived in the greater Los Angeles area and was three years younger than Woody, formed a singing duo and played around Los Angeles and Long Beach, making an occasional couple of dollars. Eventually Woody and Jack (everyone called him Jack, even though he had a more colorful nickname) managed to get a radio audition at KFVD singing cowboy and country and western songs.

To their surprise, they were offered the 8:00 a.m. slot on the air in the summer of 1937. Though they weren't paid, the exposure made Woody feel important, and being on the air each day broadened their opportunities for paying jobs at night. Mary and the rest of the Jennings could actually hear the program, which was called *The Oklahoma and Woody Show*, all the way back in Pampa when the western sky was star-lit and clear. Matt couldn't believe that his brother-in-law and old band mate in the Corncob Trio was now singing and playing on the radio in the big city of Los Angeles. It made him feel both proud and a bit envious.

When Woody and Jack weren't on the air, they'd sing wherever they could—parties, get-togethers, dances, cowboy competitions—sometimes for a wage, sometimes not. It was at this time that Woody met Maxine Crissman, a young woman who loved to sing but who had never done so in public. Jack had known Maxine's brother Roy, who had introduced him and Woody to his sister. Taken by her knowledge of country and old-timey music and her ability to sing harmony, Woody soon invited Maxine, who he christened "Lefty Lou from Old Mizzou," to sing with him and Jack on KFVD.

Crissman was twenty-three when she met Guthrie. She had been born in

Woody Guthrie and Maxine "Lefty Lou" Crissman at KFVD Radio in Los Angeles, California, ca. 1939.

Missouri. She and her family had come to California at the outset of the Depression for the same reason nearly everyone else heading west did: better work opportunities. She wasn't naturally musical, though she grew up with music in her house, mostly gospel and old-time standards, and she did learn to play the saxophone in school. Maxine was taller than Woody; she had black hair and good looks, and attracted the occasional glance from men that she passed by on the street. She also had a fine voice and knew how to use it.

When the stress of caring for his family and maintaining his construction job grew to be too much, Jack Guthrie left Woody and their radio program in September 1937. Jack liked singing and playing music; it was his dream to become a full time cowboy singer. But the duo that was he and his cousin hadn't quite developed, musically speaking, the way he had hoped. Their audience was mostly migrants from Arkansas, Oklahoma, Kansas, and Texas—nearly 100,000 of them had come to California looking for work. They wanted to hear songs and stories, told mostly by Woody, that reminded them of where they had come from, not slick sounding cowboy songs and "buckaroo ballads," made popular by the likes of singing cowboy and movie star Gene Autry, which was what Jack favored.

With the departure of Jack Guthrie, Woody and Lefty Lou changed the name of their program to *The Woody and Lefty Lou Show*. As a duo, they were an immediate hit. Daily, KFVD received dozens of letters and song requests addressed to Guthrie and Crissman. Guthrie even penned a tune he called "Woody's and Lefty Lou's Theme Song," which he crowned with a verse: "If you like our kind of singing/I'm gonna tell you what to do/Get your pencil and your paper/Write to Woody and Lefty Lou."

With their show a success, Guthrie and Crissman began earning a salary from the radio station: twenty dollars a week, plus bonuses for increased advertisement revenue that came to the station because of their show. Woody and Lefty Lou split their earnings. Guthrie, flush with cash for the first time in his life, figured he could well support his Pampa family on the money he was making. Proudly, he called his wife Mary in Texas and told her to pack her things and come to California with the kids.

Mary was only too happy to oblige. Pampa in the 1930s was an all or nothing Panhandle town. In the early part of the twentieth century, it had been a sleepy community made up largely of cowboys, small businessmen, and farming families. Pampa incorporated in 1912, the year Guthrie was born. The town grew slowly. But then in the mid-1920s, oil had been discovered on its outskirts, prompting Pampa to experience a growth spurt it never saw coming. Needing manpower to put in place and then maintain the oil drilling machinery, Pampa attracted many young men who poured into town as quickly as the oil poured from the ground. Other men found jobs in support businesses. One of those newcomers was Charley Guthrie, Woody's father, who found a job running a boarding house where many of the transplanted oil workers lived. When Woody joined him, his first job was helping his father with the daily boarding house chores.

Practically overnight, new stores were opened in Pampa and new homes were built. New banks cashed the checks of the new oil workers in town. A new Santa Fe Railway line was constructed, connecting Pampa with western Oklahoma. "There was so much activity, so many jobs, and so many people coming into town," recalled Thelma Bray, who was a child back then and who now runs the Woody Guthrie Folk Music Center in Pampa. Bray's family had come to Pampa from New Mexico in 1932. Her father got a job in a local refinery and he and his family made Pampa their home. "I remember that they were happy times. We thought they would never end."

Even after the stock market crash in October 1929, Pampa continued to prosper for a spell. The town saw the construction of a new courthouse, city hall, and, in 1934, a magnificent new post office. But gradually, the reach of the Depression extended even to Pampa, and business activity slowed down, as did the discovery of new drill sites. Then in April 1935, on Palm Sunday, a week before Easter, a great dust storm that began as far north as the Dakotas, struck Pampa. With winds fifty or more miles per hour, radical drops in temperature and humidity, and a blackened horizon, a giant dust cloud quickly engulfed the town, as it had others in its path. The storm prompted some people to believe that the Day of Judgment had arrived. No one had ever seen such a sight. In no time, the world around Pampa went dark and everything in the town was covered with a thick coat of black and brown dust.

Mary Guthrie remembered the day vividly. "We called it Black Sunday, you know. Everything turned black, dark as the night. If there was a light bulb in the room, you couldn't see it. You couldn't see your hand in front of your face. We were scared. We didn't know what to do. A lot of people just prayed."

Guthrie recalled the Great Dust Storm of 1935, as it became known, in song and in a later piece of prose that provided additional insight into that dark day in Pampa history. "We watched the dust storm come up just like the red sea [sic] closing in on the Israel children . . . a lot of the people in the crowd was religious minded . . . and they said . . . 'well, boys, girls, friends and relatives, this is the end . . . so long, it's been good to know you.'" That final phrase turned up in the Guthrie song "Dusty Old Dust," later called "So Long, It's Been Good to Know You," one of the best musical narratives of the Dust Bowl disaster and a key song in the Guthrie music treasury.

Living in Pampa, nearly two thousand miles away from Los Angeles, Mary had also grown increasingly uneasy about the relationship that Woody had with Maxine Crissman and worried that it was more than professional. Additionally, she had become envious of her husband's good fortune. There Woody was in sunny southern California, singing songs with a woman she didn't know, becoming a radio celebrity, having fun and making the acquaintance of new and exciting people, and there she was caring for their two kids in dusty Pampa, sleeping alone at night and wondering if she'd ever not need the help of her family to pay the bills and put food on the table for the young ones. Certainly, what money Woody had been sending home wasn't enough.

Mary and the two kids took the train to Los Angeles in November 1937. She was happy to see Woody, and Woody seemed happy to see her. It didn't take her long to fall in love with the California weather and the promise of better times. The appeal of Woody's and Lefty Lou's radio show broadened, so that eventually they were on the air twice a day, six days a week. However, learning new songs to sing on each show became a challenge, even for Guthrie. Despite his prolific nature, he could churn out only so many new songs before even he ran out of ideas. Guthrie often spent more time at the Crissman's house than he did his own, working on songs, then teaching them to Lefty Lou.

According to Los Angeles labor historian Darryl Holter, "In a mad scramble to generate more songs for the radio show, Guthrie began to take old songs and add new lyrics. Then he began writing songs with his own lyrics, usually borrowing melodies from older songs and adapting them as he saw fit." Writing songs was not new to Guthrie. In the spring of 1935, while still in Pampa, he had put together his first collection of songs. He called it *Alonzo M. Zilch's Own Collection of Original Songs and Ballads*. During his time in California, Guthrie would compile, mimeograph and sell two other collections of songs: *Woody and Lefty Lou's Favorite Collection (of) Old Time Hill Country Songs* in 1937, and *On a Slow Train to California* in 1939. The lyrics were there, but Guthrie didn't always write, or even suggest, melodies for them. According to Guthrie biographer Joe Klein, "the music was usually an after-thought."

Guthrie took his song inspirations from most anywhere. Things he saw, newspaper stories he read, radio broadcasts he heard, ideas spoken, and songs played by others became the lyric reservoir from which he drank. Guthrie especially loved the Carter Family, that First Family of traditional American music. The Carters— Maybelle, Sara, and her husband, A. P.—were from Maces Springs, Virginia, where they soaked up the rich musical heritage of Appalachia. In 1927 the Carter Family made its first recordings, as did another favorite of Guthrie's—Jimmie Rodgers from

Meridian, Mississippi. Together that year in Bristol, Tennessee, the Carters and Rodgers, with their seminal recordings, created the foundation for country music (Rodgers is called "the Father of Country Music") and inspired countless other musicians, including Guthrie, to absorb the same American roots music—Anglo-Irish ballads, gospel, and blues—that they did.

A number of Guthrie songs that would later come to be known as American folk masterworks were written while he was in Los Angeles in the late 1930s. "Do Re Mi," "Oklahoma Hills," "Pretty Boy Floyd," "Philadelphia Lawyer," "I Ain't Got No Home" all came from this period—as did others. Hardly a day went by in Los Angeles or in his travels around California that Guthrie didn't pen one song, or at least a piece of it. Not every verse Guthrie wrote in this period exuded genius, but clearly he had tapped into a compositional tradition that recalled the great ballads and song stories he had heard as a boy from his mother. Plus, Guthrie had a sharp eye, a clever wit, a good ear, and an honest compassion that gave life to his lyrics and elevated the power of his songs.

Guthrie's delivery of these songs and the old timey standards he sang were equally rich. Being from Oklahoma, it was not difficult for Guthrie to replicate the Southwest drawl of his mostly Okie radio audience, not to mention its humor and homesick yearnings. He had picked up these nuances the same way he had picked up song ideas. Over time, some of his friends thought he exaggerated his Okie vocal mannerisms and gave too much time to the cornpone jokes and dry humor that increasingly became part of his on air performances. But the regular folks who tuned into his and Lefty Lou's radio show hardly seemed to mind.

Guthrie was not a particularly talented singer in strict terms. He could phrase his lyrics well enough and knew how to emphasize a section of verse, or give a word or two an effective slur or slant. Yet, he had limited range and lacked the kind of vocal texture and deep soul found in naturally gifted singers. But what he sang was always more important than how he sang, and with Lefty Lou strengthening his delivery and giving it two-part harmony, folks who listened to their radio show were moved by its authentic ring. Many of those listening in thought Guthrie and Lefty Lou were husband and wife, or brother and sister, such was their synergy when singing.

Guthrie was incessantly curious, which is why he read reams of books, from philosophy and religion, to history and politics. Back in Pampa, the librarian there claimed he had ready every book on the shelf. Guthrie also devoured newspapers. But the need to know went beyond books and things in print. Inevitably, he felt an inner tug, a drive to pick up and go in order to see the land and meet and talk to the people who lived and worked on it. He was becoming more and more captivated by the plight of his listeners, many of them no better off in California than they were on the dust-plagued prairies of Oklahoma and Texas. More and more of his songs were about them or at least inspired by them.

Woody and Lefty Lou worked tirelessly and kept a schedule that would tax even the strongest souls. Lefty Lou felt utterly worn out by Woody's endless escapades and demands. He'd show up at her house unannounced and want to sing or use her typewriter to write a letter to Mary back home in Pampa or else get down on paper a new song that was bobbing around in his brain. Then he'd leave and head to who knew where, leaving Maxine wondering if he'd show up for their show. She certainly enjoyed the singing and on-air celebrity status, but not to the degree that Woody did. Finally, in June 1938, after nearly a year performing with Woody, she called it quits.

Guthrie carried on. Without Lefty Lou, who would frequently remind Woody that he sometimes talked too long between songs on their show or that he ought to temper his increasingly acidic comments about the plight of fruit pickers or striking workers, Guthrie was left unchecked to say and sing what he pleased. Fortunately, KFVD was no ordinary radio station. Its manager, J. Frank Burke, Jr., was progressive-minded and tolerated Guthrie's often excessive commentary. After Lefty Lou's departure, Burke's father, also liberal in his political views, launched a left-leaning weekly newspaper called *The Light* for which he asked Guthrie to contribute. Guthrie jumped at the offer, prompting him to embark on a journey to homeless camps called Hoovervilles that had sprouted along the main roads of California's Central Valley. (Hoovervilles were named in bitter honor of former President Herbert Hoover, who many thought brought on the Depression with his do-nothing economic policies.)

Up to this point, Guthrie's politics, though sincere, lacked depth and detail. He heard about things happening to migrant workers and strikers, and occasionally witnessed firsthand the hardship and suffering experienced by those he increasingly called his people. But by putting off doing his radio show for a spell and hitting the road—something he loved to do—he got an education in strike politics, corruption, and the growing friction between the haves and have nots in California. Best of all, he got to tell his audience all about it, through song and chat, when he returned.

It was at this time that Guthrie met Ed Robbin, a writer, who had become politicized in the 1930s after investigating a migrant worker's strike in the central California town of Salinas. Moved by the plight of the workers and the rabid, often violent response by authorities to migrant strikes in the state, Robbin joined the Communist Party and in 1938 became a staff writer for the radical newspaper, *People's World*. Soon after, Robbin became an editor for the paper.

Robbin broadened his reach by doing a radio program on KFVD and airing commentary on "the struggles of workers and unions, and against war and fascism." His show followed Guthrie's, which was now called *Woody, the Lone Wolf*. Guthrie had often listened to Robbin, and through their KFVD connection, a friendship formed. Robbin suggested that Guthrie sing at socialist and Communist rallies in and around Los Angeles. It would be good for him to meet the people working hard for economic justice, Robbin reasoned. Woody agreed. If people in need of a song or two might want to hear him sing, why Woody was only too happy to oblige.

One day Guthrie inquired as to the possibility of writing a column for *People's*

World. Robbin thought it was a good idea. If Woody wrote the way he talked and if he connected to people in print the way he did on the air, perhaps it might increase the readership of *People's World.* Robbin, however, knew Guthrie's by-line in the newspaper would raise an eyebrow or two with regular readers. There wasn't much in the way of pure or party-endorsed socialist or communist dogma that came out of Woody's mouth and it probably wouldn't come from his pen, either. But Guthrie had down pat the *spirit* of socialism as well as a keen passion for the proletarian struggle in America. That certainly counted for something.

Robbin's hunch paid off. Woody did indeed write the way he spoke on the radio, complete with deliberate misspellings, malapropisms, run-on sentences, and broken grammar. In his debut column, he described his birthplace of Okemah as a town full of "boom-chasers, drillers, roustabouts, tool-dressers, teamskinners, bootleggers, Indian guardians 'an' other tong-buckers an' grease-monkeys of the oil field work." Here was a fresh new voice in *People's World.* Woody called his column "Woody Sez," a nod to Will Rogers whose syndicated newspaper column was called "Will Rogers Says."

"Woody Sez" broadened Guthrie's popularity amongst union workers and strikers, and he was asked to sing regularly at rallies, then at fund-raising events, and union halls. He'd get paid a few dollars for his performances or sometimes nothing at all. Guthrie took it all in stride. He was happy to sing his songs, tell some stories and a joke or two, and maybe sell a couple of his mimeographed song booklets that he had put together. "I took sides with the union on all the arguments and argued for higher pay for the cotton pickers, orange grove workers, fruit pickers, cannery workers, (and) movie employees," wrote Guthrie. "I spoke out . . . for all races of people, Hindu, Japanese, Chinese, Oakies [sic], Arkies, Texans, Dust Bowl Refugees and Migratory Workers. I cussed out high rents, robbing landlords, and fake real estate racketeers, loan sharks, finance companies, and punk politicians in all offices."

Guthrie's live performance income, meager as it was, complemented his radio

We Pledge Our Alegiance. Pen-and-ink artwork by Woody Guthrie, ca. 1939.

salary. He also earned additional money from listeners to his radio show that sent in to the station a dollar here or a quarter there as a token of their appreciation for the music and stories Guthrie shared with them. Guthrie was also excited about the progress he was making as a kind of singing Will Rogers, and he particularly enjoyed the increase in requests for his singing services at union halls and workers' rallies. In his memoir *Woody Guthrie and Me*, Robbin recalled "the big problem with Woody was getting him off the stage. He loved to drawl out long commentaries and tell endless anecdotes between his songs, and it practically took a hook to pull him off the platform."

The summer of 1939 was especially fruitful for Guthrie. Another major figure had come into his life: the actor Will Geer, who had recently moved to California with his pregnant wife, Herta, to star in the film, *The Fight for Life*. Back then, Geer wasn't the warm-hearted grandfather he'd play years later in the popular 1970s television program, *The Waltons*. In the 1930s Geer was a tall, handsome actor, expressive and enthusiastic, articulate and well-educated, a dedicated social activist and a member of the Communist Party. Geer possessed a strong self-confidence and wasn't afraid to fight for causes he believed in. Guthrie and Geer: the two seemed made for each other.

Like Robbin, Geer was red all over, an unrepentant Communist who refused to stand by idly while workers were beaten and poor migrant workers and their families were broken and humiliated. Geer and Guthrie fast became best friends; the two traveled throughout California, leaving their wives behind in order to fight for workers' rights. Geer was also a singer and frequently performed with Guthrie. The two cut a fine picture of political solidarity set to music in California's agricultural areas and cities such as Bakersfield where unrest among migrant workers was running rampant.

That summer of 1939 Geer had introduced Guthrie to the writer John Steinbeck, whose book, *The Grapes of Wrath*, had been published in April. A riveting novel about the Joad family and their struggle to survive the Depression, *The Grapes of Wrath* would win both the Pulitzer Prize and the National Book Award that year. The book incited a fury of dialogue about the plight of the Okies and the political and economic oppression they encountered in California. Steinbeck had sold the film rights to *The Grapes of Wrath* and was in Los Angeles to learn about how books were made into movies when Guthrie met him.

Guthrie claimed he never read *The Grapes of Wrath*, but it is hard to see how he hadn't, given his penchant for reading, especially topics like the Dust Bowl and the migrant worker cause that was so important to him. Not only did Guthrie hear about the book, and probably read it, he also wrote about it. *The Grapes of Wrath*, Woody said, "is about us pullin' out of Oklahoma and Arkansas and down south and driftin' around over the state of California, busted, disgusted, down and out and lookin' for work. Shows you how come us got to be that way. Shows the damn bankers, men that broke us and the dust that choked us, and it comes right out in plain English and says what to do about it."

Guthrie even wrote songs inspired by or directly taken from *The Grapes of Wrath*. His haunting song, "Vigilante Man," referenced a character, Preacher Casey, from the book, while "Tom Joad," a song he would later write to secure a record contract with RCA-Victor, depicted the story of the lead character in *The Grapes of Wrath*. "Tom Joad" would later become known as one of Guthrie's most memorable masterpieces, and years later would inspire Bruce Springsteen to pen "The Ghost of Tom Joad."

Steinbeck apparently liked Guthrie when he met him and more than one Guthrie biographer has written that the novelist asked Guthrie to be the unofficial, unpaid "musical advisor" of the movie version of *The Grapes of Wrath*. According to biographer Cray, "Director John Ford asked for a song that the majority of dust bowl migrants might know; Guthrie immediately suggested one he had first heard from his Uncle Jeff." It was "Goin' Down the Road Feelin' Bad," also known as "Lonesome Road Blues." Guthrie knew the song from his Pampa days, had sung the song many times himself, and even had his own Dust Bowl-themed set of lyrics for the tune.

Because of Guthrie's recommendation, Ford used it in the movie.

During the summer of 1939, Guthrie was writing songs and gathering ideas for his "Woody Sez" columns. He was also doing his radio show on KFVD, making it increasingly political and sharp. It seemed that everything was going Woody's way until news made far from California broke up Woody's world. On September 1, Germany invaded Poland. Worse, Russia, which had been, in Woody's mind, the ideal political state with its Marxist mandate and worker-first mentality, had joined Nazi Germany in destroying the Polish army and occupying the eastern half of the country. Many Soviet sympathizers were already wary of Joseph Stalin's intentions after he signed a non-aggression pact with Germany and looked the other way as Hitler raved and ranted about the injustices the Aryan people endured in Europe. The Russian invasion of Poland was further proof that Stalin was nearly as sinister as his Nazi counterpart.

Suddenly, Guthie's and Robbin's pro-red commentary on their radio shows alarmed owner Burke, who feared significant loss of advertising revenue and alienating listeners. Since Robbin's show was more radical than Guthrie's, it was his show that was canceled first. But by November 1939, *Woody, the Lone Wolf* had suffered the same fate. Not only did Guthrie lose his daily connection to his followers and fellow Okies, but gone too was a regular paycheck, however small it was.

Mary was worried. The money Woody made by talking and singing on the radio gave their family some financial stability. Now with it gone and the family unable to save anything, she hadn't a clue as to where money to pay for groceries would come from. Her brother Matt recently had written to her about a better job situation in Texas. Matt had instructed Mary to tell Woody that there might soon be a chance to earn a good paycheck in the Pampa oil fields. Drills and derricks once again began sucking oil from Pampa ground practically everywhere you looked. And the bigger oil fields outside of town were also getting busy again. Perhaps Woody could get a real job—a steady job—and put food on his family's table like a good husband ought to, thought Matt.

Mary embraced the idea. It wasn't that she didn't like Los Angeles; who wouldn't like the beautiful weather, the beach and the warm sun? Compared to the Texas Panhandle, California was nothing short of heaven. But during the time she was there, she hardly saw her husband. Whether he was on the radio, or on the road, or playing music in migrant camps, or out raising money or awareness for this organization or that one, or out talking with strikers and fruit pickers, or traveling the rural back roads with Will Geer, Woody was rarely home.

It was a rambling, rough-edged life that Woody led in California. He'd set off with a guitar, a small sack, and his songs. He'd meet broken people holding on to broken promises, many of them hungry and barely clinging to their dignity and self-respect. He'd be gone days, even weeks. But then, seemingly out of nowhere, Woody would show up at home, greet Mary and the little ones, and act as if he'd never left. Maybe with a steady job in Pampa, Woody would be around the house more, maybe do his part in raising the three children, maybe become the husband Mary always hoped he'd be. Having Matt and the rest of the Jennings family around might help stabilize him and cure him of his restless ways. It was worth a try.

Mary and Woody talked. Not only did he lose his radio show, but Will and Herta Geer had also left California. They moved to New York City where Will had accepted the lead role in the theatrical production of *Tobacco Road*, another popular novel about the Great Depression written by Erskine Caldwell and published in 1932. *Tobacco Road* had been a theatrical hit in New York since its stage debut a year later. Geer was anxious to put his mark on Jeter, the lead character, and he set aside his political work in California to do so. With Will gone, Woody decided it was a good time to leave California, too.

Woody knew he'd miss his radio show and all the singing he'd been doing in California. But with war in Europe, the world was now a different place. It seemed as if everyone was wondering what would be America's role, if any, in this conflict?

On November 11, Armistice Day, many radio stations played patriotic music: the marches of John Philip Sousa, popular songs from World War I, military theme songs. But the one song that could be heard everywhere was Kate Smith's "God Bless America." It had been exactly one year since she had premiered it on her radio show, *The Kate Smith Hour*, and since then, it was hard to escape.

Many Americans took comfort in the song, penned by the popular composer Irving Berlin, as well as in Smith's strong rendition of it. Smith, who owned a big tenor voice, belted out the song with proud patriotic fervor, nearly turning "God Bless America" into a national rallying cry. The song's lyrics spoke of an endowed nation, privileged in its special relationship with God. The words intimated an inner national strength and resolve. As much as the song celebrated America's vitality, "God Bless America" also pinned the nation's hopes on divine benevolence.

Guthrie was not averse to bringing God into any earthly question. As a youth he had read the Bible many times. He did numerous illustrations of biblical scenes and painted portraits of Christ. He studied Eastern religion and mysticism and was intrigued by the writings of prophets. He loved the old gospel hymns and Negro spirituals that celebrated salvation and redemption. Not the conventional religious type, Guthrie even went to church when Mary prodded him. If nothing else, he enjoyed the music and the stories from the Bible and liked looking at the statues. If God was going to bless America, He'd better do it soon.

———————

The Guthries arrived in Pampa, tired and cold, but happy to see their friends and family. Baby Bill was a hit with the Jennings, and the women in the family competed to hold and feed him. The holiday season had begun and despite the economic difficulties all around, the Jennings family made the most of the arrival back in town of Mary, Woody, and the kids. The Guthries moved back into their tiny Pampa house on South Russell Street. The place was dirty and dusty, but pretty much the way Mary had left it a year ago when she and her children went to California. Despite the cramped conditions, it still felt like home to Mary.

Woody wasn't so sure. It didn't take him long to realize that Pampa was no Los Angeles. As far as he was concerned, the place offered him little when he last lived there and nothing had changed. Guthrie hadn't been in Pampa but a few days and already he was thinking of when he would leave. There would be no holding him in Texas, not with so many other places beckoning. He felt like he had gone backwards. He looked at the road leading out of town and the railroad track that ran through it and wondered which would get him on his way.

All but broke, Mary prodded Woody to find work. There were some jobs he heard about out in the oil fields, as Matt had predicted, but he wasn't really interested in them. He, after all, was a radio personality, a singer and a songwriter. Out in California, he was the voice of his people. They were striking for better pay and being beaten for it. They were fighting for decent working conditions and Woody was right there with them. He loved every minute that he was in their company. He felt important and needed. That was all any man in his shoes could ask for.

Mary prayed he wouldn't spout that socialist stuff in Pampa. She knew the local folks wouldn't stand for it. In California, with writers and actors and unions, that kind of thinking was accepted. But Pampa was a long way from the palm trees and radical sides of Hollywood. People in Pampa knew about hardship; there were plenty of men out of work. But Mary knew they weren't about to give up on the American way of life, and when some of them heard what Woody was talking and singing about on that California radio show of his, they wanted nothing to do with him.

CHAPTER 1

Woody looked for work that December and into January 1940, but not hard. Mostly he read and walked around town. He visited the library where he had spent so much time before heading to California. He chatted with the librarian there and borrowed a few books. He did put in some time behind the counter at Shorty Harris's drugstore where he had once worked. Shorty liked Woody and offered him more hours behind the counter, but Woody had no intention of making the job permanent.

Woody spoke to Matt Jennings about re-forming the Corncob Trio; Matt told him he was too busy with his butcher's job and his new wife to commit to resurrecting the group. Matt had heard that Cluster Baker, the final third of the trio, was about to get married, too and wouldn't be interested in getting the Corncob Trio going again. Disappointed, Woody next turned to his Uncle Jeff. He also was more concerned with his full-time policeman's job than about playing music around town. Woody thought about performing as a solo act, but opportunities were slim for a socialist singer. The Jennings family wondered why Woody wasn't looking for a more solid means of earning a living, with three young mouths to feed and a wife to look after. Woody wondered why he had come back to Pampa in the first place.

He wandered around town, thinking about things. Back in his little house he listened to the radio, where he'd often hear "God Bless America." Had Irving Berlin or Kate Smith ever been to Pampa? He doubted it.

2

On September 13, 1893 a crowded, immigrant-filled passenger ship, the *S.S. Rhynland*, sailed into New York Harbor. It had been eleven days since the ship had embarked on its transatlantic voyage from the busy Belgian port of Antwerp. With many of its passengers now jammed on deck, all of them struggling to catch a sight of the Promised Land, the *Rhynland* passed the Statue of Liberty, a recent gift from France, and tears welled in the eyes of more than one of these immigrants. For everyone on the *Rhynland*, this majestic statue symbolized the freedom and opportunity they hoped awaited them in America.

On board the *Rhynland* that day was a five-year-old Russian Jew named Israel Baline and the rest of his family. Tired and anxious from their journey in the steerage section of the ship, the Balines—Moses and wife Lena and their six children—felt fortunate to have escaped Russia's bloody, anti-Semetic pogroms. Traveling across Russia and then much of Europe to get to Antwerp, they left family and friends behind and had with them those few possessions they could carry onboard.

Along with everyone else who had sailed on the *Rhynland*, Israel, the youngest of the Baline children, passed by the observant eyes of customs officers at Castle

Garden in New York City's Battery section, then by more customs officials at Ellis Island. They scanned the passengers, looking for those who were sick or too weak to gain entry into America. Every week, thousands of recently arrived immigrants went through the same scrutiny. Not all of them realized their hope of a new life in America. Some were sent back to their mother countries, devastated that their journey was for naught and their dream deferred, or worse, done.

The Balines patiently stood in the long Ellis Island lines, unsure of their status. By the grace of God, none of them had gotten sick from the ocean voyage. They had some money with them, but not much, and they had plans to meet with relatives already in New York who would help them settle into their new home. The Balines spoke only Yiddish; English sounded strange to them. As best they could, Moses Baline and his family gave the Ellis Island immigration officer the information he requested. "Welcome to the United States of America," the customs officer said routinely, and waved them on.

For Moses Baline, America did not deliver in the way he had heard it would. Living conditions for the family were barely above squalid. Work was infrequent. Hope was fleeting. Buy 1901, Moses, the family patriarch, was dead, as was a sister, Sifre. Young Israel learned English quickly. Able to communicate better than the others in his family, he sold newspapers and junk, buying what little food he could for the family with the few coins he made. He went to public school, though showed little aptitude for learning. He did, however, reveal a talent for singing, something inherited from his father, who, back in Russia, was a Jewish cantor.

By the time Izzy Baline was fourteen years old, he had left home, a decision he made in part to rid the burden of having his mother feed, clothe and care for him. Despite being scruffy and poor, the boy showed remarkable resiliency. He kept in contact with his family, but spent most of his time in and out of Lower East Side saloons where he sang to half-drunk patrons for the few pennies thrown his way. It wasn't much, but at least he was surviving.

Izzy Baline's break came in 1902 when he was granted a spot in the chorus of a musical being cast called *The Show Girl*. Because the revue was a road show, Baline traveled outside New York City for the first time in his life, seeing a small part of another America and sensing the endless possibilities that existed beyond the tenements he knew too well. Upon his return to the city, Baline gained employment as a song plugger—a person hired by a composer or song publisher to promote new songs in New York City saloons. Baline worked for Harry Von Tilzer, a popular songwriter whose hit, "A Bird in a Gilded Cage," was one of the biggest selling songs of the era. Baline also worked as a singing waiter, logging hours in beer halls and gradually working toward his new passion: songwriting.

Baline had no formal training as a songwriter. He couldn't write musical notation and hadn't a clue as to how to play an instrument. But Baline was intrigued with the songwriting craft. "Once you start singing, you start thinking of songs—it's as simple as that," he once recalled. In 1907 Baline wrote the lyrics to a tune he called "Marie from Sunny Italy." A piano player, "Professor" Nick (or Mike) Nicholson with whom he worked in a Chinatown bar, wrote the melody. The song was catchy and brought to the attention of Joseph W. Stern, one of New York's prominent music publishers. Stern purchased the rights to the tune for seventy-five cents, of which Baline received half the paltry sum.

When the song saw the light of day as sheet music, the name of the lyricist was not Izzy Baline, but one I. Berlin. Seeing the song in print gave the young songwriter the impetus to try his hand at writing more pieces and perhaps becoming a true professional writer of songs. Izzy Baline was now a person of the past. He became a ghost, an immigrant image of hard times and tough luck. In his place came the person America and the rest of the world would come to know as Irving Berlin.

The songwriting genius of Irving Berlin wasn't exactly glaring in 1908, but there was enough potential, particularly in his lyric writing, that enabled Berlin to collaborate with other songwriters. At twenty years old, Berlin was eager to make his mark on Tin Pan Alley, that section of Manhattan where the offices of the city's most prominent song publishers were located. What kinds of songs were they seeking? Certainly sentimental ballads and songs with built-in humor or subtle satire were in vogue. Songs about courtship were never out of favor. The right novelty song might prove lucrative to a publishing house and songwriter, and patriotic songs were also solid bets. Berlin studied the songwriters he thought were masters: Stephen Foster, of course Harry Tilzer, and no doubt Charles K. Harris, whose song, "After the Ball," became a huge hit in the 1890s, ultimately selling over five million copies of sheet music and making Harris a most wealthy man. The remarkable story of Charles Harris provided inspiration for countless young songwriters, including Berlin.

Early on, Berlin often worked with a collaborator; he usually came up with the song's theme and wrote the lyrics, while another writer such as Ted Snyder or George Whiting might write the melody. One song penned by all three writers— "My Wife's Gone to the Country"—sold three hundred thousand sheet music copies in 1909, establishing Berlin as a rising Tin Pan Alley composer. Another 1909 song, "Dorando," Berlin wrote by himself. It earned him both critical acclaim and thousands of dollars in royalties.

Songs for musical revues and vaudeville shows came from his musical imagination, the same way pop songs did. *The Girl and the Wizard, Ziegfeld Follies,* and *The Merry Whirl* were just three shows for which Berlin composed songs. From 1907 through 1914, Berlin published 190 pop and show songs, with and without collaborators.

Hard work was Berlin's calling card in those days. Absorbing ideas, information, and inspiration like a sponge, Berlin wrote daily. One biographer claimed he had "a ferocious appetite for work." Another described him this way: "He would work on a song, when inspired or driven, through the night . . . and when he wasn't groping for

Irving Berlin, composer of "God Bless America," at the piano in 1936.

a song, he was making the rounds of cafes, bars, and vaudeville houses. . . ." Berlin enjoyed little social life outside his profession; he preferred instead to keep the company of other songwriters, music publishers, song pluggers, and singers, all of whom rounded out his inner circle of friends and associates. His life was dedicated to the art of writing popular music, and he was relentless in his pursuit of the perfect song.

There are some music historians who believe he achieved it in 1911. The rage that was ragtime in America was just peaking when Irving Berlin wrote "Alexander's Ragtime Band." Although it was the big breakthrough hit Berlin dreamed about, selling millions of copies the world over, the song was, in Berlin's words, "an accidental hit."

"Alexander's Ragtime Band" was not a straight ragtime number. The catchy song gave a nod to syncopation, the musical element most associated with the rags of Scott Joplin and other classic ragtime composers, but it emphasized more of Berlin's growing mainstream pop music sensibility. Second, Berlin knew next to nothing about Southern African–American culture from which ragtime evolved. So, the feel and story of "Alexander's Ragtime Band" was smooth and pop-polished; it didn't reference any of the early ragtime sounds that emanated from bordellos and saloons, where the music had taken shape a couple of decades earlier.

Mostly "Alexander's Ragtime Band" had simply used the *idea* of ragtime as a compositional theme. The song had begun as an instrumental, but Berlin reworked it to include lyrics and it wound up in the revue, *The Merry Whirl*, in 1910. Although the revue was a dud, "Alexander's Ragtime Band" caught on. With a magnetic melody and lyrics that celebrated ragtime as a great American pop music form, Berlin's song was so popular that people began calling him the "King of Ragtime," which couldn't have been further from the truth. However, from most accounts, Berlin did little to distance himself from the royal title.

Berlin's career was going strong, but he wasn't a bright enough star to avoid induction into the army in 1918. No sooner had he finally become a naturalized citizen of the United States—making it official in February 1918 by swearing to "support and defend the Constitution and laws of the United States against all enemies, foreign and domestic"—than Uncle Sam came calling, requesting that Irving Berlin do just that.

A little less than a year earlier—April 6, 1917—America had declared war on Germany, finally entering "the war to end all wars," as President Woodrow Wilson described it. America had resisted entering into the bloody and muddy fray for nearly three years, taking the side of isolationists who could see no point in fighting a European war and casting young men into the stench and death that came with this new modern warfare of the early twentieth century.

Already the fighting had taken the lives and spirit of so many thousands of soldiers on both sides. Many more promised to be lost. But when Germany brazenly began sinking ships with American passengers on board, a result of Germany's increasingly effective submarine fleet, Wilson, who had campaigned for reelection in 1916 on an anti-war platform, had no choice but to join the fight. America was in, and doughboys began boarding ships for England and France, eager to display American courage and do their part in bringing Kaizer Wilhelm of Germany to his knees.

Fortunately for Berlin, about as far east as he had to travel to fulfill his military service was rural Long Island. After induction, Berlin was sent to Camp Upton in the village of Yaphank, a hundred or so miles from New York City, where a U.S. army infantry division was stationed. By the time Berlin had put on a uniform, the tide of the war had changed in favor of the Allies. America's entry into the war had brought thousands of fresh troops to the front, providing the necessary firepower to force Germany to pull back. Key battles were waged and won by the Allies in the spring and summer of 1918, including the famous Battle of the Marne in July. Though the cost of victory was high, the end of the war was near.

Berlin was far enough away from the bullets and trenches to escape harm. But he still found army life all but intolerable. He hated the food, the drilling, the tight sleeping quarters, the physical regimen. It was all in stark contrast to his privileged life before becoming a soldier, a life that included a beautiful Manhattan apartment, a private cook and valet, and a profitable music publishing business. In 1967 he told *American Heritage* magazine that "I found out quickly I wasn't much of a solider. There were a lot of things about army life that I didn't like, and the thing I didn't like most of all was revile."

Private Irving Berlin was used to late New York nights; he often worked into the wee hours and slept through much of the morning. At Camp Upton it was rise and shine before the sun came up, a hideous proposition in Berlin's mind. However, like any clever composer would, Berlin put his frustration into words and music and made something of them. The result was the song "Oh! How I Hate to Get Up in the Morning," an instant classic that his commanding officer adored. Suddenly, the song-writer found himself wearing the stripes of a sergeant, with a musical secretary, more tolerable army hours, and the opportunity to do what he did best: write music.

It could have been, as Edward Jablonski, author of *Irving Berlin: American Troubador*, suggested: the commander of Camp Upton, Major General J. Franklin Bell, asked or ordered Berlin to create a musical production that would raise money for the camp or raise the spirits of his men, or both. Or that Berlin had the idea himself, perhaps to avoid the monotonous life of a camp soldier, and took the idea of a musical production to Bell.

Whatever the case, Berlin busily began writing a musical revue he'd call *Yip! Yip! Yaphank*, which would reflect Berlin's camp experiences and include the number, "Oh! How I Hate to Get Up in the Morning." The song "wasn't reminiscent of black music, or Jewish, or Italian, as so many of Irving's earlier songs had been," wrote Laurence Bergreen in *As Thousands Cheer: the Life of Irving Berlin*. It was written in "an American vernacular: simple, straightforward, masculine. Though he would continue to employ devices he'd learned from ethnic songs . . . he would write no more of them. As a soldier-songwriter, he now belonged to a category by himself."

The idea for the army to create and stage a Ziegfeld-style Broadway production wasn't novel: the navy had already done it. Earlier in the year, it ran a revue at the Century Theater in Manhattan called *Boom Boom*, complete with female impersonators and lively music. Not that Berlin was so committed to the army that he wanted to make everyone forget about the navy's theatrical accomplishments, but clearly he was motivated to make sure his revue was better written and more polished and drew the kind of attention Berlin was used to getting before being drafted. More than three hundred men worked on *Yip! Yip! Yaphank*. Berlin called every move and wrote every musical number.

Berlin's musical secretary was Harry Ruby, who was brought in from Manhattan to capture Berlin's musical dictations. Berlin worked tirelessly on the production, staying up most of the night, writing out songs and then getting Ruby to put them down on paper the next morning. In addition to "Oh! How I Hate to Get Up in the Morning," Berlin penned "Mandy," "Kitchen Police," and "Dream On, Little Soldier Boy"—all top-notch numbers. Berlin clearly was on a songwriting roll, even if it meant doing it while in boots and uniform.

"I don't believe the boys of France want sad, tearful songs about dying in the battlefield or patriotic discourses about being on duty and going to lick the Kaiser," Berlin said, "because they do these things as part of the day's work. The trouble with most of our sentimental ballads is that they haven't any real connection with the war. They are tearful songs about absent loved ones who might just as well be in Milwaukee or Hong Kong as far as any real connection with the war is concerned. I hope we shall have something better."

The songs Berlin wrote hardly recalled the patriotic flag-waving of George M. Cohan, whose masterpiece, "Over There," had become the rallying cry for American doughboys. Berlin's musical contribution to the war effort contained songs that depicted army life in a light, humorous way. They were meant to raise spirits and money for Camp Upton, not sell war bonds or inspire enlistment.

Yip! Yip! Yaphank previewed in July 1918 in a small theater in Camp Upton. In addition to the camp's soldiers, such vaudeville stars as Al Jolson, Fanny Brice, Will Rogers, and Eddie Cantor took a train to the Long Island camp to attend opening night. The positive reviews got *Yip! Yip! Yaphank* to the Century Theater in Manhattan the following month. Advertisements proclaimed "Sergeant Irving Berlin's latest musical extravaganza" and called it "a military mess cooked up by the boys at Camp Upton." The revue contained choreographed military drills, minstrel-like vignettes, and plenty of humor. Soldiers danced and sang on the stage, doing their best to entertain their audience. Most were in uniform, but some were in drag, bringing added humor of the skits.

At one point in the production, Berlin himself appeared onstage. Performing what was clearly the most memorable number of the night, Berlin was pulled from his tent, half-asleep, singing "Oh! How I Hate to Get Up in the Morning." The audience loved the song and the skit, much to the relief of Berlin. The reviews were glowing, the profits deep. According to Bergreen, Berlin and his army superiors hoped to earn $35,000; when the show closed in September because there were simply no other dates left in the theater and the boys of Camp Upton had new orders, the production had tallied $83,000. Berlin was a hero. He had brought laughs and great fun to his army buddies and demonstrated that even with the limits of army life thrust upon him, Berlin could still write a winner.

Yip! Yip! Yaphank was a tight musical production, in part because Berlin used only the music he wrote for it that was bright and light. Some songs didn't make the cut. Berlin knew how much American audiences loved songs that galvanized their patriotism. During the writing of *Yip! Yip! Yaphank*, he had penned a piece that was flowing with patriotic flair and that he hoped would be the show's finale. He called the song "God Bless America." Berlin, however, wasn't sure it worked, so supposedly he asked Harry Ruby what he thought. The secretary was said to have uttered, "Geez, *another* one?" Ruby was tired of all the patriotic songs that had been written to support America's entry into World War I, and Berlin had just added another one to the list.

Berlin let the soldiers in the cast hear "God Bless America" to gauge their reaction to the song and to see how it would fit into the revue. Berlin wrote to Ruby in 1971, recalling the decision to keep "God Bless America" out of the production. "I did let the boys hear it and decided that 350 soldiers in overseas outfits marching down the aisle of the Century Theater going off to war singing 'God Bless America' was wrong." Berlin agreed with Ruby. The country didn't need another pro-America song and thus left "God Bless America" out of the revue. "I couldn't visualize soldiers marching to it. So I laid it aside and tried other things," recalled Berlin years later. He replaced it with a song called "We're on Our Way to France."

Not thinking much else about it, Berlin placed "God Bless America" in a trunk, along with other bits and pieces of songs, perhaps to be used at another time in another production. That same year, an aspiring young singer from Washington, D.C. had just turned eleven years-old and had entertained dreams one day of being on the radio singing the songs of America's greatest songwriters. Her name was Kathryn Smith, but everyone called her Kate.

Right from the start there was something inherently patriotic about young Kate Smith. General John Pershing, commander of America's Expeditionary Force in Europe, heard her sing and invited her to the White House where she entertained President Wilson and his guests and received a medal from him. Shortly thereafter, Smith was out convincing people to buy war-bonds. She waved the American flag and sang and posed for pictures, a cute little girl, who, in her own charming way, embodied the spirit of America.

Smith continued to sing as a teen and as a young woman entered talent shows, which she often won, and did amateur engagements, where she often drew enthusiastic response. No one could deny that she had a strong, robust voice, but she lacked a shapely presence, good looks, and sexy charisma—three essentials for women to make a career in entertainment, even back then. Rotund was what Smith was; she routinely struggled with her weight, and her moon-shaped face only emphasized her chubby cheeks. Despite her obvious ability to carry a tune and then some, Smith secured only low level singing dates where occasional rowdy patrons were more apt to make fun of her portly figure than to applaud her increasingly powerful voice.

Things changed in the mid-1920s when she began securing Broadway singing engagements in New York, the result of a thick skin, hard work, and persistence. On a lark, she gave a poem she had written as a child called "When the Moon Comes Over the Mountain" to veteran songwriters Harry Woods and Howard Johnson, who wrote a melody for it, which Smith recorded for Columbia Records. Much to everyone's surprise, "When the Moon Came Over the Mountain" was a major hit in 1931, and wherever she performed, audiences called for it. CBS radio recognized a rising star in Kate Smith and offered her a radio show of her own that year called *The Kate Smith Hour*.

With Germany defeated and an armistice signed in November 1918, Sergeant Irving Berlin received his discharge papers and turned in his doughboy uniform. Hurrying back to Manhattan, Berlin was eager to resume his rise to the top of American music. And for the next two decades, he made great use of his time and talent before the war clouds returned to Europe.

During the period between the two world wars, Berlin wrote prodigiously. At first he sent most of his songs to Florenz Ziegfeld, whose *Ziegfeld Follies* remained the best place for a songwriter to showcase his songs. Ziegfeld launched the *Follies* in 1907, in the process remaking the musical revue in America and becoming the centerpiece of stage entertainment, particularly in New York. His 1919 *Follies*, considered the best of them all, featured Berlin's "A Pretty Girl Is Like a Melody," along with eight other of his songs. Seven more Berlin songs would be heard in the *Ziegfeld Follies of 1920*.

Berlin pushed himself creatively, but he didn't ignore the business side of the music. As much as he felt a need to write, it was a business after all, and the plan had always been to make money. Berlin opened his own music publishing company, Irving Berlin, Inc., and partnered with producer Sam Harris to build The Music Box, a nearly million-dollar Broadway theater that would showcase Berlin's songs—and only his songs. Berlin took what he learned from Ziegfeld and began an annual *Music Box Revue* that lasted four years. Though the Music Box was successful, Berlin had to work relentlessly to write enough good material to stock the revues. His insistence that he have a say in casting, scenery and other aspects of the productions meant much more work than he bargained for.

In 1927 Berlin was back writing for the *Ziegfeld Follies*. Despite its moderate success, both Berlin and Ziegfeld sensed that an era was coming to a close. The '27 *Follies* would be the last. Ziegfeld turned his attention to a new form, the Broadway musical, and opened *Showboat*, America's first great Broadway musical, at the end of the year. Berlin turned his attention to Hollywood. Though the movie industry was born in New York and New Jersey, by the mid-1920s it began the move west to southern California, where the weather was better and the lifestyle glorious.

The same year that *Showboat* debuted on Broadway, *The Jazz Singer*, the first "talking film," reached American movie houses. The film starred Al Jolson; one of the movie's highlights was Jolson singing Berlin's "Blue Skies." Berlin made the transition from stage to screen easy enough. Songs of his such as "Let Me Sing and I'm Happy" and "Puttin' on the Ritz" came out of the movies *Mammy* and *Puttin' on the Ritz*, respectively. Berlin liked writing for Hollywood, but he wasn't sure that musicals on the big screen would endure. Even though it starred Al Jolson, *Mammy* lost money. Other Hollywood musicals suffered the same fate.

But their loss wasn't anything compared with what the rest of the country experienced a year earlier. In October 1929, the stock market crashed; thousands of formerly well-to-do Americans, including Berlin, practically lost their shirts. With the nation in economic collapse and the future of writing songs for Hollywood musicals in doubt, Berlin returned to New York at the close of 1930, not sure what his future held as a songwriter. It wasn't as bleak as he thought. Teaming up with Moss Hart, who wrote scripts, Berlin was back writing songs for the stage. Though the productions were less lavish, Berlin's songs retained their warm charm. *Face the Music* and *As Thousands Cheer*, both from the Berlin-Hart team, were hits.

Berlin could have stayed in New York and built on the success of his two most recent productions, but something pulled him back to Hollywood in 1934. Movies had become the best distraction Americans had during the Great Depression. People filled movie houses to escape the problems of lost jobs, bread lines, and bank foreclosures. The movies sent people into a temporary world of fantasy, providing emotional relief from the rigors of the real world.

Once again writing for the big screen, Berlin scored with *Top Hat*, the Fred Astaire and Ginger Rogers movie that opened in the summer of 1935. The film featured Berlin's "No Strings—I'm Fancy Free," "Cheek to Cheek," and its title song, "Top Hat, White Tie, and Tails." Other films followed, including the Hollywood screen version of "Alexander's Ragtime Band," which was less about the song and more about Berlin's life story. Berlin was fifty years old in 1938, the year *Alexander's Ragtime Band* was released, starring Tyrone Power and Sophie Tucker. For the film, Berlin also dusted off "Oh! How I Hate to Get Up in the Morning" for a scene in which Power created a program for the army not unlike what Berlin did with *Yip! Yip! Yaphank* twenty years earlier.

While Berlin bathed in success, another Berlin, this one a German city, boiled with war fever. Adolph Hitler had created a military monster in Europe, threatening the countries around Germany and making absurd accusations that threw fear in the hearts of anyone with a sane mind. Italy and Japan, both with fascist leaders and fanatical philosophies, harbored similar visions of war. Italy had already invaded Ethiopia; Japan was already in China. In Russia, Stalin salivated at the thought of restoring Russian sovereignty in Eastern Europe and beyond.

Berlin experienced firsthand the rising temperature in Europe. He sailed to England in September 1938 to look into business opportunities there. *Alexander's Ragtime Band* was soon to make its English debut, and he had plans to attend the premiere in London at the end of the month and then explore the possibilities of opening a publishing office in the city to better oversee foreign use of his songs.

When not in meetings or socializing, Berlin took in the talk on the street and in the pubs about the increasing belligerence of Hitler and the deepening threat of war. Berlin was deeply disturbed by what he heard. On the ship sailing back to the United States, believing, too, that war was inevitable, Berlin thought about writing a song that would capture how he felt about his own country as the possibility of war increased.

"On my way back, I tried to write a song that I felt at the time," said Berlin years later. "I remember finishing a chorus of a song called 'Thanks America' which I tore up because it was very bad. It seemed a bad editorial set to music." To write a patriotic war song when there wasn't a war—yet—might be taken the wrong way, with people believing that Berlin had thrown his support behind the war hawks in Washington. Berlin was no advocate of war.

On the other hand, perhaps a different kind of song, one that might have the desired result of reminding people how blessed America was, might be better. "I'd like to write a great peace song," he had told a reporter for the *New York Journal American* before he embarked for England, "but it's hard to do, because you have trouble dramatizing peace." He later told the *New York Times* that he found "it was too much like making a speech to music."

Berlin never did say what prompted him, exactly, to recall an old song he had written years ago called "God Bless America" and had stashed away, never knowing if it would see the light of day. Either he got the idea to resurrect the song on the ship heading back to New York, or else it had come to him after Ted Collins, Kate Smith's manager, had asked if Berlin had a patriotic song Smith could sing on her popular radio show to celebrate Armistice Day. Earlier in the year Congress had made November 11 a national holiday as a remembrance of the end of World War I and the price paid by its veterans. (Years later, Congress would rename the holiday Veteran's Day.) Berlin did not know if "God Bless America" might be salvageable, or if he or his secretary, Mynna Granat, could even find it. But after searching through old clippings and contracts, and other unused pieces of Berlin-penned music, Granat located the manuscript.

On October 25, Berlin looked at the words he had written so long ago and hummed the melody. The latter met with his approval, but the lyrics needed adjustment. The original chorus had the lines, "Stand beside her/And guide her/To the right with a light from above." Berlin later recalled the alteration that needed to be done. It was "obvious that the word 'right' had to be changed because in 1918 'guide her to the right' meant the right road. In 1938, there was a right and a left and it had a different significance." Berlin was referring to the political connotations that went with the terms "right" and "left." Preferring that "God Bless America" be void of any political slant, he changed "to the right with a light from above" to "through the night with a light from above." Berlin was also dissatisfied with another line in the song's chorus: "Make her victorious on land and foam." He had to admit, "on land and foam" was simply a poor piece of lyric. He changed it to "From the mountains, to the prairies/To the oceans white with foam," which sounded much better.

After making sure the song was properly scored, Berlin had Mynna Granat send it off to Ted Collins and Kate Smith, who needed to learn the song before her radio show on Thursday evening, November 10, the night before Armistice Day.

"Hello everybody!" Most of the radio audience in America in the late 1930s knew that voice, big and husky, just like the woman behind it. Kate Smith, singer and host of *The Kate Smith Hour*, which was broadcast during the evening, and *Kate Smith Speaks*, an afternoon talk show of hers, was not only the most popular radio personality in America in 1938, but she also rivaled First Lady Eleanor Roosevelt as the most popular woman in America. Her shows were most embraced by women, especially from rural areas. Smith's simple ideas about family and homespun values were squarely in line with theirs. Plus, Kate Smith looked and sounded like everyone's favorite aunt who always had a fresh-baked apple pie on the kitchen table.

War veterans liked Kate Smith, too. She still loved to sing patriotic songs and she never forgot them on the Fourth of July and other holidays. With the threat of war in Europe filling radio news reports, and because of her longtime connection to the Great War, manager Collins figured a rousing patriotic song that celebrated America on the eve of this new national holiday might make a splash on Smith's show.

Collins believed Berlin's "God Bless America" was a great piece of songwriting, ideal for what he had in mind for Smith's upcoming Armistice Day program. Smith thought highly of the song, too, but she wasn't sure it was right for her. In her memoir, *Upon My Lips a Song*, which was published in 1960, Smith wrote that "although I loved the song and its simple, effective lyrics, I was afraid it might not be accepted. I worried that it might be considered 'too patriotic.'"

Collins pressed Smith. According to the singer, Collins said, "Look, Kathryn, America needs a song right now. And I honestly think people expect you to come up with one." Smith knew Collins was probably right, and that he possessed what she called "an uncanny judgment of the mood of the public." Finally, she agreed to do the song.

That Thursday afternoon, November 10, during *Kate Smith Speaks*, Smith told her audience that she was going to premiere that evening on *The Kate Smith Hour*, a new song by Irving Berlin. Describing "God Bless America," she said the song was "timeless—it will never die—others will thrill to its beauty long after we are gone. In my humble estimation, this is the greatest song Irving Berlin has ever composed. It shall be my happy privilege to introduce that song on my program this evening, dedicating it to our American heroes of the world war. As I stand before the microphone and sing it with all my heart, I'll be thinking of our veterans and I'll be praying with every breath I draw that we shall never have another war."

Smith couldn't have set up the song any better. Her radio audience swelled with anticipation. Everyone, it seemed, tuned in that evening. Smith waited until the end of her show and then said, "And now it is my very great privilege to sing you a song that's never been sung before by anybody, and that was written especially for me by one of the greatest composers in the music field today. It's something more than a song—I feel it's one of the most beautiful compositions ever written, a song that will never die. The author: Mr. Irving Berlin. The title: 'God Bless America.'"

And with that Kate Smith made radio history and delivered a song she'd sing countless more times in her life. She wasn't entirely accurate in the song's preface. Berlin, of course, hadn't written "God Bless America" for Smith. He did, however, make important revisions to the song and at least had Smith in mind when he did. No matter, it was Kate Smith's song now.

"God Bless America" was a sensation. When the show was rebroadcast at midnight for West Coast audiences, the response was as overwhelming as it had been three hours earlier in New York. People called CBS expressing their instant love of the song and demanding to hear it again. Others wanted to know where they could purchase a recording of it. The next day Kate Smith and "God Bless America" was all anyone could talk about.

Berlin was as surprised as anyone by "God Bless America's" incredible success. But like any great songwriter, he wasn't entirely pleased with what he had written. He had a problem with the lines, "from the green fields in Virginia/to the gold fields out in Nome," as in Nome, Alaska. Back then, Alaska was not a state, but rather a territory, and the line felt forced, thought Berlin. So he changed it. No one missed it; in fact, few people today even realize that the line was part of the original "God Bless America," sung by Smith in the song's historic radio debut.

Smith sang "God Bless America" again on Thanksgiving a couple of weeks later, and the response to it was even greater this time. President Franklin Roosevelt said he enjoyed the song and Smith's rendition of it. Congress considered making it the nation's new national anthem, replacing "The Star Spangled Banner," something both Berlin and Smith objected to. Other artists rushed to add it to their repertoire.

Both Berlin and Smith were startled by the mania. Everywhere they turned, people were raving about "God Bless America." And it didn't stop. Smith recorded the song in 1939 and it immediately became a bestseller. Right on through the year, "God Bless America" was one of the most popular songs on the radio, in the new coin-operated "jukeboxes," and on victrolas in American homes from coast to coast.

Smith was compelled to sing "God Bless America" on nearly every one of her shows through December 1940 when a temporary ban on live radio performances, due to a disagreement between radio station owners and the musician's union, halted the streak. By that time, there wasn't a person in America who hadn't heard the song many times, including Woody Guthrie.

3

The people of Pampa celebrated the start of 1940 with muted enthusiasm. The year began pretty much the way it ended; there was no sudden change of circumstance or condition when January arrived. Jobs, especially good ones, were still difficult to find. The Depression dragged on, and despite the country's New Year's joy, the brief festive feeling that many Americans had was tempered by the somber reality that another year had dawned and yet there was only faint hope that the sun would shine brighter than it did the previous twelve months.

The dust was still there. The desolation that arrived with it a few years ago was also still there, though, as Panhandle towns went, Pampa kept its community pride stubbornly intact. There were some new buildings in town and some better roads. It had oil, after all; the derricks on the horizon and even those just on the outskirts of town brought at least the promise of renewed prosperity. But even if you were fortunate to have a steady job and a family not battered by the bad times, news of the war raging in Europe and the increasing possibility that America might be pulled into it dulled most everyone's spirit.

The weather was as gray as the country's mood. Uncommonly cold temperatures, and sad skies the color of slowly moving dust, prevailed that January, and people in Pampa stayed indoors when they could. Perhaps spring would bring better weather and a few good breaks for the town and the nation. But all that was down the road. Winter had settled in this part of Texas, and there was little else to do but wait it out.

Woody Guthrie, however, had no intention of waiting for anything. After the holidays, he grew more restless and bored. The way he figured, there was nothing in Pampa holding him there, not even his family. He needed to work, but the kind of work he wanted—singing his songs, playing music, maybe landing something on the radio like he had done in Los Angeles—simply hadn't materialized in Pampa. He had been spending his days playing with his kids, rolling on the floor with them, telling them stories and singing them songs. He took walks around town, talking with whomever cared to listen to whatever was on his mind at the moment. He went to the Pampa Public Library and read more magazines and paged through some more books and chatted up the librarian.

He kept thinking about a letter he received from his actor-friend Will Geer in New York. Geer thought Woody would find the big city to his liking, even suggesting that he might find work there as part of the cast of *Tobacco Road*. The play, which Geer starred in, was receiving enthusiastic reviews and showed no signs of ending soon. If nothing else, wrote Geer, there would be more opportunities to sing and play music there, with all the rallies and fundraisers going on, than there would ever be in Pampa. Woody had never been to New York. To go there would be an adventure not unlike what California had been a few years earlier. If he could find steady work—his kind of work—then he could send for his family, just like he did when he got settled in Los Angeles, and things would be all right again with Mary and him.

Woody read and reread the letter. The more he thought about New York, the better it sounded. Finally, he spoke to Mary about his plans. Mary could have guessed that her husband would be taking to the road soon. Even she could see how little

Pampa had offered him in the way of a steady job, if Woody was even capable of holding one. She had practically given up hope of ever having what she and her folks considered a normal marriage to Woody and a stable family life for her children. But with Woody gone, how would she and the kids get by? Who would care for them?

Woody told her that he would send money home just as he did when he was in Los Angeles, once he began earning it, and he would call for her just as soon as he established himself in New York. Mary had heard this story before, and back then, Woody did send for her and the kids. She resigned herself to the idea and reluctantly told her folks, who were not surprised.

Woody sold his old Chevy, which was on its last legs and would have never been able to make it to New York, to his brother Roy and his wife Ann, who lived in Oklahoma. With the twenty-five dollars his brother gave him for the car, Woody hitchhiked back to Pampa and bought a bus ticket to Pittsburgh; it was as far east as he could afford to go with the money he had. Packing a few pieces of clothes and his songbook, Woody kissed Mary and the kids good-bye and headed to the Pampa bus station.

The trip back east was cold and gloomy, the bus ride to Pittsburgh was tedious. Woody liked movement and conversation, two things that he always seemed to be doing, which was why hitchhiking came so natural to him. With thumb out he could walk and talk with whomever he was traveling with, and when he got a ride, he could talk some more, a new pair of ears to bend with stories and songs. It was one thing to hitchhike in the winter in California; the weather usually accommodated even the most down and out drifters. But in the winter in the midst of a cold spell in Texas, it was better to take the bus.

On the way to Pittsburgh, the bus Woody was traveling in made occasional stops—for new passengers, for fuel and food, for bathroom and stretching breaks. Wherever the bus stopped, there was a chance that if the radio was on or a jukebox was playing, the song "God Bless America" might come through the speakers. The song had become the sound of America, a national obsession, and it rubbed Woody the wrong way. He was no fool; he knew why the song was so popular. It provided comfort to people—in his view, a false comfort. If God was going to bless America, reckoned Guthrie, why was He waiting so long? The nation was in desperate shape. There were poor people barely able to survive. Honest, hard-working folk were denied the opportunity to take care of their families, through no fault of their own. A war was on the horizon.

Putting faith in God might soothe the nation's soul and give hope to the masses. But was it real hope? Why had God allowed the bankers to control the destiny of the country and take from it so, in the first place? Why did He permit cops to beat workers and strikers like they did in California and other areas of the country? How could He let kids go to bed hungry? Why was the weather free to ravish farms once owned by good people who were now rootless and on America's roads looking for a fair break and a new chance at a life worth living?

Guthrie had nothing personal against Irving Berlin, the song's author. As far as he knew, the fellow could turn quite a lyric and write melodies that stuck inside your head and stayed there. So many of Berlin's songs—"Always," "Cheek to Cheek," "Puttin' on the Ritz," "Easter Parade"—were all major pop-music hits in the 1920s and '30s, and undoubtedly Guthrie had heard "Alexander's Ragtime Band" and "Oh! How I Hate to Get Up in the Morning" at some point in his young life. No one could deny the songwriting genius behind these pop songs, including Guthrie.

It's unknown if Guthrie was aware that Berlin also penned "Supper Time," which he wrote in 1933 for his revue, *As Thousands Cheer*. The song was about black lynchings in the South—taboo material for pop songs back then—and it was sung by a black star at the time, Ethel Waters, in a racially mixed cast, for a white audience. "Supper Time" was a courageous song to write; being a Russian-Jew, which in the eyes of racists was almost as low as being black, and considering the amount of anti-

Semitism running rampant in America at the time thanks to the fiery speeches of Father Charles Coughlin and others, Berlin certainly took a big risk writing it and adding it to the revue.

"If one song can tell the whole tragic history of a race," wrote Waters years later, in her memoir, *His Eye Is on the Sparrow*, " 'Supper Time' was that song. In singing it I was telling my comfortable, well-fed, well-dressed listeners about my people." Though the song doesn't get the credit it's due, "Supper Time" predated jazz singing great Billie Holiday's far better known anti-lynching classic, "Strange Fruit," by more than half a decade. (Holiday's song debuted in 1939.)

And as for Kate Smith, she was as much a part of American pop culture as anyone was in the 1930s, harmless with her mushy stories aimed at Midwest housewives, and her middle-of-the-road radio program. Guthrie seemed to have nothing personal against her, either. At least there wasn't anything in his letters or journal entries from that time that indicated such. Together, though, Berlin and Smith created something that Guthrie just couldn't embrace. Though Berlin had clearly said he wrote the song to "wake up America," the way Guthrie heard it, "God Bless America" had become a sonic elixir, a numbing narcotic that placed the nation's destiny in a God that hadn't yet figured out what to do with the nation and had given people the idea that little, if anything, was wrong with their country.

Others felt the same way about the song, or at least found fault with it. Both left- and right-wing political fringe groups criticized "God Bless America," the former believing it sappy and jingoistic, and the latter incensed that such a song could be written by a Russian-Jewish immigrant and that it was now being sung by "pseudo-Americans." Berlin countered the song's detractors in an interview he did with the New York *Herald-Tribune* later in 1940. "All that I hope for 'God Bless America' is that it will continue to be popular, especially in these days when so many people feel a need for some vocal expression of their patriotism." That summer, when both the

Democratic and Republican Parties held their political conventions in preparation for the presidential election that fall, "God Bless America" was sung at each. So popular—and profitable—was the song that Berlin created the God Bless America Trust Fund, turning royalties from the song over to the Boy Scouts and Girl Scouts of America, thus preventing critics the opportunity to claim that he was making a profit on patriotism.

Ironically, in the late 1930s and early '40s, it was the liberal left—not the conservative or isolationist right—that was more apt to embrace "God Bless America" as its own. Years later, that would, of course, change. But in 1938, for instance, one of the first public performances of "God Bless America" after Kate Smith's historic debut, occurred at a general meeting of the National Conference of Christians and Jews in New York whose goal it was to fight for "justice, amity, understanding and cooperation among Protestants, Catholics, and Jews."

But at an isolationist peace rally at Madison Square Garden in 1941, the leader of the musical program, Robert Crawford, according to the *New York Times*, "asked the audience if it wanted to sing 'God Bless America.' He was drowned out by a chorus of 'No's' and said 'Let's drop it.' A spokesman for anti-war groups said it was regarded as an interventionist song." Charles Lindbergh was at that rally. He, too, refused to sing "God Bless America."

Certainly, mainstream America was willing to sing "God Bless America" and embrace it warmly. The song was incredibly popular with the average American as well as politicians not on the far edges of American political thought. Eleanor Roosevelt sang it and loved it. New York Mayor Fiorello La Guardia sang it and loved it. America's exciting new actress and singer, the young Judy Garland, who in 1939 starred in the Hollywood classic *The Wizard of Oz*, sang it and loved it.

The movement to make "God Bless America" the new national anthem, replacing "The Star Spangled Banner" lingered in 1940. Smith went so far as to record "The

Star Spangled Banner" on the flip side of her rendition of "God Bless America," and Berlin voiced his support for keeping America's national anthem "The Star Spangled Banner," reminding its citizens that "a national anthem is something that develops naturally through age, tradition, historic significance, and general recognition. There is no such thing as a new national anthem. We can't legislate one. They arise alone and stand the test of time. We've got a good national anthem. You can't have two."

Sometime during the trip from Pampa to New York, or perhaps it occurred to him earlier, or maybe even when he got to New York, Guthrie planned to write a song that answered "God Bless America" or at least told a different American story and described the country in a different way. Guthrie's idea of a good song was one that told the truth, and from what he had seen in his travels, "God Bless America" was nothing but a musical mirage. Over the past few years he had been on a songwriting binge, turning out dozens of tunes that mirrored what he had seen in Texas, Arizona, Oklahoma, and California. To sugarcoat a song was not in Woody's make-up. A good song was something that shed light on the way things were, or maybe the way things ought to be. The plight of the Dust Bowl victims, not just the people he knew personally from Pampa or Okemah, but those he met on the road and on the rails, had affected him greatly and he felt a responsibility to document their plight in song.

Some of his songs—"Do Re Mi," a sarcastic, edgy account of the plight of Okies as they tried to cross the California state line without the necessary money in their pocket, and the "dust songs" "Dust Storm Disaster," "Talking Dust Bowl Blues," "Dust Bowl Refugees," "Dust Pneumonia Blues"—all resembled musical newspaper stories and editorials. Guthrie loved writing such topical songs. He knew that a song could carry a story, teach a lesson, motivate some action, stir the soul, make a man have a change of heart. The power of a good song was unlimited. He recalled how people back in California reacted to his songs when he sang them at migrant camps and under railroad bridges. He could see how people reacted to "God Bless America" too.

And he figured he'd do something about that.

By the time the bus Guthrie was riding on pulled into Pittsburgh, the weather had turned colder and nastier. Guthrie was nearly broke and anxious to get to New York. Rather than scrounge some money to pay for another bus ticket or hop a freight train going east, Guthrie opted to hitchhike the rest of the way to New York City. He stayed in the bus terminal long enough to warm up and grab a bite to eat and then walked out into a western Pennsylvania snowstorm looking for a free ride and some good conversation.

Guthrie got a ride or two, but no one that had picked him up was going very far. On the outskirts of Harrisburg, the weather had grown worse. Blizzard conditions discouraged most drivers from venturing out on the highway, forcing Guthrie to stand shivering on the side of the road in the hard-falling snow and whirling wind with nary a car in sight. The wind had blown away his hat. This was a serious storm that Guthrie was stuck in, the worst in years in those parts. Guthrie was numb with cold and flirting with frostbite on his hands and feet; his fear of being left out in the storm heightened, and deservedly so.

Then Guthrie got lucky. Miraculously, a forest ranger had come along in the thick white swirl of snow, moving cautiously down the road. He picked up Guthrie, and "yanked me into the rear seat of his car full of steel traps, cameras, and all kinds of skins and feathers from wintering birds and varmits." The ranger took him to the home of his parents, who gave him hot clam chowder, something Guthrie had never tasted before. "I will never forget how good that hot clam juice tasted as it slid down my throat," recalled Guthrie later on. "I had really given up all hopes of ever seeing any human beings alive on this planet any more."

Feeling sorry for Guthrie, who must have looked pathetic, wet from the snow and hardly outfitted to deal with an East Coast blizzard, with no money and few possessions, a perfect portrait of a Depression era hobo, the forest ranger's parents let

---

Guthrie stay the night in order to thaw out and regain his strength. The next day, they gave him money for a bus ticket and had their son drive him to Philadelphia where he caught the next bus to New York.

It was still snowing when the bus pulled into Manhattan. They were fortunate to make it. Roads had been closed due to the storm; the strong winds caused large snow banks that had to be plowed before cars and such could pass. At the area airports, planes were grounded. Off the New Jersey coast, a tanker lost power and was dangerously drifting in open water. For Woody, it was a rude welcome to New York in the winter.

Guthrie got directions to Will Geer's apartment on 56th Street and Fifth Avenue and made his way there in the snow from the midtown bus terminal. Geer lived there with his wife Herta and their baby daughter, Katie. The apartment was clean and spacious—especially considering places Guthrie had lived—and it was warm. However, despite the size of the apartment, there wasn't a spare bedroom, so Woody would have to sleep on the couch.

The Geers were happy to see him, but surprised, too, given the treacherous weather conditions. Guthrie told them of being stuck on the Pennsylvania highway during the worst of the storm and how he thought he was going to freeze to death. But he was there in New York now, and ready to get to know the place. He had no money in his pocket and no plans, but he looked forward to whatever might come next.

Guthrie had arrived in New York in mid-February, so the weather remained cold and the days were short, while the sky yearned for a warm sun. For the next week or so, he spent most of his days writing lyrics to new songs on Herta's typewriter and figuring chords and melodies on her Martin guitar. He gazed out the apartment's windows and realized there was a whole new world out there to explore. Los Angeles had some skyscrapers and other tall buildings, but little of what New York had. Certainly nothing in New York compared with Pampa, except, of course, the people out of work and the constant talk of the war raging in Europe.

Will Geer was anxious for Woody to learn New York and get him to the point where he could get his own place. It wasn't that he had worn out his welcome so soon with the Geer family. But Woody was messy and not very considerate, and his sleeping on the family couch began to grow old after only a few days. During the evening, when Geer wasn't appearing onstage in *Tobacco Road* or else rehearsing, he showed Woody around the city. When Will wasn't free, Woody roamed New York, with Herta's guitar for company, usually winding up in a Bowery bar where he sang his songs and earned a few coins for his efforts.

Guthrie memorialized his sentiments about the Bowery in a song called "I Don't Feel at Home on the Bowery No More." The song spoke of hard times in Bowery flophouses—"The beds are so small that your feet touch the wall/The bedbugs so big that they swallow you whole/The lice are so thick that they cover the floor/I don't feel at home on the Bowery no more."

Another verse, however, praised the comfort of the Geer's apartment without admitting that he'd been staying there: "I seen an apartment on 5th Avenue/A penthouse, and garden, and skyscraper view/A carpet so soft, with a hard-wood floor/I don't feel at home on the Bowery no more." The lyrics were typed, but he had handwritten the words: "Written February 18, 1940, in the city of New York on West 56th Street in Will Geer's house, in the charge of his wine and the shadow of his kindness."

Geer had promised to introduce Woody to his New York friends. One event Geer was sure Woody would enjoy and make some friends at was "A *Grapes of Wrath* Evening," which was to occur at the Forrest Theater on 49th Street (now the

Eugene O'Neill Theater) the following month. Guthrie knew John Steinbeck, the author of the exciting new novel about the plight of the Okies. He had met him in California. Guthrie was an Okie himself, so Geer was sure that the singers and musicians set to play the show, which would benefit the John Steinbeck Committee for Agricultural Workers, would find Guthrie's authenticity quite exciting. Guthrie was added to the bill.

Geer also got Guthrie appearances on a couple of other upcoming benefits, and Guthrie was playing Bowery bars at night, earning some money to live on. Things seemed promising enough that Guthrie thanked Will and Herta for their hospitality, packed up his few things, and moved to a cheap boarding house a few blocks away on West 43rd called Hanover House. He asked Herta if he could borrow her guitar, a gift from her mother. Reluctant at first because of its sentimental value, not to mention that a Martin was a prized, well-crafted instrument, Herta sighed and lent it to him, knowing full well the only way Woody would survive in New York was with a guitar. Woody took the instrument, but left the case.

Woody booked himself into Hanover House on February 22. Filled with itinerants, merchant seamen, hustlers, and hookers, the Hanover House was a long way from the cleanliness and comfort of the Geers' apartment and Herta's good cooking, but it was closer to Guthrie's way of living. It also was all he could afford and he so he settled into the badly lit, sparsely furnished room, admiring the view of Times Square from his dirty window.

There is no evidence that Guthrie heard Kate Smith sing "God Bless America" on the radio those first couple of weeks in New York. But her show, *The Kate Smith Hour*, which aired weekly, was broadcast every Thursday evening in New York and the rest of America, and it still was the most popular radio show on the airwaves. February 22, the day Guthrie got his room at the Hanover House, was a Thursday. Radios everywhere were tuned to her show that night, and like on all her preceding

Kate Smith's recording of "God Bless America" was heard on radios everywhere in 1940, prompting Woody Guthrie to write "God Blessed America," which he later re-titled, "This Land Is Your Land."

programs since Armistice Day, 1938, Kate Smith sang "God Bless America" in front of a live radio audience.

Wherever the inspiration came from, on the following day, February 23, Guthrie decided to write his rebuttal to Berlin's "God Bless America." He preferred to write lyrics on a typewriter, but he hadn't asked Herta Geer to borrow that, too. Instead he put pen to a piece of three-holed binder notebook paper and in his best penmanship, wrote the words to a song he called "God Blessed America," which, later on, would come to be known as "This Land Is Your Land."

Guthrie didn't describe the song in any letters he sent to Mary that February. He didn't comment on it in any journal entry. To the best of anyone's knowledge, he didn't play it for Will or Herta Geer or perform it anywhere other than in his Hanover House room for an audience of one—himself. He may or may not have thought the song good enough to play for friends or fellow drifters at the local bar. He might have used the song simply to get the frustration he felt over "God Bless America" out of his system, and that was that. Whatever the case, a great American folk song had been written and no one knew about it.

Of the six verses he'd write, most of the first verse to "God Blessed America" became the most popular. It would also eventually become the song's chorus. "This land is your land, this land is my land" went the first line. The second originally read, "From the California to the Staten Island." It's probable that the word "the," which preceded "California," was simply a mistake and quickly crossed out by Guthrie, as indicated in the song's original manuscript. And at some point, Guthrie also replaced "Staten Island" with "New York island," so that the line later read, "From California to the New York island."

The third line, "From the Redwood Forest, to the gulf stream waters," remained untouched then, and later. Berlin had a similarly styled line in "God Bless America"— "From the mountains, to the prairies/To the oceans white with foam." Was Guthrie intentionally imitating Berlin to make a point? Or did the line come to him naturally? One way or another, there clearly was a lyrical connection to Berlin that Guthrie created with the line. As much as Guthrie disapproved of the overly patriotic intention of "God Bless America," he was impressed enough by the cleverness of the lyrics to mimic them.

For the fourth and final line of the song's first verse, Guthrie wrote "God blessed America for me." But at some point, probably a couple of years later, he drew a line through it and everywhere else in the song that the phrase appeared. With "God blessed America for me" deleted, Guthrie would write the line, "This land was made for you and me" as the closer, and, in the process, altered the entire attitude of the song.

"God Blessed America's" second verse—"As I went walking that ribbon of highway/And saw above me that endless skyway/And saw below me the golden valley, I said/God blessed America for me."—remained permanent, except for the "I said" in the third line, which was eventually removed, and the final line, which, as already stated, Guthrie later crossed out in pencil, most likely after he decided to retitle the song "This Land Was Made for You and Me." (As we will see, the song experienced other changes, including another title change, until Guthrie was satisfied with its message, or grew bored by it.)

In early 1940, Guthrie couldn't have claimed to have seen all of America. He'd been born in Oklahoma, traveled through Texas and most of the Southwest, explored much of southern, central, and northern California, and had bused and hitchhiked east to New York by this time. Few other American songwriters could boast such mileage by their late '20s. But there were still great swaths of the country Guthrie hadn't seen: the deep South and southern Atlantic seaboard, New England, the upper Midwest, the Rocky Mountain region, the Pacific Northwest.

Nevertheless, with the second verse to "God Blessed America" as well as the third—"I roamed and rambled and followed my footsteps/To the sparkling sands of her diamond deserts/And all around me, a voice was sounding/God blessed America for me."—Guthrie painted a majestic lyrical portrait of his country, even if he hadn't seen all of it yet. These lyrics represent some of most elegant and poetic Guthrie would ever write.

"God Blessed America" became overtly political in the fourth verse, and the mood of the song changed dramatically. What began as a veritable love song to America's vast natural riches and beauty became a defiant poke at capitalism and greed. Guthrie wrote: "Was a big high wall there that tried to stop me/A sign was painted said: Private Property/But on the back side it didn't say nothing—/God blessed America for me." Guthrie's America was not perfect, not like Berlin's. Amid the idyllic visions described in the earlier verses, there were man-made objects—ugly signs with uglier warnings—that corrupted the grand portrait, and, in the process, made the song more real and more meaningful.

The rhyming scheme was awkward and the meter bumpy, but the message was clear: some of America's most prized land and most precious resources were in the hands of a privileged few—not the masses—who jealously guarded what they owned with walls, signs, fences, and even guns. Over the years, as we'll see, this verse often was intentionally or unintentionally deleted by those afraid of its message or unaware of its existence, surfacing only when radical folksingers recalled in the late 1960s Guthrie's adamant leftist views. But in early 1940, fresh from his travels through California where he regularly witnessed labor strife and injustice and saw large plots of land owned by rich people who employed poor people to reap its harvest, these lyrics were both real and important to Guthrie.

"God Blessed America" continued with a fifth verse that, in effect, was a more guardedly optimistic description of the America Guthrie knew and gave the listener a brief respite from the criticism of the country that would follow in the sixth and final verse of the song. "When the sun come shining, then I was strolling/The wheat fields waving, and dust clouds rolling/The voice was chanting as the fog was lifting/God blessed America for me."

There is sun, and the wheat fields are robust and healthy, but there are also the dreaded dust clouds that are ready to roll over the image of agrarian allure. The dust clouds, of course, are a direct reference to the Dust Bowl and its consequences to the farmers that tend to the "wheat fields waving." Ominous in spirit, there is no beauty in dust, just destruction of the land and the families that work it. And perhaps Guthrie also meant the dust clouds to suggest a foreboding future. War was certainly on everyone's mind in early 1940. Walking around New York, he could feel the tension in the air and hear the talk in the saloons.

The sixth and final verse of Guthrie's "God Blessed America" was as barbed and as choppy as verse number four. "One bright sunny morning in the shadow of the steeple/By the relief office I saw my people/As they stood hungry, I stood there wondering if/God blessed America for me." Its message was unmistakable: the American utopia that Berlin wrote about didn't exist for all of its citizens. Though an immigrant who knew firsthand poverty and squalor, Berlin chose not write about it in "God Bless America." But Guthrie did in "God Blessed America." He too loved America— or at least the promise of America—and he had faith that it would right itself; but not blind faith. When he wrote "God Blessed America," Guthrie didn't whitewash the country's imperfections. Rather what he did was tell it like it is, as indicated by what he wrote at the end of the page: "All you can write is what you see."

Berlin had written both the music and the lyrics to "God Bless America." Guthrie could claim true ownership of only the lyrics to his song, since he used much of the melody to a song recorded by the Carter Family, "Little Darlin', Pal of Mine" as the musical inspiration for "God Blessed America." Guthrie routinely took melodies from other songs and, consciously or not, used them in his own songs. Woody once said when questioned about the possibility of another songwriter appropriating one of his song ideas. "Aw, he only stole from me; but I steal from everybody. Why I'm the biggest song stealer there ever was." He probably meant that in jest, but lifting ideas, particularly melodies, was something Guthrie did often. It was a practice not uncommon in American roots music before World War II, especially in folk and blues circles.

The Carter Family did its own borrowing. "Little Darlin', Pal of Mine" could be traced back to the old Baptist hymn, "Oh My Lovin' Brother." Later, Bob Dylan, a direct musical descendent of both the Carter Family and Woody Guthrie and the author of "Blowin' in the Wind," a landmark folk and civil rights song of the '60s, got much of its melody from an old slave song, "No More Auction Block." It has been written that Dylan learned about "No More Auction Block" from the Carter Family. And when Dylan wrote his tribute to Guthrie, "Song to Woody," he used the melody from Guthrie's own "1913 Massacre."

Legendary bluesman Robert Johnson, who died at age 27, a couple of years before Guthrie penned "God Blessed America," had taken liberty with the melodies from earlier blues greats Lonnie Johnson and Leroy Carr. And later, the slide blues guitarist Elmore James, whose main influence was Johnson, borrowed riffs and melodic lines from Johnson. Invention and reinvention, interpretation and reinterpretation, creation and revision, were all components of American roots music before World War II and the emergence of music-copyright watchdogs ASCAP and BMI.

Guthrie said little, if anything, about "God Blessed America" to Will Geer or anyone else when the two met at the Mecca Temple in Manhattan on February 25 for

Guthrie's first official onstage performance since coming to New York two weeks earlier. The show, a benefit for Spanish Civil War refugees, featured a wide range of singers and musicians. According to Guthrie biographer Cray, Guthrie was "added at the last moment and introduced as just in from Oklahoma, was buried deep in the program, between the workers' chorus singing Russian folk songs and classically trained baritone Mordecai Bauman." Guthrie sang yet another new song, this one about Franklin Roosevelt, called "Why Do You Stand There in the Rain."

Guthrie had gotten the idea for the song after reading an article in the *New York Post* that described the President's speech to the left-leaning American Youth Congress in Washington, D.C. The song was clever and funny and painted FDR as a pawn of war hawks and their push to get America into the European conflict. In a letter sent shortly after the benefit, Guthrie wrote, "The song New York has liked best so far that I made up is called 'Why Do You Stand There in the Rain?' " Clearly Guthrie was pleased with the song and the response it had received at the Mecca Temple, which gave him confidence that other songs of his might experience a similar New York applause.

For most New York intellectuals, Guthrie was an exotic species. Part of his attraction stemmed from the fact that there just weren't many other singing and topical songwriting Okies in New York at the time. When contemplating their Oklahoma exodus, few, if any, Okies thought it wise to head east, all the way to New York City. California was closer and warmer and the prospect of work there brighter. Most Okies were farmers; New York, to them, represented the epitome of the American urban metropolis—big buildings, long crowded avenues, factories, and swarms of people everywhere you turned, none of whom looked, dressed, or talked like them. Except for Woody Guthrie. He played the part well. Authenticity was prized among this crowd, and Woody Guthrie, in their eyes, was as Oklahoma Dust Bowl authentic as you could get in midtown Manhattan.

Guthrie spent the rest of the month and most of March at Hanover House. During the day, he walked to the New York Public Library on 42nd Street, where he read the newspaper, thumbed through books, and wrote more songs, including the wonderful "Talking Subway Blues," about his recent experiences in New York's underground trains. As good as the song was, it paled in comparison to "Jesus Christ," one of Guthrie's finer writing efforts that year. Guthrie had always been fascinated with the story of Christ. In his teens, he often painted portraits of Jesus and read whatever he could about him. Guthrie saw Jesus Christ as a philosopher, a venerable sage with the highest principles. "It ain't just once in awhile that I think about this man," Guthrie wrote, "it's mighty scarce that I think of anything else."

Being in New York City had clearly stirred his creative senses as indicated by the number of songs he was turning out. Hanover House looked out over Times Square, with its bright lights, urban noise, and endless activity, and he soaked it all in. During the evening, there were benefits to play or jaunts to the Bowery, guitar in hand. Nearly everywhere he went, he seemed to see a song.

Will Geer kept in touch with Woody; he was anxious for him to play the March 3rd benefit he and the rest of the cast of *Tobacco Road* had arranged with John Steinbeck. Calling the event "A *Grapes of Wrath* Evening" was a wise move; the film version of Steinbeck's recent best-selling novel had just opened in New York at the Rivoli Theater. It was directed by John Ford and starred Henry Fonda. Despite Woody's California relationship with Steinbeck and that he claimed never to have read the three hundred-plus page book, he did admit to seeing the film.

Guthrie was only too happy to play the Forrest Theater event. Geer told him that many of New York's most important activists would be there, as would other social and political protest singers like himself, folks that Geer thought he ought to know, including the wife of a miner whom everyone called Aunt Molly Jackson; the black songster, Hudie Ledbetter, better known as Lead Belly; and a tall, young, banjo-playing Harvard drop-out with an endless appetite for American folk music. His name was Pete Seeger. Will promised to introduce Guthrie to all of them and the others on the bill—a veritable who's who of New York folk music in those days.

The concert was presented by the "Theatre Arts Committee and Will Geer of the *Tobacco Road* Company." Another featured artist on the bill, Alan Lomax, helped with the musical production. Not only was Lomax a folk performer, but he also was a musicologist, recently named the assistant in charge of the Archive of American Folk Music at the Library of Congress. If that wasn't enough, Lomax also was the host of a CBS radio show, during which he played American folk music. Lomax already had most of the performers on the Forrest Theater bill as guests on his show, save Guthrie, who he had heard for the first time a few days earlier at the Mecca Temple benefit.

Guthrie showed up at the Forrest Theater wearing a pressed work shirt, a necktie, and a sweat-stained hat that he wore high on his head, along with the guitar he borrowed a couple of weeks earlier from Will's wife, Herta. Aunt Molly Jackson opened the benefit. Now living in New York, she had left rural Kentucky, her home, after she and her husband received death threats from mining officials who saw their strike activities as dangerous and subversive. Like Guthrie, she was the real deal. Feisty and fast with a pro-union song, Aunt Molly Jackson knew hard times in a different part of America than the one Guthrie came from. Appalachia was poor before the Depression hit. In the '30s, it hit rock bottom.

Woody Guthrie was next. He ambled out onstage, strummed his guitar a few times and then, as he was more and more prone to do when he had a captive audience, launched into an Okie-flavored monologue. Pete Seeger, who was standing in the wings recalled the memorable evening in an essay he penned on Guthrie in 1996: "He'd tell a joke and sing a song, and then he'd tell another joke. I remember him saying something like this: 'You know, Oklahoma is a very rich state. You want oil in Oklahoma, just go down a hole and get it. If you want coal, why, we've got coal in Oklahoma. Jus' go down a hole and get it. You want lead, we've got lead mines. Go down a hole and get you some lead. If you want food, clothes, groceries, just go in a hole . . . and stay there.' And he'd go right into 'Do Re Mi.' He must have been onstage for twenty minutes, more than any other member of the cast. Backstage, he was still singing, so I got to accompany him with my banjo. We got well acquainted that night."

The Forrest Theater audience loved Guthrie and clapped approvingly. Seeger didn't have as successful a night. By the time he got the chance to perform onstage, it was very late. Seeger wasn't even sure he wanted to perform, but his mentor and friend Lomax insisted that he do one song. "I wasn't entirely welcome," recalled Seeger; "it was a full program and there were a lot of dependable performers already part of it. . . . I remember walking out to the front of the stage and singing, very amateurishly, the outlaw ballad, 'John Hardy.' I got a smattering of polite applause."

After the show had finally ended, Lomax sought out Guthrie. With a personality that exploded with passion for American folk music, Lomax was like a kid in a candy store backstage, vividly and loudly proclaiming his excitement for what he had just heard. Later, he'd call the Forrest Theater concert a turning point in American folk music, the moment when, as Lomax biographer John Szed wrote, "the folk revival in America was born."

For Guthrie, too, the March 3 benefit was a life-changing evening. Not only did he turn in a memorable performance, but he also met Seeger, Lomax, Aunt Molly Jackson, composer Earl Robinson, Lead Belly, the Golden Gate Quartet, and others. By the end of the evening, Guthrie was the talk of radical New York and Lomax would invite him to travel to Washington, D.C. to make his first recordings. Things would never be same for him, or for American folk music.

Alan Lomax was on a mission. His burning desire was to capture the songs, the styles—the veritable soul—of authentic American folk and roots music. He had been born into this work. His father, John Lomax, was a respected and tireless collector of songs, mostly western and cowboy songs, for which he had a special fondness. From an early age, the young Lomax had accompanied his father on song collecting expeditions down South. He'd watch and listen, and then as he grew older, assist his father in searching out singers and songs and setting up the large tape machine that recorded right there in the fields or on the back porches and even in prisons, the indigenous sounds of American music.

For a nation with such a rich music heritage, it had done a meager job of preserving it, at least up until the twentieth century. There were only a handful of song collectors and trained musicologists working in America when John Lomax came into the picture. Unfortunately, most of them had all but ignored the African–American music tradition, especially the blues, the foundation of nearly all American pop music in the twentieth century, including jazz, rhythm & blues, rock and roll, and even hip-hop. The blues came out of the Deep South, a not especially welcome region for white musicologists from the North looking to preserve and celebrate the music of former slaves and old sharecroppers. It was easier and more productive to concentrate on the music of the Appalachian Mountains where the Anglo-Irish tradition had slowly been transformed into a homegrown American sound.

The Lomax father-and-son team had done much to preserve some of the nation's most important folk songs. But as Alan Lomax was just 24 years old in 1940, he considered his life's work—beyond the shadow of his father—to be ahead of him. Coming across Woody Guthrie was a big step in that direction and a most fortunate one, too. According to Guthrie biographer Ed Cray, Lomax was quite taken by Guthrie at the Forrest Theater. "Guthrie was not only singing folk songs, he was writing his own, songs that reflected Lomax's own belief in a 'New America,' a nation in which the working people expressed themselves through folk culture. Never one to stifle his enthusiasms, Lomax was frankly excited."

Since Guthrie had only been one of many performers at the Forrest Theater, playing just a few songs, Lomax hadn't a clue as to the extent of Guthrie's growing catalogue of songs, including one of his newest, "God Blessed America." Back in Los Angeles, when Guthrie and Lefty Lou had their radio program and were pressed for new material, Guthrie would write something, Lefty Lou would learn it quickly, and the duo would perform it on the air, often that same day. The catalogue of songs that Guthrie knew and kept in his head and his notebooks was large, and growing.

For some reason, Guthrie didn't choose to perform "God Blessed America" that night at the Steinbeck benefit. "Do Re Mi" had always gone over well wherever and whenever he performed it, and it fit nicely with his clever Oklahoma monologue that preceded it, so he opened with that song. However, he did do two new songs, "Why Do You Stand There in the Rain?" and "Talking New York Subway Blues," which was preceded by a hilarious account of Guthrie's first few days in the big city. Why didn't he play "God Blessed America" too? It's possible that Guthrie thought the song lacked a catchy prelude, or maybe he believed the song was not fully fleshed out. Whatever the case, Lomax hadn't any idea the song existed, and it would stay that way for a long time.

Guthrie and Lomax spoke backstage at the Forrest Theater, Lomax barely controlling the enthusiasm for his new folk music discovery. Lomax spoke quickly and excitedly and overwhelmed Guthrie with all that he wanted to do with him. He made Guthrie promise to be a guest on his radio show, *American School of the Air*, and repeatedly told Guthrie how much he wanted to record him down in Washington, D.C. Lomax asked Guthrie if he had any more songs he might sing for him, and Guthrie played "Pretty Boy Floyd," a tune about an Oklahoma outlaw who had turned into a folk hero in those parts. "Pretty Boy Floyd" only elevated Lomax's excitement. Before the evening ended, Guthrie agreed to meet Lomax in Washington, D.C. for a recording session and interview, even though he was uncertain of Lomax's overall intentions. Guthrie had come east to make some money and broaden his chances at becoming a folksinger and entertainer of some note. Going to Washington, D.C. seemed like the right thing to do.

Guthrie arrived in Arlington, Virginia—just across the Potomac River where Alan Lomax and his wife, Elizabeth, lived—a little more than two weeks after the Forrest Theater benefit. Alan insisted that during his time spent recording in Washington, D.C., Guthrie would be a guest at his house, which was just a couple of miles from his Library of Congress office. Guthrie accepted the offer, but instead of staying in the spare room, he preferred the couch. Alan and Elizabeth lived in a nice place, but Woody paid it no mind, preferring to be a messy guest much like he was at the Geers. If it was authenticity that people wanted from him, then Woody would give it to them straight and not bother to pretend his social habits were anything but unrefined.

On March 21, 1940, Woody Guthrie entered a recording studio for the first time, and with Lomax acting as producer, proceeded to empty himself of the many stories and songs he had been carrying around with him—traditional tunes, originals, and traditional/original hybrids. Guthrie recorded for three days at the Department of the Interior. When he was finished Lomax had captured a batch of Guthrie's best songs to date: "Do Re Mi," "Pretty Boy Floyd," "Goin' Down that Road Feeling Bad," and "So Long, It's Been Good to Know You," among others. "God Blessed America" was not one of them.

There were no plans to release the Guthrie songs Lomax recorded. Back then, neither the Library of Congress nor the Smithsonian had outlets to make their recordings commercially available. Lomax recorded Guthrie simply to get his music into the national archives and to preserve the rich collection of folk songs he knew.

Lomax also recorded conversations with Guthrie. What resulted was something of a living or oral history. The questions Lomax asked were often sophomoric and even silly, but Guthrie answered them anyhow, like he had done this many times before. Here was Lomax, the budding folk-music intellectual, schooled at the elite private school Choate and later at Harvard, asking questions of the singing Okie, with whom he had become unabashedly fascinated. All the time spent with his father, recording indigenous songwriters and musicians, and he had never come across anyone as intriguing as Guthrie.

What is particularly interesting about the Lomax sessions is the easy flow of Guthrie's monologues. He told stories about his early upbringing, his family, and his songs and did so with remarkably rich language and his often exaggerated Okie drawl. It was obvious that Guthrie had a way with language. Whether or not all this was a put-on for Lomax's sake is something that is today still debated by Guthrie scholars. But all it takes is one good listen to the Lomax Library of Congress recordings to realize that Guthrie, like Will Rogers before him, spoke like he grew out of the Oklahoma ground.

To cap off the visit, Lomax asked Guthrie to write out a small biography that

Lomax could use later on his radio show. Giving Guthrie a typewriter and sheets of white paper—two of his favorite things—Guthrie unleashed a stream of stories and anecdotes that, according to Lomax, read like literature. Some twenty-five pages in all, Guthrie wrote and wrote, as was his custom, words and sentences rolling from his brain to his fingers that quickly produced so many thoughts on a page. Lomax was stunned. Not only was Guthrie an authentic folk performer, storyteller, and songwriter, but he was also an accomplished writer. Lomax couldn't help but believe that Guthrie was his great American folk find.

Pete Seeger, the lanky young folksinger that Guthrie had met at the Forrest Theater benefit, also worked in Washington, D.C. and was a good friend of Alan Lomax. It was Alan who insisted that Seeger be part of the Forrest Theater program, and though his performance was memorable for all the wrong reasons, Seeger was thrilled to be in the company of such singers and musicians and especially to have met Guthrie, who, like Lomax, he considered a rare folk music talent.

Seeger, too, had a folk music pedigree. His father, Charles, had been a professor of American music at the University of California in Berkeley and young Pete was exposed at an early age as to how American history and culture was reflected in song. Originally, Seeger set out to become a journalist and enrolled at Harvard, but his increasing fascination with folk music and the five-string banjo led him to drop out of college in 1938 and take a job with Lomax and the Library of Congress.

Lomax had invited Seeger over to his house when Guthrie was there. He thought the two might become friends, and they did. Seeger, in fact, had known about Guthrie before meeting him backstage at the Forrest Theatre. Seeger had met Will Geer in 1938 in New York, just before Geer had moved to California. Geer taught an acting class at Stage for Action, a small New York arts group and Seeger had wandered in, having just moved to New York. The two became friends and corresponded after Geer headed west. While in California Geer mailed Seeger a copy of Guthrie's mimeographed collection of songs, *On a Slow Train to California*. Seeger thought the songs especially interesting and the concept clever, since he knew the origin of the collection's title. According to Seeger, "*On a Slow Train to California* . . . was a takeoff on a book of jokes back then called *On a Slow Train through Arkansas*. They used to sell it on railroad trains and in stations to people who got bored with traveling. Woody's little book of songs and jokes cost 25 cents."

Where Woody Guthrie was rough-edged, Pete Seeger was polished. Where Woody was small—five-foot-four or so—Pete Seeger was tall, well over six feet. While Woody perfectly represented the look of the wandering musician with rumpled clothes and hair and guitar in tow, Pete portrayed a picture of poise and intellect. The two couldn't have been more different in background, education and style. Yet, over time, they became good friends, road mates and band mates, sharing box cars and stages, and ending up the two most important American folk music figures of the twentieth century.

Politically, Pete Seeger rejected the privileged status that came with his family's lineage. He could trace descendents all the way back to the Mayflower. He had a Puritan heritage and work ethic and a New England upbringing. He could have chosen an easy road in life. Instead, Seeger embraced socialism and music, and sought to see how the two could improve the world. He was eager and idealistic and spoke incessantly about the need for change in America and the value in having folk music play a part.

Woody was puzzled by Seeger. For starters, Seeger was a few years younger than Guthrie, having just recently turned twenty-one—Guthrie was twenty-seven when they met. Seeger hadn't traveled much; nearly all he knew about life came from reading books. According to Guthrie, "He doesn't look at girls, he doesn't drink, he doesn't smoke, the fellow's weird." The common denominator in their relationship was music, and it didn't hurt that Seeger saw Guthrie as a mentor, much like he saw Lomax. To Pete, Woody was the living embodiment of all that was exciting about

American folk music. Alan Lomax felt the same way.

It was Lomax who solidified the friendship between Seeger and Guthrie and the musical bond they'd share from then on when he suggested the two of them work on a project that would come to be called *Hard Hitting Songs for Hard Hit People*. Lomax had Guthrie, with Seeger's help, annotate a collection of American social and political protest songs. The job was way out of the reach of Guthrie, who had certainly demonstrated a penchant for writing and knew a lot about folk songs, but did not possess the scholarly chops or the research acumen to assemble a series of fully constructed essays. Guthrie wrote from the heart, with a colloquial cadence that was entirely improvised. Facts were not as important as feeling. Seeger provided what he could, drawing on his Harvard experience. But as song collections go, it was truly a work in progress.

Seeger and Guthrie worked on *Hard Hitting Songs for Hard Hit People* (Woody's title) for a number of weeks, often working at the Library of Congress, with Lomax playing recorded folk songs and Guthrie reacting to them on his typewriter. Seeger tried to fill in the gaps where he could. It was an unbalanced piece of work, full of holes and partially completed ideas and anecdotes. Seeger, for one, was not especially proud of the work. Guthrie, on the other hand, felt otherwise. He loved sitting and pecking away on the keys to a typewriter, rarely running out of things to write. One thing Woody had was something to say, and although it often rambled out of him, as evidenced in the writing he did for *Hard Hitting Songs*, his narrative style was irresistible and original.

Lomax thought *Hard Hitting Songs*, written in an authentic folk vernacular, was ready for publication, but no book publisher was interested in releasing it, despite the fact that the Foreward was written by John Steinbeck. In it, Steinbeck described Guthrie: "Woody is just Woody. Thousands of people do not know he has any other name. He is just a voice and a guitar. He sings songs of a people, and I suspect that

Woody Guthrie and Pete Seeger, ca. 1943.

he is, in a way, that people. Harsh voiced and nasal, his guitar hanging like a tire iron on a rusty rim, there is nothing sweet about Woody, and there is nothing sweet about the songs he sings."

For years, the manuscript for *Hard Hitting Songs for Hard Hit People* lay dormant. If, during the 1940s, publishers thought the songs too incendiary, with their socialistic themes and working man ethos, publishers in the 1950s, a more politically conservative era with McCarthyism and the Cold War in play, weren't about to touch it either. Over time, pieces of the manuscript were misplaced or lost, further lessening the chances of it ever being published. But then, miraculously, a carbon copy of the complete manuscript surfaced, and Irwin Silber, founder of the folk music magazine called *Sing Out!*, was charged with giving it life. Silber organized the songs, wrote the Publisher's Foreward and included Depression era photographs by Dorothea Lange, Walker Evans, Ben Shahn, and others. Finally *Hard Hitting Songs for Hard Hit People* was published in 1967.

After his stint in Washington, D.C., Guthrie returned to New York. Lomax, ever the idea man when it came to promoting folk music, next asked Guthrie to be on a radio show produced by Norman Corwin called *The Pursuit of Happiness*. Guthrie performed on the show in late April and was paid fifty dollars for singing just one song. Guthrie couldn't believe his good fortune. Back in California, during the best of times on the air, he and Lefty Lou were paid twenty dollars a week for doing two shows a day, and they had to split that. Fifty dollars for one show and one song was certainly something Guthrie could get used to.

Guthrie's good luck continued. RCA Records approached Lomax, whom the company considered an expert in American folk music, with the idea of him releasing an album of folk songs, in part to capitalize on all the attention first the book and then the movie, *The Grapes of Wrath*, was receiving. Lomax had doubts about his voice, which he didn't consider strong, and politely refused the invitation to make an album. He suggested to RCA's R. P. Wetherald that he record Guthrie instead. In late April 1940 Guthrie entered a recording studio in New York to record his first collection of songs for commercial release for RCA. A second session occurred in early May. Guthrie recorded thirteen songs, all of them with a Dust Bowl theme, which is what Lomax suggested and RCA wanted. Guthrie recorded "I Ain't Got No Home," "Do Re Mi," "Pretty Boy Floyd," "Vigilante Man," and one of his newest numbers, "Tom Joad," an amazing musical narrative of the lead character in Steinbeck's *The Grapes of Wrath*. Guthrie had penned the song for the session, apparently at RCA's request. The long, 17-verse epic was set to the melody of the Carter Family's outlaw song, "John Hardy." So long was the song that RCA had to break it into two tracks, "Tom Joad—Part One" and "Tom Joad—Part Two."

Dust Bowl Ballads, as the RCA collection would come to be called, would be the most successful and critically acclaimed recording Guthrie ever made. As music historian Dave Marsh wrote in the liner notes to a 2000 release of *Dust Bowl Ballads*, "So these songs are not only historical; they are history itself, history being that which links present to future. That is why, sixty years after they were recorded, Woody Guthrie's *Dust Bowl Ballads* still deserve their place among the greatest American stories and songs."

Dust Bowl Ballads would come to influence a whole corps of Guthrie-styled singers and songwriters, including Seeger, Bob Dylan, Phil Ochs, and Bruce Springsteen. As much impact as the songs had, so did the collection's original liner notes, penned by Guthrie. Once again, Guthrie's flair for language flourished in the words he used to describe the roots of the songs and the rationale for singing and recording them. It was beautiful, homegrown prose, plain and simple and wonderfully descriptive. "This business of such awful and terrible dust storms," wrote Guthrie, "so black you can't see your hand before your eyes, or a light in your room, or a dollar in your pocket, or a meal on your table—that's what's new, that's what the old timers can't figger out . . . and you might be able to stand the dust, if it was dust alone, 'cause you're made out of dust, and can take a lot of it for a little while, or a little of it for a long time, but when things just sort of fly loose and all happen at once, like an old clock, why—everything goes haywire. . . ."

For his services RCA paid Guthrie three hundred dollars, an astounding sum for someone who just a few months earlier was basically broke. Guthrie sent some of the money back to his wife Mary in Pampa, and then promptly purchased a new car. Despite his recent spate of good luck and high earnings, Guthrie was growing restless again. He had been on the East Coast, in New York and Washington, D.C., for four months and he was ready to run again. Clearly, there was something in his soul that prevented him from taking root in a town or in a job or anything that might curb his wanderlust or freedom to roam whenever the desire struck him. He moved and rambled when he felt the road tugging at him, and there was no person or prospect that could stop him.

Pampa was on Guthrie's mind after he bought his car, a 1939 Plymouth. Looking for companionship on his planned trip west, Guthrie convinced Pete Seeger to drive to Texas with him. Seeger, thirsty for adventure and the kind of experience that Guthrie wrote about in his songs, jumped at the chance to spend more time with Guthrie and to see America. It was a quick trip. Guthrie and Seeger spent but a few days in Pampa with Mary and the kids, playing music with Matt Jennings and sharing a drink or two with his in-laws. Then it was back on the road for the two folksingers, winding up in New York City just in time to attend the national convention of the American Communist Party in Madison Square Garden.

So much speculation has been written in biographies and essays as to whether or not Woody Guthrie was a card-carrying communist. It's been grappled with at academic conferences and presented in lectures and on the op-ed page. Woody was often non-committal. He'd say something to effect that he didn't know what it meant, exactly, to be a communist, but that he'd been in the red all his life. According to Seeger, "Woody considered himself a Communist. Was he a member of the Party? Not really. The Party turned him down. He was always traveling here and there. He wasn't the kind of guy you'd give a Party assignment to. He was a valuable fellow traveler."

There is no doubt that he supported the party platform. He wrote for Communist periodicals and sang at Communist rallies. In 1940, even after Russia had signed its non-aggression pact with Germany and had invaded Poland, he still supported its policies, though he had grown increasingly skeptical about Stalin's overall intentions. Yet, there is no evidence that Guthrie was an official member of the Communist Party. There is, however, plenty of evidence that he thought like one and wrote like one and probably would have been one had he owned even a tiny bit of personal affinity for organizations and committees, other than those of American unions, which, at the time, certainly had their share of socialists and communists.

That September he wrote to Lomax and expressed dismay at the criticism he received in the New York media for his communist connection, whatever it may have been. "They called me a communist and a wild man and everything you can think of but I dont [sic] care what they call me. I aint [sic] a member of any earthly organization. My trouble is I really ought to go down in the morning and just join everything. I registered in California as a democrat and changed it one day to a progressive just because I was passing the lady[']s house. I done that on a dare more or less from a girl I was out walking."

Despite the controversy, Guthrie's presence in the New York folk community grew. In leftist intellectual circles, the communist hoopla that swirled around Guthrie only fortified their positive view of him. In the meantime, throughout 1940, he continued to sing at benefits and parties. He played Bowery bars when he had nothing to else to do. And he did more radio dates, appearing again on *Pursuit of Happiness* as well as on a new Alan Lomax program, *Back Where I Come From* and another CBS show, *We, the People*. Some of his most memorable radio performances came on WNYC's weekly program, *Adventures in Music*. He even got an endorsement deal with Model Tobacco and briefly became the host of its radio show, *Pipe Smoking Time*.

On all of these programs, Guthrie came across an original Okie in the big city, a dusty troubadour full of stories and songs and dry humor. He was paid well for his services, often making three hundred dollars a week. With all that money coming in, anyone looking closely at his financial success might have grown skeptical of the down and out Okie persona that Woody cultivated. No one bothered to check, though. Woody Guthrie was a fine entertainer and a prolific songwriter and came to New York with the right kind of cultural credentials. He had what Pete Seeger later described as "the genius of simplicity."

He also had real money in his pocket, which is why that fall he decided to send for Mary and the kids, buy another new car, this time with only minimum down and the promise of monthly payments, and rent an apartment in upper Manhattan. For a couple of months, Mary and the kids enjoyed their new life in New York City. Woody took Mary to parties and social events where he'd often wind up playing a few songs, or else the Guthries threw their own get togethers and invited the likes of Lead Belly, Alan Lomax, Seeger, and a couple of recently arrived bluesmen from the Carolinas, Sonny Terry and Brownie McGhee.

However, as quickly as this new life started, it ended. Despite the money he was making, he grew to hate his radio job with Model Tobacco, mostly because of the way they tried to control his creative output. Eventually, Woody had had enough. In late December 1940 he told Mary it was time to leave New York. She was shocked, but she did what she was told. She packed up the kids and their things and just like that, the Guthries were gone. Good-bye New York, hello (again) Los Angeles.

Woody took his dazed family on a zig-zag car trip back to southern California. They wound up living in Pasadena, a pleasant community north of downtown Los Angeles, next door to Woody's old writing and radio friend, Ed Robbin. The house next to Ed's home was vacant, which the Guthrie family promptly inhabited, sometimes paying rent, sometimes not. Woody went back to doing what he enjoyed most: playing music in migrant camps, and talking and telling stories to families from Oklahoma and Texas who had come west to California looking for a new start.

On the outside, Woody was the same old Woody. Most people saw him as a kind soul, one who truly cared about their sorry condition and used music—simple, down home, old timey-style music—to heal their hurt and inspire their heart. He was a friend who understood, and he turned that understanding into songs that reflected the way they felt. If nothing else, he made them laugh with his jokes and tales and remember better times with his songs.

On the inside, however, the story was different. When angry, Guthrie's temper spiked, and he was not averse to getting roaring drunk when the spirit moved him. The liquor only made the temper burn hotter. Woody seemed torn by his stature back east as a folk-singing, blue collar philosopher and radio personality, and his need to stay connected to the road and the people he wrote his songs about. The drinking only made things worse. Mary and the kids saw him grow apart from them, and they were afraid of the outcome. Woody sensed it too. Rather than confront the issue head on, he lost himself in a world of writing: songs, letters, journal entries, more songs, and even a book about his life, something that Alan Lomax suggested back in Washington, D.C. It was as if by writing and setting down his thoughts, he released some of his inner angst, providing himself with much needed relief. Guthrie wrote that the act of writing was "a conversation with yourself . . . just a quiet way of talking to yourself." Of which he was doing plenty.

With Woody in an agitated state, the Guthries were soon back on the road in late spring 1941, this time heading north to Portland, Oregon where the federal government was constructing the Grand Coulee Dam and officials there were making a movie about it. The director of the film, Gunther Von Fritsch, had visited Guthrie in Los Angeles after the songwriter had been recommended to him as the one who ought to write the songs for the film's soundtrack. However, by most accounts, no official offer was made to Guthrie to join the project during that meeting.

Intrigued by the dam and curious about the film, Guthrie nonetheless packed his family into their car and drove north like gypsies on an endless journey. He got the job, and that meant much needed income. Yet Mary worried about how all this instability would affect her children. Where, exactly, was home? How would they ever make friends? Where would they go to school? When Mary brought up these concerns, often they'd lead to loud quarrels with her husband that frightened the kids. The Guthrie marriage was badly strained and the domestic family life that Mary wanted with Woody, or thought she did, was badly fractured. The end to both was near.

All the traveling proved to be hard on Guthrie's family, but as a songwriter Guthrie was about to enter one of his most prolific songwriting periods ever. The month Guthrie spent in the Pacific Northwest resulted in another notebook of songs, some of them Guthrie classics—"Pastures of Plenty" and "Roll on Columbia"—among them. Inspired by how big and complicated the construction of the dam turned out to be, Guthrie grew excited by turning it all into song. With a typewriter as well as a chauffer and car at the ready for his use, Guthrie turned out, on average, a song a day. In all he wrote twenty-six songs; some of them were brand new compositions, others were adapted from earlier songs he had written, or restructured with new themes. The work had earned Guthrie $266 in government pay.

Despite the sense of satisfaction that Guthrie enjoyed after picking up his pay-check, two other problems cut short any celebration. First, the Guthrie car was repossessed. When he bought it in New York, he agreed to pay it off monthly, which Guthrie either forgot about or ignored. Now the family was without transportation. Second, Mary announced to Woody that she thought it best if they parted ways.

Woody now wanted to go back to New York after getting a letter from Pete Seeger about a folk singing group he had formed and how he wanted Woody to be a part of it. Woody was excited by its prospects. But Mary knew her children would be hard-pressed to make another journey across country, ultimately winding up back in New York . . . for who knew how long this time?

Mary realized the marriage was over, and Woody probably did too. Mary also knew that her primary responsibility was to her children and that her husband would never be the settling-down type, no matter how much she wanted him to, or how much he tried. She resigned herself to accepting the fact that she would be alone with her kids and began making plans to go back to Texas where she'd finally make a home for Teeny, Sue, and Bill. Woody agreed that her plan was a good one. And then Woody was gone again, destination New York City.

That Guthrie spent the past few months traveling the country meant that he had seen much of the natural beauty he had written about a year and a half ago in "God Blessed America." He had been through the redwood forests, had seen pretty much of all California, had marveled at "that endless skyway." And yet still the song sat in one of his notebooks, buried amongst the other songs waiting for their chance to be sung and heard. With all the moving around he did, it's a small wonder the song never got lost to history. Yet, as messy as Guthrie could be with his personal hygiene and small amount of material possessions, he treated his notebooks and songbooks with care. "God Blessed America" was neatly written on loose-leaf paper. It was numbered—page 178—suggesting it was in a notebook with plenty more songs. Guthrie even thought enough of the song to at one point to attach hole reinforcements to the paper, so the sheet wouldn't tear away. For a largely unkempt individual, Guthrie kept his song notebook in remarkably tidy order.

In late spring and early summer of 1941, the war in Europe had grown larger and bloodier. France and the Low Countries were in Nazi hands. England had been brought to its knees during the Battle of Britain, its cities badly damaged by German air power. British forces in North Africa suffered a string of defeats at the hands of one of Germany's best generals, Erwin Rommel. And in the North Atlantic, epic sea battles raged.

America had created a lend-lease program with England, offering ships and other war material to support her in the war effort. President Roosevelt called what Germany was embarking on, militarily speaking, a quest for "world domination," and sought support for what he believed was inevitable: war with Germany. America was split on whether or not to go to war. Interventionists believed it was the right thing to do. Isolationists believed otherwise. In newspapers and on the radio, in speeches and at rallies, both sides sought to sway the country, each rallying celebrities, civic leaders, and politicians to help make their case.

On the other side of the world another tempest was blowing. The aggressive and often brutal policies of Imperial Japan had prompted Roosevelt to divide his attention between Europe and Asia. China had been overrun by the Japanese army; in the takeover of the country, hundreds of thousands of innocent civilians had been slaughtered. In mid-1941, Japan was threatening nearly every other country in Asia that had precious natural resources or provided strategic geographic vantage points from which to launch further acts of aggression. It was also beginning to plan an attack on U.S.-held Hawaii, home to the American Pacific fleet. Japanese military brass believed that if it could knock out the American aircraft carriers and battleships while in port in a major surprise attack, the United States could do little to interfere with Japan's imperialist ambitions. A date of infamy was fast approaching.

Americans looked for comfort wherever they could, and once again, they found it in "God Bless America." In fact, if anything, the patriotic song had grown in popularity. Kate Smith made it her hallmark song, singing it on her radio show, but also in live appearances, patriotic rallies, and in concert. And now, others had embraced the song as well. Marching bands, choirs, other singers—they all felt the song's patriotic pull and included it in their repertoire.

Why Woody Guthrie had not resuscitated his response to the song at that point remains a mystery. Surely he would have gotten a reaction anywhere he had sung "God Blessed America." Guthrie was certainly not afraid of controversy. As a songwriter, he thrived on it. Had he simply forgotten about the song? He had written so many since February 1940 that it was entirely possible that the song on page 178 was, in his mind, just another song in his notebook. So, in the middle of 1941, what would turn out to be his most famous song was nestled among dozens of other writings and lyrics that Guthrie kept in a notebook that by this time was bulging.

Woody hitchhiked his way back to New York just in time to read in the newspapers about the most staggering war news in the first half of 1941. Germany, which had signed a non-aggression pact with the Soviet Union, nearly two years earlier, had invaded its former ally on June 22. The European war now had two fronts: Eastern and Western. In the end, it would be this one fateful decision by the madman Hitler that had more to do with the eventual defeat of Nazi Germany than anything save the U.S. entry into the war, which would occur by year's end.

It was shocking to think that Hitler would cross Stalin so and risk the wrath of such a potentially fierce enemy. The Soviet Union lacked the war material that flowed from German factories and the spit-polish precision of its war machine. But it had millions of men under arms who would be scratching and clawing for the Motherland's survival. It also had another thing: weather. Brutal winter weather. The Germans would find out just how brutal in a matter of months.

Ever since Stalin signed the non-aggression pact with Hitler, American leftists were in a quandary. How could they support the political policies of a nation that shook hands with the fascist Nazi monsters and looked the other way as the German army began its conquest of Europe? Some American socialists and even communists grew disillusioned with the proletariat propaganda coming out of Moscow. Others, like Guthrie and Pete Seeger, tried to see a bigger picture in the non-aggression pact. Both folksingers had remained anti-war. Things now changed.

Guthrie decided to come back to New York after Seeger invited him to become a member of his loosely knit folk group, the Almanac Singers. But he had arrived a month too late to take part in the group's biggest performance: Madison Square Garden. That May the city's Transport Workers' union had called a strike and produced a massive rally at the Garden, Manhattan's largest venue, holding up to 20,000 people. When the union went looking for musical entertainment, one of the acts it contacted was the Almanac Singers. Banjo-playing Seeger and the rest of the group, which included singers Millard Lampell, Lee Hays, and Pete Hawes, were thrilled with the chance to sing to so many people, but they were apprehensive as well. The Almanac's largest audience up to that point added up to a few dozen friends, and they were listening in small clubs or Greenwich Village lofts. The Garden stage was many times bigger than the places the Almanac Singers were used to singing their radical songs. What if things didn't go so well?

As it turned out, Pete Seeger and the Almanac Singers were a hit. Opening with "Talking Union," a funny, yet hard-hitting number that celebrated the virtues of union solidarity, the Almanac Singers used the power of song to celebrate the power of the union and to inspire it to stay the course and win the battle for better pay and working conditions. The union men in the audience appreciated the musical support. Their families listened and clapped their hands. Seeger and the rest of the group, which had been together only a short time, had proved their worthiness. People listened and got something from the songs. That was the point, more than money or fame, of which there was none or little. Inspire people through music, that's what the Almanac Singers hoped to do.

Seeger was glad to see Guthrie, who, according to Seeger, greeted him by saying, "Well, [I] guess we won't be singing any more peace songs, will we?" Up until that point, the Almanac Singers had both anti-war and pro-union songs in their repertoire. But with the sudden turn of events in the war in Europe, with Russia now the victim of Nazi aggression and the worker's revolution there in danger of being destroyed by fascism, Seeger and the rest of the Almanac Singers had the same change of heart that Guthrie did.

Seeger thought Guthrie would measurably add to the group. With his songs and his wit, plus his New York reputation, Guthrie, thought Seeger, would give the Almanac Singers more clout and draw for the group more performance dates. As for Guthrie, he was glad to be back in New York and had plenty of stories to share with Seeger and his other friends, not to mention the new batch of songs in his notebook. Without having to worry about Mary and the kids, he would be free to build on what he had earlier in New York and he was ready to get started.

But being in a group wasn't natural for Guthrie, especially a group in which he wasn't absolutely in charge. Out in California with Lefty Lou, there was no doubt who ran the show, and when he played with Will Geer and others, they were sure to take their musical cue from Guthrie. He'd have to go all the way back to the Corncob Trio with his brother-in-law Matt Jennings to recall how it felt to be simply one of the boys. And the Almanac Singers weren't the kind of musicians he sang and played with in Texas, where everyone had grown up on hillbilly music and cowboy songs. Woody aside, and with the exception of Lee Hays, who at least was from Arkansas, the Almanac Singers were a cast of young, East Coast intellectuals, who hadn't tasted dust in their mouths and who knew about the Dust Bowl and the travails of the Okies in California only by what they read and what Guthrie told them.

Before Guthrie arrived, in addition to playing Madison Square Garden, the Almanac Singers recorded their first album, *Songs for John Doe*. On it was anti-war

The Almanac Singers (l to r): Woody Guthrie, Millard Lampell, Bess Hawes, Pete Seeger, Arthur Stern, and Agnes 'Sis' Cunningham, 1941.

songs and pro-red ones. No record company would release it, so the Almanacs released it themselves. The album's pacifist nature made it especially controversial after Germany had invaded the Soviet Union. Only the staunchest pacifists were still calling for peace. It was one thing to sing for peace when Stalin signed the non-aggression pact with Hitler. To pacifists, non-aggression was good, even though the deal Stalin cut was with the devil himself. But now that the Soviet Union was betrayed, all bets were off. It was time to fight.

The Almanacs had based much of their live repertoire on an anti-war message. Now, Mill Lampell and Seeger, the two principal tunesmiths in the group—along with the new guy, Guthrie—began writing a brand new kind of song, one they never dreamed of writing just a few months earlier. Now the songs were fight songs about defeating the Nazis. Hitler and the fascist machine provided plenty of songwriter fodder. All the Almanacs had to do was open the page of any newspaper and they'd find plenty of anti-Hitler song ideas just begging to be put to music. Guthrie was the master of the topical song. He could write two or three a day, and often did. Seeger tried to write his share, but he simply didn't have Guthrie's gift.

The Almanacs, being devout leftists, also continued to sing about American workers and unions. It was a grand year for strikes. Everywhere you turned, it seemed as if a strike was in process. Guthrie biographer Joe Klein wrote that there were more union strikes in 1941 than in any other year since 1919; some two and a half million workers walked picket lines that year. All of this would change once America finally entered World War II. But until the Japanese attacked Pearl Harbor on December 7, 1941, there were plenty of striking union workers willing to hear the Almanac Singers play their songs of union solidarity, and those workers that weren't striking, welcomed their musical support nonetheless.

Guthrie's union songwriting topics shifted as he focused on more urban labor issues than those suffered by fruit pickers and Okies. Back East, where he now was, steel workers were striking for better pay and safer working conditions. Subway workers in New York City were clamoring for the same. Miners in Appalachia sought to improve their working conditions. On the other side of all of these struggles were company owners and corporations that loathed the idea of workers' rights and increased benefits. They tried to paint striking workers in a portrait that was red all over.

Guthrie had plenty of new material to put to music, and when the Almanac Singers decided to hit the road to provide musical inspiration for the union men (and women, one of their most popular songs was "Union Maid") in their struggle with the boss men, Guthrie was in his element. In California, he had seen firsthand how a good song could get a crowd of striking workers going. He loved that power of the protest song, and he and the Almanac Singers intended to make good use of it.

The Almanac Singers piled in a car that Millard Lampell had bought in New Jersey with the money the group earned from the recording session that would result in another set of albums, *Sod Buster Ballads* and *Deep Sea Chanties and Whaling Ballads*. How strange this group of folksingers must have looked squished in a beat up Buick, showing up at union rallies, instruments in hand, playing songs, passing the hat, and jumping back into the car, off to the next city and the next union hall. That summer, the Almanacs went to Pittsburgh and Cleveland and other Midwest cities, where serious strike action was taking place. They pushed on to Chicago and Milwaukee, moving west. Eventually they hit the West Coast, playing San Francisco and Los Angeles.

It would be some time before another group of visionaries seeking to foster change in America would cross the country in such vagabond nature. Jack Kerouac, Allen Ginsberg and the other writers of the Beat culture would do it a decade later, but instead of singing protest songs, they recited poetry, and their preferred music was jazz, not union songs. In the '60s Ken Kesey and His Merry Pranksters hoped to change America—with hallucinogenic drugs. You'd have to time travel all the way to the 1970s when punk bands—kids crowded into old beat-up vans, going from grimy club to grimy club, playing not exactly political music but music that was designed to shake up the Establishment and instigate a new way of thinking, culturally, would in any way compare to the Almanac Singers.

The Almanacs' tour took a toll on the group. Both new members Pete Hawes and Lee Hays got sick. Hawes contacted pneumonia and dropped out early; Hays had a number of ailments. Rather than ride home with Guthrie and Seeger, he took a bus back to New York. Lampell, ever the playboy, met up with a woman he knew in Los Angeles and told his friends he'd be along eventually, which didn't happen. The Almanac Singers were now a duo: Pete Seeger and Woody Guthrie, and they did their best to carry on the group's tradition of singing for striking workers and union members. Heading up to the Pacific Northwest, they played in Portland and Seattle, then turned east, driving through Idaho and Montana and the Dakotas.

Seeger, who had admired Guthrie, emulating him onstage and off, now found that he could be a difficult friend. With the rest of the Almanacs around, Seeger didn't have to deal with Woody one on one so much. But on the trip back from the West Coast, neither musician was ever alone. Traveling in the car together, braving snowstorms and dangerous mountain roads with poor brakes and nearly bald tires, the stress and the fatigue gnawed at their relationship. Yet, Seeger valued their friendship and tolerated Guthrie. Seeger confided in Hays, "I can't stand him when he's around, but I miss him when he's gone."

In an interview with Seeger biographer David Dunaway, Hays recalled that "Woody kind of jarred Pete's regular way of life, made Pete feel unnerved when he was around. Woody was hard to take, he was *not* housebroken. If he drank too much, he was obnoxious and rude, at best an unruly child."

The two folksingers returned to New York that fall. The future of the Almanac

Singers was in doubt; too much tension had caused fractures musically and socially. They rented a place in Greenwich Village they dubbed Almanac House that turned into a musical commune, with musicians coming and going, girlfriends moving in and then moving out. Pete played the role of house mother, Guthrie and Hays the incorrigible kids. Guthrie had grown close to Lead Belly, who would come over to the townhouse to play music, along with blind harmonica player Sonny Terry and guitarist Brownie McGhee. Another visitor was Josh White, an increasingly popular black folksinger, and new members of the Almanac Singers: husband and wife Gordon Friesen and Sis Cunningham, and Arthur Stern, who replaced Lee Hays after he was asked to leave the group for not being dependable and healthy enough to go on.

The problem with the Almanac Singers was that there now was more music being made at home than on any stage or in any union hall. Dates dried up and Seeger grew frustrated. Guthrie, on the other hand, was content to play music and share a bottle with his blues friends, preferring their company to Lampell and the others whom he increasingly grew irritated with as they tried in vain to assume the authentic folksinger credentials that Guthrie already thought he had in spades.

In order to pay the rent and buy groceries, the musicians living in the townhouse often produced house parties or "hootenannies" on Sunday afternoons, a term Guthrie and Seeger were introduced to in the Pacific Northwest describing folk music get-togethers. The challenge was that the same people seemed to come time and again: New York intellectuals and young, middle class wannabe intellectuals, some of them from the suburbs. They enjoyed the music and the wine, but at best, could only imagine the sweat and the toil of the men being sung about in the songs.

On December 7, 1941, Japan attacked Pearl Harbor. America declared war on the Japanese Empire and then Adolf Hitler and Nazi Germany. The country was now at war in Asia and Europe. The surprise attack not only shocked America but also deeply angered it, and almost overnight, the country came together. Most striking workers went back to work and the appetite for protest music and union songs withered, making the Almanac Singers less and less marketable, even though they had inserted into their set more and more pro-war songs.

But America was now a different place. Out in California, where the nascent aircraft industry was rapidly gearing up to make airplanes for the war effort, Okies who couldn't find jobs picking peaches were finding employment on aircraft assembly lines. Guthrie, like everyone else, was taken by the colossal change of events in America, and as a songwriter, he began to churn out even more war songs, the most notable being "The Sinking of the *Reuben James*," about an American destroyer torpedoed by a Nazi submarine that October, even before war between America and Germany had begun. In his original version of the song, Guthrie named nearly all one hundred and fifteen sailors killed on the *Reuben James*, carefully rhyming last names and using the Carter Family's melody to "Wildwood Flower," one of its most popular tunes. Seeger suggested that he might approach the song using less names in the verses, since it was too tedious to sing them all. Surprisingly, Guthrie took the advice, altered the lyrics, and the song became one of the Almanac Singers' most popular songs that season.

The Almanac Singers relied on Seeger's banjo as much as they did the direction he carved for the group. Aside from Guthrie, he was also the group's most convincing singer; Hays might have had a better pure voice, but he often sounded like he should have been in a men's chorus than in a political protest folk group. The others provided ample back up, but their contribution made the Almanacs' delivery more formal and stiff. Guthrie was used to ragged vocals, hardened by the road, as well as rough-edged guitar and banjo picking. Seeger and the rest of the bunch might have possessed the proper spirit and intention, but more times than not, the Almanac Singers lacked the scars and scrabble that Guthrie owned. Guthrie endured as an Almanac Singer, but he was not in his element.

With a repertoire that blended pro-war and pro-union songs, the Almanac Singers also put traditional American folk songs in the mix. Seeger was anxious to keep the group connected to the American songbook that was housed at the Library of Congress, hence the recording and performing of sea shanties and whaling songs, among other traditional tunes. Sometimes the group sang the traditional songs straight, other times they gave the old songs a facelift. In the early 1940s, there were no other groups like the Almanac Singers. The uniqueness of their make-up and the manner by which they could move from pro-union to anti-fascist numbers, followed by old American folk songs, was rather remarkable.

But it was still the group's topical songs that gave the Almanac Singers their edge. In the group's early days, President Franklin D. Roosevelt was a popular target, principally because of conscription and the path toward war. The group's union songs were its best, though, with "Union Maid" and "Talking Union" always good for rabid response in union halls and bars where longshoremen and the like drank their whiskey. Not surprisingly, the Almanac Singers' second album, *Talking Union*, which was recorded in mid-1941 and preceded both *Sod Buster Ballads* and *Deep Sea Chanties and Whaling Ballads*, became its most popular and durable recording effort.

The Almanac Singers enjoyed one last round of glory before it all came crashing to an end. When things looked as if they couldn't get any worse—the commune was evicted from Almanac House just after the first of the year in 1942—seemingly out of nowhere came an offer from CBS radio to appear on the *We, the People* program, followed by a performance of "Round and Round Hitler's Grave" on a series called *This Is War*. Suddenly, things looked bright for the Almanac Singers—but it was fleeting. In mid-February a newspaper reporter writing for the *World-Telegram* did a feature on the group titled "Singers on New Morale Show Also Warbled for Communists." The *New York Post* did a similar piece. The content of both pieces and the fallout that result from them was predictable. As quickly as the Almanac Singers' prospects had picked up, they had fallen down. The group's bookings were cancelled, and despite one final recording session from which came the album *Dear Mr. President*, the Almanac Singers were all but finished.

It didn't help things that Uncle Sam came calling for Pete Seeger in the spring of 1942. Without Seeger, the heart and soul of the Almanac Singers, the group had little chance at carrying on. The Almanacs played a couple more gigs that spring, capitalizing on Seeger's last days as a civilian-musician and hoping to promote *Dear Mr. President*, but the fire had faded and only embers were left in its place. In June, Seeger, who had mixed feelings about being in the army, was off to boot camp. It wasn't that he didn't want to serve his country. On the contrary. It was just that Seeger thought he'd be much more effective combating the Germans or Japanese by carrying a banjo rather than a rifle and by singing rather than shooting.

Guthrie was sad to see Seeger, his friend, head off to war, but he didn't much care about the probable demise of the Almanac Singers, although for a while he did try to keep the group going by having Lead Belly and Sonny Terry and Brownie McGhee fill in, even if it was only a half-hearted attempt. By this time he was deep into writing his autobiography, *Bound for Glory*, spending hours and days at the typewriter. And there was something else: he was in love.

Marjorie Mazia was young and bright, a dancer with Martha Graham, one of the best and most innovative dance companies in New York, if not all of America. Her black hair and supple body matched her warm smile and self-confidence. Not yet twenty-five, she was a beautiful woman with a promising career. The world might have been at war, but Marjorie Mazia kept the horrors of it at a distance. When she danced, it was as if each move was a celebration of life itself.

Marjorie was from Philadelphia and married to Joseph Mazia, but lived much of the time in a small apartment in New York's Greenwich Village, away from her parents and husband. It was a matter of geography and convenience that caused the separation and Marjorie did her best to cope with it. There was a lot of going back and forth across New Jersey on the train, which didn't help her marriage grow deep, but dancing meant the world to her and she would do pretty much anything to make a career of it.

Woody Guthrie was still married, too. Mary and the kids were now settled in El Paso, away from his unpredictable rambles and aversion to creating a normal life for him and his family. He certainly cared about them, and loved Mary for all they'd been through and as the mother of his children. But the heat in their relationship never hit the right temperature, as Woody always seemed to be running from her and domesticity.

Guthrie met Marjorie in New York in early 1942. Surprisingly, Marjorie knew of Guthrie; she was familiar with *Dust Bowl Ballads* and admired its contents, especially the song "Tom Joad." When Sophie Maslow, another Martha Graham dancer, had suggested that the company create a dance piece called *Folksay* based on *Dust Bowl Ballads*, Marjorie accompanied her friend to meet Guthrie and explore the possibilities. A deal was struck, as was a romance. Though Guthrie had a difficult time with the musical precision and timing necessary for the dancers to master their routines, *Folksay* was performed in March, with Guthrie providing the accompaniment on

Woody and Marjorie Guthrie, ca. 1943.

guitar and Marjorie and the others physically expressing the music with avant garde motion and fluidity.

By the time Marjorie left New York that spring to tour with the Martha Graham Company, Woody and she were deeply in love. Marjorie later found out that she was also pregnant. While Guthrie was excited, Marjorie was confused, concerned, and scared. How to tell her parents and, worse, her husband, that she had fallen hard for an unkempt folksinger from Oklahoma who failed to bathe regularly, had no job to speak of, and wasn't exactly a pillar of propriety.

Guthrie often presented a pretty pathetic portrait to people from the normal confines of Eastern urban society. He often spoke like a country hick, his words drawn and easy. His clothes were often wrinkled and dirty, his hair unwashed and uncombed. His boots were scuffed and worn. Yet, when he cleaned up, most women saw him as cute, someone to cuddle and hold, even take care off. But he'd rather not take the time or effort to fit in. Instead, he'd be looking to drop out and head out. Simply put, he was what he was: a restless, rootless, folk poet with a driving need to express himself, be it in verse or prose. Woody Guthrie was a free spirit if there ever was one. Marjorie accepted it, even admired that in him.

While in New York, another important person altered Woody's life: Gilbert Vandine Houston, whom everyone called Cisco. Guthrie had first met Cisco Houston in 1939 in California where Houston, the handsome young man that he was, secured acting bits and scraped his way through the Depression. The two had hit it off immediately; Woody taught Cisco the rudiments of the guitar, and it wasn't long before the two of them were playing and harmonizing together. Guthrie later said that Cisco sang "a high cowboy kind of coyote, snifting, drifting harmony that seems to bring a gleam of wrangling to the eyes of many girls. He's a big cuss, with a mixed walking gait that comes from being by nature a western desert rat and an expert at walking with high waves rolling against a ship."

The latter part of Guthrie's wildly colorful description of Houston came from the fact that Houston, in addition to being an actor and budding folksinger, was also a merchant marine, having gone to sea at the outset of the war. He had turned up in New York at a time when Guthrie needed a friend and an outlet for his Marjorie-inspired blues. Despite her feelings for Woody, Marjorie had decided for the baby's sake to go back to her husband so that it would be born in a proper household. Guthrie, who'd been writing imaginary letters to what he was certain would be a son—he playfully referred to him as Railroad Pete—was shocked and angry at her decision. Cisco's friendship helped soothe Guthrie's pain.

When he could think straight, Woody turned inward and wrote. In a letter to Marjorie, he reflected: "I have already found out that the only thing that keeps me from going completely screwball is just to keep at work every minute of the night and day, and maybe this is a good thing, maybe the best thing that can happen to anybody. To keep at work."

Guthrie had been working on *Bound for Glory*, which he seemed to turn to whenever he needed to be introspective. The pages of the manuscript seemed to fly from the typewriter as Guthrie sat at the kitchen table, pecking away at the keys. He worked in long stretches, often to the point of exhaustion. Rather than plop into bed after hours at the typewriter, Guthrie often folded his arms into a pillow and slept with his head on the table, or he slid under it and slept there like a dog.

Alan Lomax had been the one who first encouraged him to set his life down on paper, and it was he who had passed along information on Guthrie and his book to editor William Doerflinger of the publishing house, E. P. Dutton. Doerflinger met Woody and read some of the manuscript and saw much promise. It meandered and bounced along unevenly, but it owned an original voice and had a distinct American spirit that Doerflinger liked. Doerflinger decided to sign Guthrie to a contract and give him an advance to live on. Then he got his wife, Joy, also a writer and editor, to help Guthrie organize the manuscript, a tall order given the fact that the manuscript was well over one thousand pages long—single spaced.

Not everything in the book was true. Guthrie regularly employed an artistic license when he felt like it, omitting people and scenes, changing names, creating dialogue, and embellishing events for the sake of the story. It all just gushed out of him. According to biographer Ed Cray, Guthrie covered himself by calling his book "an autobiographical novel." It was indeed just that.

Guthrie's prose was naturally rich and full of wonderfully descriptive detail of the places he'd been and the people he'd met. He also had an uncanny ear for dialogue and a compelling sense of story, so that *Bound for Glory*, which would be published in 1943, read like a work of fiction more than a conventional memoir. The book's first chapter began: "I could see men of all colors bouncing along the boxcar. We stood up. We laid down. We piled around on each other. We used each other as pillows. I could smell the sour and bitter sweat, soaking through my own khaki shirt and britches, and the work clothes, overhauls and saggy, dirty suits of the other guys." Clearly, Guthrie had prose power. Upon publication, *Bound for Glory* was critically acclaimed and sales were strong; the *New York Times* and the *New Yorker* magazine both wrote enthusiastic reviews. Other glowing reviews in other newspapers and magazines followed. In some literary quarters, Guthrie was being hailed as an exciting new voice in American letters.

Guthrie also had another thing for which to be proud. In February 1943 Marjorie gave birth, not to Railway Pete, a son, but to Cathy, a daughter, who Guthrie promptly nicknamed "Stackabones." A month later, Mary, his wife, sent him divorce papers, which he was relieved to receive. He had not forgotten about her or his kids, but his life in New York had taken him in a direction where there was little hope that they all could be reunited. Mary wouldn't have wanted it anyway. She had a decent job in El Paso and her kids were happy in their new home. They needed stability in their lives and that was something she knew Woody would never be able to provide. Divorce was the logical end of their relationship. Mary knew it and acted on it. Guthrie was happy to accommodate her wish. He signed the papers and thought about how he could bring Marjorie and Cathy into his life in a permanent way.

For one of the few times in his life, Guthrie was not short of cash. Instead of recklessly blowing the money from the book advance, he watched how he spent it as best he could and even sent some of it back to Texas to Mary to help with the kids. Dutton, his book publisher, was also interested in a new book project from him, which would mean another advance, and whenever a gig with Sonny Terry and Brownie McGhee or Lead Belly or Cisco Houston—or all of them together—was offered, he took it, adding more money to his pocket.

It all seemed so good for Guthrie. But there was one problem: now that he was a single man, it meant he was eligible for the draft. The war was in a critical stage in early 1943. The tide had begun to change in both Europe and the Pacific, but the big push to end both conflicts was just gearing up and new recruits were desperately needed. There were few men Woody's age—he was thirty years old—not in a branch of the service or in a job that serviced the American war machine. Men up to age 38 were being drafted on a daily basis.

Guthrie knew it was only a matter of time before he got his draft notice. Cisco Houston encouraged him to take control of his own destiny. Join the Merchant Marine and serve with me, he said. That would keep him away from the regimented ways of the armed forces, something Cisco knew Guthrie would have trouble with, no matter what branch of service got him. Woody thought Cisco's advice made sense. He hated to leave his young daughter and the woman he deeply loved behind, but there was no way out of his predicament unless Marjorie got divorced and quickly married him, something she was not yet willing to do. Rather than roll the dice with his future, Guthrie joined the U.S. Merchant Marine, and shipped out in

June 1943 with Cisco Houston and a new friend, Jimmy Longhi, on the *S.S. William B. Travis*, a Liberty ship named after one of the heroes of the Alamo. Their destination was the North Atlantic where German U-boats awaited their arrival.

———————

The image of Woody Guthrie as a rugged sailor—a merchant marine calloused to the bone, able to carry his weight (which wasn't much) and responsibly fulfill his duties on the ship—was a comical one. Since living in New York, Guthrie might have been writing about tough times and the hardships that he and the American working man endured during the Depression. But the only calluses now on his hand were at the tip of his fingers where they met the strings of his guitar. It had been a while since Guthrie had done hard manual labor. Even Cisco Houston thought Woody had gone soft. Getting him on a ship would do him a world of good, Houston believed. It would bring back the old Woody, the one in California that tramped around and roughed it and slept under railroad bridges—the Woody that Cisco so admired.

From most accounts, however, Guthrie was a pretty fair seaman and he enjoyed being a member of the National Maritime Union, the pro-union man that he always was. He did his part, although he struggled with some tasks, as he confessed in a 1944 essay. In it Guthrie describes the challenge he faced when his duties included work in the mess hall: "I can strain and get through the job on time but I cannot do the work as it should be done. I can't keep tables clean, wash extra silverware and sweep and mop up my deck as it should be. The boys get sore and think that I'm in favor of filth and all this mess. The truth is that I am just forced to work through each meal as best I can. They get nervous and impatient and yell orders all at once. I get all mixed up. . . ."

Guthrie also continued to write songs. One of them, "Talking Merchant Marine," is a lighthearted account of how Guthrie came to be in the Merchant Marine. But before the song is done, he made certain it did its part to support the war effort, as evidenced by the lyrics: "This convoy is the biggest I ever seen/It stretches out across the sea/An' the ships blow their whistles and ring their bells/Gonna blow them fascists clean to Hell/Win some freedom, liberty/Stuff like that."

Guthrie's stint in the Merchant Marine didn't mean he was safer than being in the armed forces. Although the Merchant Marine didn't actively seek combat, the ships the men sailed were often thrown in the thick of it. The *William B. Travis* was an explosion waiting to happen; it carried as its cargo bombs and fuel headed to Palermo, Italy.

Guthrie's first dash across the Atlantic in the "Willy B.," as he called his ship, occurred without incident, save the sinking of a nearby Liberty ship that was hit by a torpedo and sunk. However, after unloading their dangerous cargo in Palermo, the *William B. Travis* steamed out of port into the Mediterranean where it was torpedoed. Crippled, it made its way back to port. The event revealed just how vulnerable Woody and Cisco were in the Liberty ships and how their next breath could easily be their last.

Guthrie was less afraid of being sunk than having the ship catch fire. The sensitivity to fire was understandable. All he had to do was recall the death of his sister Clara, who died at age 14 from burns suffered when her dress caught fire. Or the tragedy of his mother Nora, who suffered from deep depression and one day poured kerosene on her sleeping husband, Charley, and set him on fire. Charley survived, but was never the same man. Woody's mother was sent to an insane asylum where she eventually died. Guthrie didn't talk about this part of his life much. He buried it way back in his soul where it stirred on occasion, and when it did, it brought him a new round of gloom to go with the anxiety of sailing across the Atlantic on a potential ball of fire.

Woody's first voyage as a merchant marine lasted eight months. When he returned to New York, Marjorie had divorced her husband and moved from Philadelphia to Coney Island in Brooklyn, just a stone's throw from the beach. Nearby also were the arcades, amusement rides, and concession stands for which Coney Island was famous. Marjorie had Cathy with her, and when Woody saw her, he broke down. Guthrie had matured much since he first became a father back in Pampa. Teeny, Sue, and Bill never got Woody's full attention, except for bursts of it during the short stints that he was home. But Woody couldn't seem to get enough of Cathy. While Marjorie was at work, Woody spent much of his time pushing Cathy in a stroller and walking along the Coney Island waterfront, a proud papa. At night he'd tell Marjorie all about their day, making it so that Marjorie badly wished she could join the two most important people in her life instead of going to work.

It wasn't long before the pleasant home life that Guthrie was truly enjoying was interrupted by a letter from his local draft board, informing him that he'd been drafted. Rather than report for his physical, Guthrie, Cisco Houston, and Jimmy Longhi shipped out again in January 1944, this time on the *William Floyd*, enabling Guthrie to once again steer clear of army regimentation. Their destination was North Africa, without a stop this time in Sicily. On board were oil workers whose job it was to bring oil out of the ground to be turned into aviation fuel. With North Africa won, the Allies turned their attention to Europe, which they bombed from the air incessantly.

On the trip home that spring, Woody and Cisco played music whenever they could, and they continued back in Brooklyn. With no place to go, Cisco took Woody's and Marjorie's offer to stay at their Mermaid Avenue apartment, providing even more music time for the two friends. All that jamming had a positive effect on Guthrie's musicianship, which included playing the guitar, fiddle, mandolin and harmonica. It might have been the best that Guthrie had ever sounded. The only problem was, with Marjorie at work during the day, he and Cisco were mostly playing for an audience of one: young Cathy.

Moses Asch had neither the name nor the look of an American folk music giant. He wasn't named for an American president, statesman, or great man of commerce. Instead, at his birth in late 1905, his father Sholem bestowed upon him the righteous name of Moses, which came straight from the Old Testament, and, one would assume, cloaked with certain responsibilities and expectations. But, like Woodrow Wilson Guthrie, whom everyone called Woody, most people who knew Moses called him Moe, thus ending all biblical implications and divine connections.

With a beak for a nose and a moustache that made his countenance into a caricature, with a receding hairline and stern eyes that stopped just short of piercing those in his sight, Asch, a devout curmudgeon, looked like what he was: a Jewish immigrant from Poland, who just so happened to have a wonderful taste and a talent for recording music. And, like a couple of other Polish Jews, Leonard and Phil Chess, who owned Chess Records in Chicago in the 1950s and recorded some of the earliest and best rock and roll and electric blues records of the era, Moe Asch made his mark in American music by recording Woody Guthrie, Lead Belly, Pete Seeger, and other major folk artists. Asch also singlehandedly recorded hundreds of other songs and singers that are now a permanent part of this nation's music treasury.

His father was a prominent Polish writer who often wrote about Jewish life in Europe. The Asch family left Poland in 1912 and for two years lived outside Paris before coming to America at the outset of World War I in 1914. At an early age, Moses developed an interest in communications and technology. He became a ham radio operator, and in the early 1920s, his father sent him to Germany, which was at the vanguard of sound reproduction. It was there that he studied audio engineering and got involved in music preservation, particularly folk music, a passion that would shape his career and remain with him the rest of his life.

While abroad, Asch came across the most important book of his young life. John Lomax, father of Alan, had written the seminal book at the time on American cowboy music called simply *Cowboy Songs and Other Frontier Ballads.* Asch found it in a Parisian bookstore and immersed himself in it. Eager to learn more about the music culture of America, his newly adopted country, Asch devoured *Cowboy Songs and Other Frontier Ballads,* reading and rereading the Introduction by that great American Teddy Roosevelt. For Asch, the book inspired a growing interest in music as culture. When he returned to the States in 1926, he vowed to dig deeper into his new passion.

Unfortunately, there wasn't much money to be made as an amateur musicologist in the late 1920s. Thus, Asch worked for companies that dealt with another love of his: electronics. Eventually he started a small radio repair business of his own called Radio Laboratories or simply Radio Labs. Being a Jew in Germany in the mid-1920s, Asch witnessed firsthand the growing rise in anti-Semitism as well as budding socialist movements against the backdrop of fascism. His father saw it too and wrote about it, particularly the Jewish dilemma as it exploded in Germany in the 1930s.

Living in New York, Moe Asch married his love of electronics and ethnic music with progressive political causes and began recording radio programs for WEVD, one of the city's liberal radio stations. He loved his work, believing that to create a recorded body of work was a way of preserving national and ethnic culture. Asch spent his days and nights engrossed in the music and the matter of recording it. He soon got a reputation in New York as someone to turn to when it came to ethnic music, particularly Yiddish music.

If Lomax's *Cowboy Songs and Other Frontier Ballads* was a defining book in Asch's life, meeting Albert Einstein in 1940, was a defining moment. He had already begun Radio Labs and was already involved in ethnic music. But now, inspired by what Einstein and his own father had told him about the importance of music and music culture—and his role in recording and preserving it—Asch opened up Asch Recording Studios and debuted Asch Records that year.

Asch couldn't have picked a better—or worse—time to enter the ethnic music business. The large record companies of the time—Columbia, Victor, and Decca—had either recently abandoned or had cut back on the recording of ethnic music, including Yiddish music. Asch was happy to fill the void if, for no other reason than his association with WEVD, which led him to record groups like the Bagelman Sisters for the station. WEVD had a large Jewish listening audience, but few records to play for it. There was not enough revenue in ethnic music in the early 1940s to keep the big record companies interested, but for an upstart like Asch, recording Yiddish music kept his business afloat, if barely.

Asch, however, didn't see the shellac rationing coming. Back then in the pre-vinyl period, 78 rpm records were made with shellac, a natural resin which came from Asia and was needed in the war effort. Even the large record companies had difficulty securing it during World War II. For tiny labels such as Asch Records, it was virtually impossible to get any more shellac than that amount that was due you, which in Asch's case, was next to nothing, considering the size of the company. In order to survive, Asch merged Asch Records with Stinson Records in 1943. Stinson distributed throughout the U.S. recordings made in the Soviet Union, but also recorded Russian artists on its own. Together, the two labels were able to secure enough shellac to make enough recordings to ride out the war.

Asch might have known how to engineer a recording session and he was learning how to sell records, even if it was in small amounts, but he was neither a musician nor a talent scout, though he often considered himself the latter. In other words, he really didn't know the difference between a good and not-so-good singer or musician, as evidenced by the dozens of artists that would record for Asch over the years, many of whom would never have gotten the chance to record with any other label. What Asch had, however, was some luck, and it came knocking on his door in April 1944.

There are different accounts as to how Woody Guthrie first heard about Asch Records. Most likely, it was either Pete Seeger or Alan Lomax who told him about Asch and his fledgling folk music label. Guthrie had been itching to record again; he missed making the kind of money that Victor gave him for *Dust Bowl Ballads*. And now with a young mouth to feed, he was determined to show Marjorie that he could provide for her and baby Cathy.

Guthrie knew exactly where the Asch office was. Located at 117 West 46th Street in mid-town Manhattan, the area was where Guthrie lived when he first arrived in New York more than four years ago. As recording studios go, even back then, it barely made the grade. Simple and barely adequate, Asch had built the studio himself. According to Asch, it only measured fifteen by ten feet and it connected to his office, so that he could slide from his desk to his recording board with ease. "All I had to do was get off [sic] the desk and put the equipment on and record," remembered Asch. "Nobody ever had to call beforehand to make appointments, because they all knew I was there twelve to fourteen hours a day."

Like most everyone else, Guthrie showed up without an appointment and announced that he was there to record some music. Asch professed not to know who

Guthrie was, and perhaps he really didn't know. But recently Asch had recorded Pete Seeger; earlier in 1941 he had recorded Lead Belly. It's hard to believe that Asch hadn't at least heard of Guthrie, since both shared a love of folk music and traveled in the same political and music circles in New York. It's also hard to fathom that Guthrie hadn't known of Asch, given Guthrie's relationship with Lead Belly, Seeger, and Lomax.

Despite his professed ignorance of Guthrie, Asch wasn't about to kick him out. As the years went by, Asch rarely turned anyone away from his recording studio. In an interview Asch did with Guthrie authority Guy Logsdon in 1974, Asch recalled his first meeting with Guthrie:

"One day, Woody comes in and squats himself on the floor. He squats himself before the office door and just sits there—very wild hair, clean shaven, and clothing one would associate with a Western person. . . . He started to talk . . . the simplicity of his speech was so deep that you start to remind yourself of Walt Whitman. The words were clear, simple, but the meanings were deep and very well thought out and philosophized. So we became friends. . . ."

And collaborators. Not only did Guthrie record literally dozens of sides for Asch Records over the next few months, but he also listened to the crop of recordings Asch had in his office and gave his detailed opinion of them, meticulously stressing what he liked about them, and what he didn't like, all in typewritten prose that could stand alone as respected music criticism of the day. Asch was so impressed with Guthrie's musical knowledge and ideas that he paid Guthrie for them. According to Asch, Guthrie had a clear view of the value of folk music, and it matched perfectly with his. Asch knew not to fool with any of Guthrie's music, either. He let Guthrie record at will, the way he wanted, the songs he wanted. If Guthrie asked for advice, Asch gave it to him. But Asch wasn't interested in messing with folk music genius.

During that first visit Asch had Guthrie record two songs—"Hard, Ain't It Hard" and "More Pretty Gals than One." Asch was stunned with what he heard. He was used to the Jewish artists on his label and the ethnic music he'd been selling. Like Lead Belly, Guthrie, reasoned Asch, was an authentic American artist. He didn't perform cowboy music, the kind that Lomax spoke about his book, but there was something distinctly western about the way Guthrie sang his songs, and compelling too. After the session, the two men spoke about future sessions. Guthrie said he'd be back in a few days and this time he'd bring along a friend or two.

Guthrie was true to his word. On April 19 he came back to the Asch studio, guitar in hand and folksinger friends in tow. Cisco Houston was certainly there; it's quite possible that Bess Lomax and Sonny Terry also accompanied Guthrie to Asch's studio. Over a number of hours, according to Asch's recording log, Guthrie and Houston recorded sixty-three songs. The next day they locked in twenty-five more. Before the month was over, Guthrie, Houston, or both together recorded still more tracks.

It was an incredible body of work that Asch had presided over, watching and hearing American music history being made sitting behind his desk in his makeshift control room. Exhausted, he could have only thought what to do with all the tracks. This was as full and as complete a body of American folk music as anyone had ever recorded in a month's work, to be sure. Where did all these songs come from? Guthrie was a music machine; the songs poured out of him. Asch could only shake his head in amazement.

For most of the sessions, Guthrie went through his songbook, selecting tunes he had written while at sea and pulling others from his past, songs he had written or learned years ago, months ago, weeks or days ago even. One of them, "Talking Merchant Marine," (also known as "Talking Sailor") was so new that Guthrie fumbled the words to the song more than once and had to do a number of takes before he got it right. One can't help but wonder why Guthrie insisted on recording so many songs in such a short burst. There was no deadline that he was facing. Asch hadn't a clue as to what he'd do with all the tracks. There was no big pay-off. Asch told Guthrie that he couldn't pay him for so much effort, at least not until he started releasing the songs commercially.

Perhaps Guthrie thought that if something happened to him at sea, at least his songs would survive. During his time in the Merchant Marine he would have two close calls—one with a torpedo, the other a mine. Perhaps the third time, if there was a third time, he wouldn't be so fortunate. Or maybe Guthrie had found himself in a folk music zone where things felt right and the songs sounded good, and there was nothing to do but record each and every one of them that came to mind.

A number of Guthrie classics came out of these first Asch sessions, including "Philadelphia Lawyer," "Hobo's Lullaby," "Grand Coulee Dam," "Jesus Christ," "(The) Sinking of the *Reuben James*" and "Going Down the Road Feeling Bad" (aka "Lonesome Road Blues"). However, a majority of the tracks Guthrie recorded were folk standards and old-timey numbers like "John Henry," "John Hardy," "Turkey in the Straw," "Stagger Lee," "Old Dan Tucker," "Old Joe Clark," "Old Dog a Bone," "House of the Rising Sun," and "Frog Went A-Courtin'," among others.

Some of these Guthrie likely learned from Alan Lomax when Alan introduced Woody to a cross-section of the best recordings that the Library of Congress had collected up to that point. Others Guthrie had learned from other folksingers he had met in his travels, or from previously recorded works. Sometimes Guthrie altered the song's delivery, but mostly he recorded them like he had learned them, with just a bit of original phrasing and lyric twisting to make them his own.

There is one Guthrie original that stands out in the big batch of songs Guthrie recorded for Asch that spring of 1944: "God Blessed America." Finally, the song Guthrie had written more than four years earlier at Hanover House in Manhattan, just a few blocks from where he stood in Asch's studio, had been preserved for posterity. The date was April 25, 1944, and instead of calling it "God Blessed America,"

Some Drunks Run Up. Pen-and-ink drawing by Woody Guthrie for his autobiography *Bound for Glory*, 1942.

Asch put down the title as "This Land Is My Land." It apparently was done in one take, like so many others that day. Guthrie didn't seem to pay it special mind, at least not in the way he sang it or in the order it was recorded. (It was the tenth song he cut that day; he'd lay down twenty-four more tracks before he was finished.)

One thing Guthrie did do, however, was change the line that ended each verse. Instead of the original line—"God blessed America for me"—Guthrie sang "This land was made for you and me." It's unknown when, exactly, in the song's life did the lyric change occur. Did Guthrie do it on the spot at the Asch studio? Probably not. He was moving through his songs much too fast to stop for verse alterations. A look at the original lyrics, written February 23, 1940, reveals a penciled cross-out of the title "God Blessed America," replaced by "This Land Was Made for You and Me," not "This Land Is My Land" as Asch called it. There is no documentation that ascertains when this revision took place. All we know for sure is that for Guthrie's original recording of the song, Asch wrote it in his logbook as "This Land Is My Land" and Guthrie included what would become the song's most recognized line: "This land was made for you and me."

As we'll find out, this revision to "This Land Is My Land"—which ultimately, of course, would be called "This Land Is Your Land"—wouldn't be the last. Nor would it be the only time Guthrie recorded it. For years, it was assumed that a later recorded version of the song—done without Guthrie singing the two controversial verses about "private property" and people at "the Relief Office"—was the earliest version that survived. However, in 1997, the Smithsonian Institution released the first of a four-volume series called *The Asch Recordings* that included this 1944 version of the song. On the Smithsonian set's "This Land Is Your Land" are the two verses—the fourth and the sixth—that most people in America who love the song, never knew existed.

Everyone knew an Allied invasion of Europe was imminent, including the Germans, but no one knew exactly where or when. As it turned out, it occurred on the beaches of Normandy, France on June 6, 1944. Known to history as D-Day, the pivotal battle began the Allied push to the Rhine and then into Germany where every American hoped the Nazis would finally be crushed and the war in Europe would finally end.

When news of D-Day broke, Woody, Cisco and Jimmy Longhi were on yet another ship, the *Sea Porpoise*, transporting American soldiers across the Atlantic to partake in the battle for France. Longhi, who would later write a book about his experiences in the Merchant Marine with Guthrie and Cisco Houston called *Woody, Cisco, and Me*, described how Guthrie and Houston entertained the crew and the troops.

"Woody stood in the center of the hold, quietly tuning his guitar, his other instruments at his feet," wrote Longhi. "All six hundred men in the hold, those who could see him and those who couldn't, waited silently for him to begin. . . . Then he turned to the soldiers. 'Like to start off with a little song I helped write which I think is appropriate to the occasion—it's 'The Sinking of the *Reuben James*.' " It was the song he had written a couple of years earlier and that had become one of the Almanac Singers' most popular numbers.

The event wouldn't have been so noteworthy had not Guthrie decided to sing a song about a ship that was torpedoed by a German U-boat at *precisely* the time the *Sea Porpoise* was under attack. Guthrie had the tense crew and troops sing the chorus of the song loudly and with feeling, and they responded, in the process taking their minds off the depth charge explosions all around the ship. When Guthrie finished the song, the crew demanded more. "And how he sang," continued Longhi. "He soon had the hold jumping with hillbilly hoedowns, Woody Guthrie war songs, and anything else of a spirited nature that could possibly be sung."

The *Sea Porpoise* had good luck in getting the soldiers on board to their destination in one piece. In a short while they'd join the fight raging across France. But just after it began its return voyage, the *Sea Porpoise* hit a mine and struggled to stay afloat. After its crew stabilized the hole in the hull, the *Sea Porpoise* limped across the English Channel to safety in an English port. It was the second time that a ship Guthrie crewed on had been hit. He commemorated his fate by writing "Drunk once, sunk twice."

Not only was Guthrie serving America by carrying out duties in the Merchant Marine, he had also turned his guitar into what he considered a "lethal" weapon, playing songs on it about the war effort, and in his mind, killing the Nazi spirit and uplifting that of the Allies. Guthrie and Cisco Houston sang their songs to the men on board ships they sailed on and in the ports he and Cisco visited. Guthrie was proud of the anti-Nazi songs he was writing, and to make sure everyone knew the music was both potent and dangerous, he put a hand painted sign on his guitar that read "This Machine Kills Fascists." An acoustic Gibson, it would become Guthrie's most famous guitar.

A number of photos of Guthrie playing guitar have survived and are located in the Woody Guthrie Archives, the Smithsonian, and other libraries and agencies. Looking at the photos, one is surprised at how many different guitars he had. Not all of them were his. Some he borrowed, like Herta Geer's Martin that Guthrie used when he first arrived in New York in 1940. Others he bought or were given to him.

As important as music was to him, Guthrie didn't care for his instruments with much love. It was quite common for him to carry his guitar slung over his shoulder, shunning protection for it in favor of easy access to the strings and lighter weight when he traveled. He rarely, if ever, put his instruments, which in addition to the guitar also included a fiddle and mandolin, in proper cases. As of 2011, only two known Guthrie guitars have surfaced. One is located at Experience Music Project in Seattle, the Paul Allen-financed music museum that opened in 2000. The other is in the hands of a private collector, but is often seen on display at the Grammy Museum in Los Angeles, the music museum that spearheaded Guthrie's centennial celebration in 2012. Neither guitar is the one that contained the "This Machine Kills Fascists" sign on it, nor is either one a later Guthrie guitar that contained a similar message. The whereabouts of the "This Machine Kills Fascists" guitar is unknown. If it ever were discovered, it surely would become one of America's most valued folk music instruments.

Guthrie returned to New York in August 1944; a month earlier he had celebrated his 32nd birthday. Time at sea had weathered him. He had lost some of his youthful looks. Lines appeared on his face and his unruly hair was minus some of its luster. He had hoped to write a novel about his time at sea that he planned to give to Dutton, the publishing house that had released *Bound for Glory*. But Guthrie often faced writer's block on the mornings he sat down to write, possibly for the first time in his life. He suffered from too many distractions, whether they came from visiting friends and musicians, Marjorie and young daughter Cathy, or people he'd met at the local Brooklyn bar he frequented. Finally, he gave up, figuring he'd return to it when he was more in a writing mood.

In the meantime, Guthrie contemplated a return to radio. In July, while in England, he had performed on the BBC, doing children's songs and other numbers from his growing repertoire. In New York that fall he played some on local radio. But it was his appearance in early 1945 on WNYC's sixth annual *American Music Festival*, and a new program on WNEW called *The Ballad Gazette*, that made American folk

Woody Guthrie, ca. 1943.

music history.

Begun by folk enthusiast Oscar Brand in 1940, the *American Music Festival's* aim was to celebrate the richness of American music culture at a time when dark war clouds threatened the nation and sapped its spirit. The show was a success, each year presenting a wide cross-section of American music on the air, including that of Leonard Bernstein, Benny Goodman, Lead Belly, Josh White, and many other artists from all corners of popular, folk, and classical American music. Brand was educating his listening audience to the diversity of American music at the same time he was lifting the nation's mood. The two-week festival, heard live on WNYC each February, consisted of a series of live concerts in New York, the music and media capital of America. "It was obvious that something should be done to fill the gap that was a serious hindrance to the furthering of the cause of native American musical genius," wrote WNYC station director Morris Novik. "There were no provisions for encouraging and fostering this talent, and only a very limited means of presentation of American works that deserved to be heard."

Guthrie's 1945 appearance on *American Music Festival* wasn't his first (he also appeared in 1942), but it was the most significant. With host Ralph Berton setting the stage for Guthrie's set, telling listeners that he would play "songs the people sing," in the background Guthrie sang and played "This Land Was Made for You and Me," or simply "This Land Is My Land," Guthrie still unsure of what he wanted the title to be. It was, quite possibly, the first time that the song was played over American airwaves.

A short time later Guthrie secured a slot on WNEW. The program was called *The Ballad Gazette* with "your editor-in-chief, Woody Guthrie." As was the case on WNYC's *American Music Festival*, the show's producer and Guthrie used "This Land Is My Land" as its theme song and opening and closing number. Guthrie never indicated in letters or journal entries why "This Land" was selected to represent the program, but it is clear that he was finally beginning to see the value of the song as a sort of musical calling card. It also was the perfect song for the program, which described Guthrie as a great American troubadour, dusty from some hard traveling and anxious to share the good music that he heard and wrote along the way.

With Guthrie singing "This Land" in the background, the un-named host introduced Guthrie this way: "A guitar and a song is your musical introduction to a man who is as American as the forty-eight states to which he has traveled by foot, freight train, and freighter. A man whose eyes have seen America as it really is—the city streets, the country lanes, mountains, plains. A man who knows Americans as they really are, the big folk and the little ones, and who sings the songs that all America sings. Meet Woody Guthrie and his guitar, editor of *The Ballad Gazette*."

The program occurred once a week—on Sunday—and it lasted for only fifteen minutes. On it, Guthrie told a brief story or two, or described how or where he had heard a folk song, or why he had written one, before playing three or four songs, and that was that. He hated the limited radio time so much that he asked listeners to write letters to the station's management requesting a longer show. It didn't work, and three months later, Woody was off the air.

Like he did in Los Angeles back in the late '30s on KFVD, Woody sought to make available to his radio audience a book of his songs. What was officially titled as *Ten of Woody Guthrie's Songs, Book One*, but became known as *Ten Songs for Two Bits* was self-published by Guthrie. He had mimeographed the words and music to a handful of his songs and provided brief commentary for each one. Originally published in January 1945, Guthrie included "This Land Is Your Land" in the collection. On the cover, he called the song "This Land." In the commentary he called it "This Land Is Made For You and Me." Clearly, he hadn't settled on a permanent title.

"After we built the Coolee [sic] Dam," wrote Guthrie in the booklet, "we had to sell the people out there a lot of bonds to get the money to buy the copper wire and high lines and pay a whole big bunch of people at work and I don't know what all.

We called them Public Utility Bonds, just about like a War Bond, same thing. (And a lot of politicians told the folks not to buy them but we sold them anyhow). The main idea about this song is, you think about these Eight [sic] words all the rest of your life and they'll come a bubbling up into Eighty Jillion all Union. Try it and see. THIS LAND IS MADE FOR YOU AND ME."

It wasn't Guthrie's best piece of writing. In fact, it hardly made sense. There is no mention of Berlin's "God Bless America" or the 1940 origins of the song. Guthrie tied "This Land Is Your Land" to his time spent up in the Pacific Northwest, which occurred after he had composed the song. Since it was the theme song of his radio show, it was a good idea to include "This Land Is Your Land" in the song booklet, along with "Biggest Thing," "True Love," "Grand Coolee (Coulee) Dam," "Jackhammer John," "Talking Blues," "Ship in the Sky," "East Texas Red," "Bed on Your Floor," and "Hard Traveling."

Even more interesting is the fact that inside the booklet, where the lyrics to the songs were, Guthrie left out what would become the two controversial verses—one about private property and the other about people on relief. He also had significantly altered the song's other four verses, and he now acknowledged a chorus, but even that had some new words and images. Also, in this most recent version of "This Land Is Your Land," Guthrie typed out in all capital letters as he often did, the chorus as "THIS LAND IS YOUR LAND. THIS LAND IS MY LAND./FROM THE REDWOOD FOREST TO THE NEW YORK ISLAND/THE CANADIAN MOUNTAIN TO THE GULF STREAM WATERS/THIS LAND IS MADE FOR YOU AND ME."

A few things about the song were obvious. One, Guthrie didn't feel the original lyrics were good enough to remain as he first put them on paper. Revising the words and even deleting full verses meant "This Land" was still a work in progress. At least it now had Guthrie's attention, after he let the song lay dormant in his notebook for a few years. The second thing is that based on the song's notes in *Ten Songs for Two*

Bits, Guthrie still hadn't finalized what, exactly, he hoped to convey with the song. If "This Land" was originally a rebuttal to "God Bless America," he certainly wasn't selling it that way.

Throughout the war, "God Bless America" had become one of the nation's most popular patriotic songs. Guthrie might still have been annoyed with the song's ubiquitous presence on the radio, at baseball games and other athletic events, at Boy Scout and Girl Scout meetings, at political rallies, and wherever else Americans gathered, but he wasn't proclaiming it in print. Also, omitting the original verse about "the relief office" made sense in 1945 since nearly everyone who wanted to work was now employed due to the war effort at home, or else was in the armed forces. And, finally, as for the song's original contention that the idea of "private property" somehow was an affront to him and the rest of America's common folks, Guthrie didn't think enough of the idea anymore to keep it in "This Land."

In March, 1945 Moe Asch finally found the time and money to release a fraction of what Guthrie had recorded for him in his mid-town Manhattan studio a year earlier. Asch released six songs—"Ranger's Command," "Gypsy Davy," "Grand Coulee Dam," "Jesus Christ," "New York Town" and "Talking Sailor," his early merchant marine song. The songs were on three 78 r.p.m. discs (one to a side) called *Folksay* (no apparent relation to the Martha Graham dance routine) and were packaged together as one collection that included a self-portrait by Guthrie on the cover.

In later years, Asch often said that he thought "This Land Is Your Land" was one of Guthrie's best songs. Yet, when the opportunity occurred to release the vast treasure trove of material that Woody had recorded for Asch a year prior, he failed to include the song on the debut collection, even though Guthrie was using the song as the theme of his radio show.

Reviews of *Folksay* were generally good, but the album did not sell well. *Billboard* might have summed up the collection best in its review when the critic wrote that the songs on *Folksay* "appeal to the man in the back street." The album stood little chance of tapping the pop music market. America was listening to Kate Smith, the Andrew Sisters, and big bands such as those led by Glenn Miller and Benny Goodman. In the midst of the war effort, Americans used music and dance as a means of entertainment and escape from war stress. They did the Lindy, and they turned on the radio to feel good. Guthrie's songs didn't have a chance with mainstream American music audiences. The only people interested in Woody's recordings were the same small circle of intellectuals and folk music fans that had always been his base.

Guthrie didn't have time to celebrate the release of *Folksay* or to promote it. Rather than return to the Merchant Marine with Cisco Houston that spring, Guthrie opted to stay home with Marjorie and Cathy and take his chances with the draft board. The gamble failed. Guthrie received his induction notice in the mail just as *Folksay* was being released. He was told to report for service in May.

With the war winding down—the day Guthrie reported for basic training, May 7, was the day the Nazis finally surrendered—Guthrie couldn't understand why America needed his help at this late stage of the conflict. Surely he had done his part with time spent in the Merchant Marine. He had risked his life in the Atlantic and nearly lost it twice. He supported the war effort with songs, too. Why draft me, Woody wondered.

The answer was simple. The war in the Pacific still raged, and with the Japanese army showing no signs of capitulation, it was generally presumed that American forces would have to invade Japan in order to bring it to its knees. That Guthrie was in his early thirties when he was called for service indicated just how many more men the army figured it would need to win the final battle with Japan. No one believed Japan would cave easily. Many army strategists thought the invasion of Japan would mean hundreds of thousands of casualties on the American side alone.

Woody wasn't a very good soldier. Pictures of Woody in a too-large uniform revealed a sad sack private, hardly a warrior or killing machine. Rather, he was an undisciplined free-spirit caught in a culture where discipline and rules made up the day, every day. At first Guthrie sought to fit in. Then he gave up and waited to get out. He missed Marjorie. He missed his old life. In a word, he was miserable.

Marjorie sensed his desolation, which is why she finally agreed to marry Woody in November, 1945 while Woody was on furlough. Her divorce had gone through and by the tone of Woody's many letters to her, Marjorie was certain Woody's love for her was real. Many of the letters expressed intense feelings: "I love you more away from you because I can feel afraid, worry, wonder, and imagine you," wrote Woody in October. "I can see you walk and ride and dance as I read your letters or as I wander around the field here. I know that I must love you because I think so much about you. Us."

Other letters described in embarrassing detail the sex he longed to have with Marjorie. Guthrie wasn't afraid to pour out his feelings and desires on paper and the longer he was away from Marjorie, the more he craved her. The army, of course, was filled with sexually starved soldiers, but few were writing in often embarrassing detail just how hungry for intimacy they were. Woody had no problem in airing out his sexual frustration. He bided his time, fantasying away the days, in between painting signs—one of his official army duties—and playing guitar and writing letters and more songs.

But there was something else. Woody optimistically thought that with the surrender of Japan in August after the release of a pair of terrifying atomic bombs on Hiroshima and Nagasaki, respectively, he'd be immediately discharged. Thankfully, there was no longer a need to invade Japan, so why did the army still need his services? When his discharge papers failed to materialize, he grew despondent. Such a feeling was understandable given his deep distaste for army life. Marjorie could accept that, but she grew worried over letters in which Woody described a growing ailment. "It seems like a hundred pound sack of frogs and snakes are tied to each of my arms, my mouth is full of rabbit hair and my brain is caught in a net it can't get out of," wrote Woody. "Confused states of mind, a kind of lonesomeness, a nervousness stays with me no matter how I set myself to reading, painting, or playing my guitar. Without trying to make it sound too serious, it never does get quite right in my head."

But it was serious, very serious. What Woody described to Marjorie was the early signs of Huntington's disease, the disease that would eventually rob him of everything, including his life.

———— • ————

Woody Guthrie was finally discharged on December 21, 1945. With the war over, a new world began, a world that was very different from the one that existed before the bombs began to fall and the German army began to march in the fall of 1939. The Depression was over. America was now a super-power, a new word in the world's vocabulary and a new international category amongst nations. But peace was short-lived, as was what should have come from the peace, namely a world free of serious ideological and political tension. What would quickly become known as an "Iron Curtain" separated East from West shortly after the end of World War II and made the Soviet Union America's newest rival and "cold war" enemy. Many observers wondered if World War III wasn't on the horizon.

Musically, America also changed. Almost overnight, interest in Swing, the sound America danced to during the war years, quickly waned. Glenn Miller, the nation's most popular big band leader, had been killed while serving his country. Colonel Miller's plane went down somewhere over the English Channel in December 1944,

Bob Dylan's personal copy of Woody Guthrie's book, *Bound for Glory*.

its wreckage never found. Miller's death shocked America. With hit songs such as "In the Mood," "Moonlight Serenade," "Little Brown Jug," and "Chattanooga Choo Choo," Miller and his band filled dance floors across the land and on army bases throughout England. He was America's best-selling recording artist during the war years, and though artists such as Duke Ellington, Benny Goodman, and Count Basie were more musically creative, no one was more popular than Miller.

In black communities a new sound, rhythm & blues, was shaping up to be the next hot music. Played by five- and six-piece combos instead of big bands of more than a dozen members, the beat of R&B was harder-edged and sexier than its precedessor. Led by Louis Jordan, who mixed these new rhythms with light-hearted lyrics and flash, R&B began to settle in as one segment of America's new popular music spectrum.

In New York, another new sound, bebop, a type of jazz, was as radical as anything ever heard in American music. Stellar musicians from the big band world that had grown tired of its creative confines, rebelled and created bebop, with little regard to melody or conventional structure. Saxophonist Charlie Parker was the prince of this new form of jazz. Dizzy Gillespie, Thelonious Monk and others added their musical signatures to it.

A new breed of pop singers led by a handsome young Italian-American from Hoboken, New Jersey named Frank Sinatra, made young women swoon with a voice that ranked with the best that America ever produced. Sinatra was suave, sexy, and singular in his ability to phrase a lyric. There would be others who walked in Sinatra's shadow, but none would match his vocal genius.

Down South, in the mountains of Appalachia, a new kind of country music was evolving called bluegrass. Led by Bill Monroe and His Blue Mountain Boys, bluegrass featured charged rhythms and exceptional musicianship, matched with old-timey, traditional themes. Solos from Monroe's mandolin, along with those of banjo player Earl

Scruggs and guitar picker Lester Flatt, set the standards by which all other bluegrass bands would be judged.

Woody Guthrie most likely was aware of this creative American music explosion in the years after World War II. He might have even wondered where he could fit in with his many songs. He would have difficulty finding a spot. Topical songs had seemingly run their course now that both the Depression and the war were over, and except for small folk song circles in New York and other urban areas, most Americans were looking forward rather than backward. They embraced material things like television, bigger and better automobiles, automatic washers and dryers, and a new place to live that folks called suburbia.

None of this riled Guthrie, though. All he knew was that with Pete Seeger also discharged from the army, the two would pick up where they left off before the war began.

Pete Seeger was a dreamer. He saw the world fueled by music, a place where singers and songwriters were near the apex of culture, potential leaders of a great societal shift in America and the rest of the world. He addressed nearly every American problem—political, social, economic—as if music could cure it.

Seeger had been discharged from the army around the same time Guthrie had, and it was inevitable that the two would meet shortly after becoming civilians again. While Woody used his brief time in uniform to write long love letters to Marjorie and anxiously await the day that he'd be released from the torture of military life, Seeger, ever the planner, outlined what he envisioned to be a vast musical network stretching from New York to Los Angeles called People's Songs. The organization would bring together musicians of different styles, sounds, and stripes around common causes, especially those connected to labor. Seeger's intent was to use music to ensure that gains made by labor just before and during the war were preserved and that new victories be won through the power of song. He wrote to his wife Toshi from the South Pacific, where his unit was stationed during the war, "I want to organize a very large chorus of untrained voices."

Seeger was serious. As soon as he was discharged and arrived in New York in December 1945, he rolled up his sleeves and got to work on People's Songs. He contacted his old folk music mentor, Alan Lomax, and quickly got him on board. Lee Hays from the Almanac Singers was in. Seeger went beyond the parameters of folk music, enlisting classical music composers Aaron Copland and Leonard Bernstein. He worked feverishly, as if he was bound by a time limit or narrow window of opportunity. He had come out the army more mature and more convinced of his beliefs that without a vibrant movement based on song, the common laborer in America didn't stand a chance against its big bosses. If this all seemed tied to socialist principles, so be it, reckoned Seeger.

Seeger signed up supporters in the early months of 1946. He was energized by the response. Hundreds of dues-paying music people became members. Seeger did everything he could to promote People's Songs. He spoke of it at meetings, sang about it, dreamt about it in his sleep. He became the ultimate music organizer in America. Everyone was watching Pete Seeger perform music magic, including the FBI.

Naturally, Woody Guthrie jumped onboard People's Songs. He wasn't much on making the details of the organization a priority, but he loved the collective sound of their possibility. He also enjoyed playing music with his old friends again. Although People's Songs embraced Woody and knew his presence was important, few key members, including Seeger, relied on him to push the organization's agenda forward. Guthrie had always been a lone wolf; he did things his way. In People's Songs his inability to follow a general strategy was tolerated because "Woody was Woody." Hardly anyone who knew him well expected anything else.

Guthrie was living in Brooklyn, on Mermaid Avenue, with Marjorie and daughter Cathy. Though Woody was again playing out, most of the dates paid little or nothing, making Marjorie the family's primary breadwinner. During the day, when she went to work, teaching dance, Woody stayed home with Cathy, working on new songs and his off-again, on-again novel. He had reentered a deeply creative space; whether it was because he was free from army regimentation, or reunited with Marjorie and Cathy, or because of his connection to Pete Seeger and People's Songs, Guthrie was turning out songs again in a steady cadence.

He was also thinking about turning "This Land Is Your Land," which he was now calling "This Land Is Made for You and Me," into a movie score. In July 1946 he saw the film, *Banjo Pickin' Boy*, at the Preview Theater in New York. It wasn't a good film by Hollywood standards, but according to Guthrie, "it come [sic] the closest to bringing the people their songs of any film, or book, or play, or picture painted, that I have ever seen."

Guthrie wrote a letter to filmmaker Irving Lerner in which he suggested that "This Land" or "Goin' Down This Road" be the theme for a movie about an itinerant ballad singer. "He would travel by box car, by cushion, by ferry, by truck, by limousine, jalopy, by shoe leather, and would cross fields, orchards, rivers, mountains, swamps, and all of the uplands and the lowlands and the downlands." In essence, Guthrie was hoping for a movie about himself using a song to carry the story, a story in which "he is a mystery to everybody except to his own self." The letter went on for seven double-spaced type-written pages. He ended by writing "I will stop now because I can smell Marjorie frying something in the kitchen and I've not had no breakfast yet."

Nothing came of Guthrie's movie idea. But it didn't matter. For the first time in his life, Guthrie behaved like a father should. His three children with first wife Mary rarely got the attention Cathy got from Woody. Back in Texas and California when Woody was with Mary, he was young, wild and reckless; he didn't really know the meaning of fatherhood. Immaturity and a constant thirst for adventure and music always seemed to get in the way. Had Guthrie experienced a conventional childhood and a strong relationship with his parents, things might have been different, but as they were, he was hardly a model husband or father the first time around.

Spending so much time with Cathy, it was natural that their bond and Woody's fascination with her would find a way into song. Woody began writing children's songs and spoke to Moe Asch about recording them. Some were nonsensical, but others were irresistible gems, the simple kind of song that kids love. Asch thought these new tunes had merit. He invited Woody to come to his studio to record them, then released them as *Songs to Grow on: Nursery Days*, which included two of Guthrie's very best kids' songs: "Put Your Finger in the Air" and "Car Song."

As a children's songwriter, Woody found a new way to express himself. He had always enjoyed simplicity in a song. With kids' songs, he could take a simple idea and express it in the simplest terms. It was easy for him to think like a child and with Cathy, he had someone to give him endless song ideas. Also, the fact that so many servicemen now home from the war were starting families meant that there would be a need for new children's songs, believed both Guthrie and Asch.

Guthrie took his children's songwriting seriously. In his notes to *Songs to Grow on for Mother and Child*, another album of kids' songs written by Guthrie and released by Asch, Woody wrote, ". . . I don't want to see you use my songs to divide nor split your school nor your family all apart. I mean, don't just buy this record and take it home so your kids can listen to it while you go off and do something else. . . . I want to see you join right in, do what your kids do. Let your kids teach you how to play and how to act these songs out. . . ." He ended his essay by saying, "I don't want the kids to be grownup. I want to see the grown folks be kids."

Despite the occasional argument with Marjorie and the frustration he sometimes experienced when ideas in his mind seemed to clog his thought process—the same kind of thing he complained to Marjorie about while in the army—life was generally good for Woody Guthrie. But that all changed in February 1947.

Guthrie had been at a union hall performance in New Jersey. When he returned home he found a note on the Mermaid Avenue apartment door instructing him to go quickly to the hospital for there had been an accident. Not knowing much else, a frantic Guthrie raced to Coney Island Hospital where he found a hysterical Marjorie who told him what happened: their Cathy had been badly burned in an electrical fire in their apartment. Woody couldn't believe it. The thing he feared the most in life; the thing that ruined his childhood, killed his sister, destroyed his mother and nearly killed his father, struck again. What was it with Woody Guthrie and fire? Why had fate so fooled with his fear of fire and then made it real all over again? Finally, a doctor came out to see Marjorie and Woody and tell them to say their final good-bye to Cathy.

The weeks and months after Cathy's death were tough on the couple. Marjorie blamed herself for leaving the four-year-old child alone in the apartment, if only for a couple of minutes. Woody mostly sulked and privately wondered whether it was his fault, given his history. The couple argued more. Woody drank more. Ocasionally, he found solace in song, but what he wrote often lacked the poetic power of earlier efforts and its emotional spirit.

Earlier, Moe Asch had fronted him money to write a series of songs about Nicola Sacco and Bartolomeo Vanzetti, the Italian immigrants involved in labor battles in Massachusetts and convicted of murder and robbery in 1921. Many liberals and leftists thought the two immigrants wrongfully framed and innocent of the charges. Sacco and Vanzetti died in the electric chair and became martyrs to America's labor and leftist movements. Guthrie struggled to write their story in song, eventually producing a series of songs that did not rank with his best work.

In addition to *Ballads of Sacco & Vanzetti*, the twelve song collection that Woody composed about the immigrants, Asch released other Guthrie albums in the late 1940s and early '50s. Guthrie's best sellers were his children's songs, yet these sold sparingly, even with a "baby boom" underway in America. One of the problems was that Guthrie clearly was not the songwriter he used to be, though there were exceptions and still moments of sheer genius. But whether it was because of all the personal pain he was suffering, or the lack of new topical issues that could rile his spirit, or the early onset of Huntington's disease, Woody Guthrie no longer was turning out the great songs—one after another—like he had done before the war.

Though labor issues in America continued in the postwar period—a usual source of song inspiration for Guthrie—many of the young men without jobs or hope before war went into the service, got discharged, and enrolled in college, courtesy of the G.I. Bill. Rather than head to the picket line after the war, many of them married and headed to the bedroom, eager to start families.

The left-leaning American labor movement also had to be careful not to incite mistrust, now that the Soviet Union had replaced Nazi Germany and Imperial Japan as the nation's number-one enemy. Possession of the atomic bomb had given Americans comfort. Should war break out with the Soviets, we had a distinct weapons edge. But when the Soviets announced that they, too, now had an atomic bomb in 1949, the comfort quickly disappeared. As the 1940s gave way to the 1950s, a growing red fear that in some quarters bordered on hysteria emerged in America. It would have disastrous results for the left-of-center American folk music scene.

The gloom that engulfed Woody Guthrie began to lift in July 1947 with the birth of his son, Arlo. A year later, another son, Joady, was born, followed by a daughter, Nora, in 1949. Gradually, the pain of Cathy's tragic death eased and then began to fade, but never entirely. He had a full family again. He had a loving wife in Marjorie who bravely tolerated his drinking binges, bouts of depression and increasingly odd mood swings. But Marjorie grew more and more concerned about Woody's mental health; she saw the slow transformation of her husband who once was vibrant with songs and thoughts and the driving need to express himself on paper to a person who seemed lost in a lonely, dark place.

Ideas that were once clear and crisp and easily translated into song began turning up on the notebook page as a jangled mess of words. Guthrie was always a sexually charged man who seemingly could never get enough sex to calm his libido. But what was once erotica that occasionally came out of his pen now turned into unabashed, embarrassing pornography. It was easy to blame such instability on his personal loss and especially the drinking, and most of his friends did just that. No one knew yet that the real cause of his strange behavior was Huntington's disease.

Guthrie wasn't the only folksinger in his New York crowd that was suffering from a serious ailment. Lead Belly, whom Guthrie admired perhaps more than any other folk musician with whom he played, had been struck with Lou Gehrig's Disease. Lead Belly, proud and strong, withered physically, yet fought to remain a performing musician. Steadily he lost muscular control of his body and was unable to walk without a cane. Then he struggled to complete the most mundane tasks. By December 1949, he was dead.

People's Songs also died. Pete Seeger, who had heavily invested his time and talent in the organization, couldn't prevent its demise. Early on, idealism flowed from the organization's meetings and performances. But it wasn't sustained. In the end, People's Songs was the right organization in the wrong era. Had Seeger hatched People's Songs in the years before World War II, rather than after it, it might have stood a chance of succeeding. But when in-house bickering and second guessing robbed People's Songs of its energy and then when it caught the attention of the FBI, which monitored its actions and events and kept files on many of its musicians, anxiety amongst its members mounted. A crushing blow occurred when People's Songs enthusiastically endorsed Henry Wallace, the Progressive Party candidate in the presidential race of 1948—won by Democratic incumbent Harry Truman. The mounting bills and external pressures got to be too much, even for the ever-optimistic Seeger. People's Songs ground to a halt in March 1949.

That didn't slow Seeger down any, but it did send him spiraling into temporary depression. He loved singing at union halls and worker's meetings. Seeger believed with his heart that he and his songs could change things, inspire people, rally them, and before World War II, they did. But the postwar era in America was significantly different from the prewar era. Folk music had lost much of its connection to the American labor movement. Given the increasingly hot anti-red climate in America in the years after World War II, many union officials sought to distance themselves from prewar communist and socialist ideologies. The way union leaders saw it, folk music and the musicians who played it were still believed to be under the Soviet spell. Therefore, any endorsement of their music or having them play at rallies was risky business.

Seeger experienced firsthand the new America. In September 1949 in Peekskill, New York, he and others were viciously attacked by right wing veterans' groups and vigilantes determined to stop a concert by the African–American political activist/actor/singer Paul Robeson. It was an ugly America that threw stones and fists and screamed racial slurs while the police and many local residents looked the other way. The event became known as the Peekskill Riots, and it sent a clear message to Seeger and anyone else with real or perceived communist affiliations: go away.

Seeger was also sick of New York City and of being broke. With kids to feed and raise, Pete and his wife Toshi said good-bye to Greenwich Village and bought some property in upstate New York on the Hudson River, ironically, not too far from where the Peekskill riots happened. Seeger built a log cabin for his family to live in, grew a big garden, and made his life less complicated. Gradually, he began to feel better about himself.

There was still a matter of money. Seeger needed an income. He considered a factory job or one as a folklorist, but playing music was what he loved most. Instead of punching a time clock, Seeger chose to sing. Before moving out of New York City, he and Lee Hays had started another group. They called it the Weavers and in addition to Seeger and Hays, it included singer Ronnie Gilbert and singer-guitarist Fred Hellerman. Seeger saw the Weavers as a group that could "give a big solid warmth to the songs of Lead Belly and to many songs which had seemed ineffectual with one voice." The Weavers hadn't much of a political agenda, not like the Almanac Singers had, and Woody Guthrie wasn't asked to join the group. His erratic behavior kept even Seeger from endorsing his involvement. Plus, recalled Seeger, "Woody was amused by the Weavers. He really didn't approve of us; we got a little too fancy for his tastes."

The Weavers played a few parties and social events in New York City. Encouraged by the positive response, Seeger got the group some dates at the Village Vanguard, one of Greenwich Village's hip nightclubs, which led to a six-month stay. At first, attendance was light, but gradually the Weavers began to draw a regular crowd and some newspaper interest, and then the attention of record scouts. The Weavers signed a record deal with Decca in 1950. As a tribute to the recently departed Lead Belly, the group closed its live show with a version of his song "Goodnight, Irene," which became the B-side of its debut single, a rendition of the Israeli folk song, "Tzena, Tzena, Tzena."

Pop music was in poor shape in 1950. In just a few years, America and then the rest of the world would discover Elvis Presley and rock and roll and everything would change. But as the new decade rolled out, "race" records still sold primarily to blacks, while whites listened to and bought safe, homogenized popular music in the form of hits by Perry Como, Doris Day, Sammy Kaye, Gene Autry, and the Ames Brothers. However, the number one singing group of 1950 with the biggest-selling song of the year was none other than the Weavers. The song was "Goodnight, Irene."

Sung by Lead Belly, "Goodnight, Irene" was bluesy, rough-edged, and sad. By comparison, the Weavers' version was polished and pop-flavored. Much of that had to do with the song's arrangement created in the studio by Gordon Jenkins, a Decca artist himself who was a big fan of the Weavers and who knew how to turn a song into a pop hit. Giving "Goodnight, Irene" a soft, sentimental feel, Jenkins made it and the Weavers palpable to American pop audiences. Suddenly an old folk song written and originally sung by a recently deceased bluesman and now interpreted by a new folk group, "Goodnight, Irene" had become the number one song in America, selling an incredible four million copies.

The Weavers were hardly one-hit wonders. They followed the success of "Goodnight, Irene" with more hits: "(The Wreck of the) John B," "Kisses Sweeter Than Wine," "On Top of Old Smoky," and the South African chant, "Wimoweh," among others. The Weavers became pop stars, playing nightclubs and ballrooms across America and living a privileged life that couldn't even have been imagined a couple of years earlier. Here were Pete Seeger and Lee Hays, founders of People's Songs and fighters against Big Business and the Establishment, now soaked with success and stardom. Seeger, in particular, was torn by it all. Often he felt as if he had somehow betrayed principles that just a few years ago meant the world to him, namely keeping folk songs and work songs sacred, not allowing them to be polluted by popular tastes or demands. And yet here he was in the biggest group in America, making money, staying in top hotels, eating gourmet meals and traveling in style. It made him happy and sick at the same time.

Whether it was out of guilt or simply the result of a search for more great songs to record, the Weavers went to Woody Guthrie's catalogue and selected "So Long, It's Been Good to Know You" and "Hard, Ain't It Hard" to sing and make into singles. Before recording the former in late 1950, Seeger invited Woody to come down to a club the Weavers were performing in to hear the group's version of his song. Woody liked what he heard and told Pete to record it. Guthrie went with the group to the recording studio to listen to the Weavers turn his song into theirs. Though Jenkins liked the song's melody, he thought the Dust Bowl lyrics were passé. Guthrie took the cue and quickly penned an alternate set of lyrics, which satisfied Jenkins enough to record the song.

Giving a nod to the Weavers to record "So Long, It's Been Good to Know You" was one of the smartest business decisions Guthrie ever made. The Weavers' version of the song was another pop hit for the group, reaching number four on the charts and giving Guthrie a royalty check of ten thousand dollars. The money more than made up for his lack of income and gave Marjorie the opportunity to open up her own dance studio in Brooklyn called Marjorie Mazia's School of Dance, which became the family's main means of support.

Though Woody was performing less and less, and his prose writing had lost its edge, there was some hope for Guthrie continuing as a recording artist. Pete Kameron, the Weavers' manager, persuaded Decca talent scouts to give Guthrie an audition. Why not see if he, too, could move into the mainstream like the Weavers had, bringing more of his folk songs onto the pop charts. Guthrie happily agreed to the audition, which occurred in early 1952. One of the songs he sang for the Decca scouts was "This Land Is My Land." It is not known if Decca actually offered Guthrie a contract and then later retracted it, or he simply failed to impress the Decca people at the audition. Whatever the case, though, "This Land Is My Land" and a second song, "Kissin' On," were recorded by Decca engineers that day, but neither was released by the label.

The Decca recording of "This Land Is My Land" marked the third time Guthrie recorded the song, this one coming nearly eight years after the original version he cut for Moe Asch in New York in April 1944 and a second version he cut for Asch later on (see below). The rights to the Decca version of "This Land Is My Land" were purchased by Bear Family Records and released in 1996 on the compilation, *Songs for Political Action*. In the set the song is called "This Land Is Your Land."

Nothing exists to explain why Guthrie chose "This Land Is My Land" to play for Decca. However, performance song lists from this era suggest that Guthrie was playing the song in concert as early as 1947. Referring to the song simply as "This Land," Guthrie often buried it in the middle of his set, not giving it the special role of closing concerts or using it as an encore as would be the case later on for many artists interpreting the song, including Seeger. But Guthrie had recognized "This Land Is My Land" as one of his best, as indicated by its number ten slot on a list he created in 1952 of his "Twenty Best Songs." (Number one on the list was "Hard Travelin'." Interestingly, few other early songs of his made the grade. Not on the list: "Pretty Boy Floyd," "Pastures of Plenty," and "Tom Joad," all recognized as Guthrie classics today.)

Had Decca released the "This Land Is My Land" version from the January 1952 session, it wouldn't have been the first time the song appeared for commercial consumption. A year earlier, Moe Asch had been the first one to offer "This Land Is My Land" on a recording. Asch released the song on the third volume of his *Songs to Grow On*, the children's song collection. This volume of *Songs to Grow On* was called *This Land Is My Land* and was released on Asch's new Folkways label. It had come out as a ten-inch long-play recording (three 78s could fit on this new long-play, or LP, recording disc), but "This Land" included only three verses. Missing from this version were the Depression-era lyrics about "private property" and the "relief office." The inclusion of such verses wasn't necessary, since the song was billed by Asch as a children's sing-a-long song rather than one with social and political messages kids wouldn't understand.

Asch's Folkways label evolved from Asch Records after risks he took in the record business went bad. In the late 1940s Moe Asch became enamored with jazz, seeing the music as both folk and art music. Asch had met Norman Granz, who'd been producing jazz concerts in California. Granz convinced Asch that not only should his label include jazz, but that he could save money by recording it live rather than in the studio. After all, reasoned Granz, jazz was largely improvisational music anyway, and there was no better place to celebrate the music's improvisational spirit than in front of a live audience. Asch hired Fred Ramsey and Charles Smith, avid jazz record collectors who knew the music from the inside. Ramsey and Smith gave Asch Records a jazz sophistication that enabled Asch to attract and record such major jazz artists of the time as Mary Lou Williams, James P. Johnson, Art Tatum, and Sidney Bechet.

When Asch took a chance with a Nat King Cole recording, spending a considerable sum to press and distribute it, bad weather prevented the disc from getting to distributors and stores in time for Christmas, according to Richard Carlin, author of *Worlds of Sound: The Story of Smithsonian Folkways Records*. Asch lost considerable money on the mishap. Other financial woes widened the gap between expenses and profits and soon Asch had no choice but to declare Asch Records bankrupt.

Asch was determined, however, to remain in the record-making business. In the summer of 1948, he and Marion Distler, his former assistant, began Folkways Records. The music Folkways recorded and released was very similar to what Asch Records put out. What was different was the name and the way the ownership of the label was presented. (Because of bankruptcy, Asch had to cleverly cloak his role with the label, officially calling himself a "consultant" and "production director.") With Folkways, Asch paid out less up front money than he did for jazz recordings, thereby minimizing potential loss should a release stiff or encounter problems beyond his control. He also went back to concentrating on the music he knew best: folk music.

The first batch of Folkways Records to be released included the first volume of Guthrie's *Songs to Grow On*. Other releases in the debut of the label included recordings by Pete Seeger (*Darling Corey*) and Lead Belly (*Take This Hammer*). Each of these was an actual album in the contemporary sense—one ten-inch, 33⅓ rpm disc, as opposed to "albums" that contained several 78 rpm discs in a single package with an attractive cover.

Songs to Grow On: This Land Is My Land didn't break any sales records, but it did begin a new life for the title song. Woody Guthrie might have written it as a response to "God Bless America," now a fully embraced patriotic anthem that was beloved and sung nearly as much as "The Star Spangled Banner." But "This Land Is My Land" no longer packed the political protest punch that Guthrie intended in 1940. Now his song was being promoted as a children's song due to the irresistible allure of the chorus and the lyrics that celebrated America rather than criticized it. It was easy to learn, easy to sing—two essential elements in all kids' songs—and without the original protest lyrics about "private property" and the "relief office," the song was completely benign in the new age of McCarthyism in America.

Guthrie, meanwhile, struggled. Good songs came out of him less and less frequently; the ideas simply weren't there and his lyrics lacked luster. He had turned to prose, namely autobiographical novels with names like *Ship Story*, *Study Butte*, and *House of Earth*. Marjorie had even given him his own special writing space in their small apartment, but what resulted from all this were rambling storylines, unfocused characters, and a general lack of focus.

Guthrie had also created a children's songbook, *Twenty Songs to Grow Big On*, but no publisher wanted it, despite the wonderful artwork that Guthrie included with the manuscript. Ever since his days as a sign-painter, Guthrie had often livened his writing with cartoons and illustrations, some of them as good as the songs he penned. The illustrations that were contained in *Twenty Songs to Grow Big On*, were considered some of Guthrie's best, but still there were no bites from New York publishers.

When Guthrie grew frustrated with his writing, he roamed New York. Harold Leventhal, who once had been a song plugger for Irving Berlin, and now acted as the agent and eventually the manager for the Weavers, recalled a humorous Guthrie incident at a Weavers show.

According to Leventhal, Woody would occasionally go to a Weavers' show in Manhattan. "One evening the Weavers were headliners at a trendy East Side nightclub, the Blue Angel. Just before the show started, the club's doorman came looking for me. 'Hey, there's this guy looking to get in, says he's a friend of the Weavers and he's expected. Trouble is, he looks kind of beat and unkempt.' I knew it was Woody. I brought him down through the cellar and up to the kitchen where I borrowed a jacket and bow tie, put a white dishtowel over his arm and had him masquerade as a waiter while watching the Weavers perform."

The respect that fellow folksingers and people in New York folk circles had for Guthrie never wavered, but increasingly, they saw him as a tragic figure. Most blamed alcohol. At parties, Guthrie often sat alone, seemingly in his own world. At home, Marjorie witnessed wild mood swings; sometimes there was no alcohol involved, which at first puzzled her, then frightened her. The worst part was that Woody was growing violent, and more than once she feared for her life and the welfare of their children.

With his great songwriting flame all but extinguished and his soul in turmoil, Woody turned to drink. Many of his days were wasted affairs made up of wandering the streets and trying to find his focus. People that once embraced him and were happy with his presence now avoided him. In their eyes, he was pathetic. How could he treat Marjorie that way? A saint by any standard, Marjorie was the only one that could endure the physical and emotional abuse he handed her, yet still love him so.

Marjorie sought help for Guthrie. She begged him to see a doctor and get in a program to curtail his drinking. Woody resisted. He decided to take a trip to Florida to visit a friend. Marjorie was both relieved and worried. At least she and her children were temporarily free from the stress Guthrie brought upon his family. However, when he returned, the same old problems returned with him. Finally, after more wailing arguments at home with Marjorie, more threats, more fear instilled in his young children, and more deep bouts with depression and confusion, Woody Guthrie admitted himself into Brooklyn State Hospital in July 1952.

What Marjorie heard from the doctor, a neurologist, was what she feared most: Woody had Huntington's disease. The disease was incurable and eventually fatal. He would grow worse, week after week, month after month, year after year. The confusion Guthrie suffered would get more intense and he'd begin to lose muscular control of his body until he was incapable of doing much for himself. Guthrie was already dealing with the mental and emotional symptoms, and now he was beginning to experience the physical ones. Later that year he wrote, "Face seems to twist out of shape. Can't control it. Arms dangle all around. Can't control them. Wrists feel weak and my hands wave around in odd ways I can't stop." It wouldn't be long before Woody realized it was the beginning of the end of his life as he knew it.

Woody Guthrie was never any good at facing his problems full on. After being diagnosed, Woody signed himself out of the hospital that fall. When he came home, the arguments with Marjorie grew louder and more intense; she knew Woody was taking his fear and frustration out on her and the children. Now that she knew the truth of what ailed him, she sought to protect him from himself, but it did no good. Guthrie fought her and frightened her children to the point where she could do nothing else but throw him out. Guthrie took the rejection as a cue to run, and that's what he did. He remembered his days out in California when he was healthy and free, and longed to return to them.

The Weavers had been out on the road, performing regularly and solidifying their reputation as America's greatest folk group. It had surprised most everyone in folk music circles with how easy its members had embraced the money and the fame that came with their record sales and sold-out shows. Though the Weavers were as much a pop group as a folk group, and quite conscious of what was needed to stay popular, at least one of them, Pete Seeger, sought to stay connected with his original folk roots and old way of life.

Seeger was a walking and singing paradox. He tried to enjoy the attention the Weavers got and rationalized his success by telling himself it was a way to populate the pop charts with traditional folk music. The Weavers' songs could broaden the nation's knowledge of its musical heritage and at the time ensure the best folk songs lived on and were enjoyed by future generations of Americans. Yet, when it was obvious that singing more politicized songs would damage their career, the Weavers agreed to hold back and concentrate on songs less controversial and more mainstream.

Some old left hardliners saw Seeger and the other Weavers as a sell-out. Why hadn't they used their success and acclaim to further political causes, as had always been the case with Seeger's music? The use of song as social and political protest was evaporating. Why hadn't the Weavers, with all their commercial clout, prevented such? Guthrie personally enjoyed the success of the Weavers. He was proud that they did some of his songs, and certainly didn't mind the royalty monies that came with it. But that had nothing to with the simmering resentment in some intellectual circles caused by the Weavers' commercial success and widespread popularity.

In late 1952 Woody Guthrie went to California for the last time. Marjorie was for the trip. Getting him away from the kids and giving her some emotional rest was just part of the reason. She also knew that Guthrie loved California; he loved the memories of living there and singing his songs there, of being on the radio, and feeling like his music mattered. She thought the trip would be good for him. It would also give her time to consider what to do with him when he returned. If Guthrie's temper could not be controlled and if his actions became completely unpredictable, she was told by friends and doctors that she had to take into consideration the safety of her children more than any marital responsibility to the man she still loved.

Woody's trip to California didn't turn out the way Marjorie hoped it would. Upon arriving, he settled in with Will and Herta Geer, sleeping in a storage shed and acting as crazy as he'd acted back East. The Geers had returned to California when work ran out and the promise of getting back to the land began to consume both of them. They tolerated Guthrie's erratic behavior; the hardest part was the pornographic nature of the way he wrote, spoke, and thought. To a bystander he might have come off as a pervert. But the Geers knew that underneath the disease and the never ending sexual talk and advances was a man in personal torment.

Guthrie had heard from Marjorie only occasionally. Though he still loved her, at times intensely, he craved female companionship and sought to get it wherever he could. Relief came from a Topanga neighbor of the Geers, a light-haired young woman named Anneke Marshall. She was married to David Marshall, an actor, but once Woody had entered her life, the relationship with her husband was doomed. In typical Guthrie fashion, he turned a fascination Anneke had with him into unrequited love. In reality, she was young enough to be Woody's daughter, but that didn't bother him, or her. For his part, Guthrie was happy for the company in bed, and out.

Even California couldn't hold Guthrie. He went back to his old rambling ways as he and Anneke took a bus to New York and then to Florida where they stayed through the spring. Then fire and fate came together and struck Guthrie yet again. While camping one day, Guthrie carelessly lit a kerosene soaked log. The flame caught the log and then the kerosene that Guthrie had unknowingly splashed on his shirt sleeve, igniting it and burning his right arm, from hand to shoulder.

Guthrie was largely incapacitated for much of the summer. Aside from the continuous pain, there was the Florida heat and humidity to deal with, along with the unceasing buzz, hum, and bite of insects. And then there was the fact that Anneke was pregnant. Knowing that their predicament in Florida was all wrong for bringing a baby into the world, Woody and Anneke headed back to California, stopping along the way in Juárez where Woody got a Mexican divorce from Marjorie.

The return to California, as it turned out, was just one more stop on a wild Woody ride in which Anneke was a willing passenger. They did, however, stay long enough to get married, so the baby would not be born illegitimate. All the traveling made it hard on Anneke, who had grown big with child. But it was even tougher on Guthrie. His arm was healing, but the new skin was tight and tender. Instead of regularly exercising it, he simply didn't use it. His muscles contracted, so that the arm resembled a dead branch on a tree. Not having use of his arm meant no writing and no playing the guitar. Guthrie was miserable. And he was broke.

Anneke gave birth to a baby girl in February 1954; they called her Lorina. In better times, a new baby might have brought happiness to the couple. That was not the case this time. Now back in New York with no income to speak of, Anneke took a job as a telephone operator while Guthrie babysat. Friends of Guthrie who knew of his desperate situation tried to help. More than one organized a rent-party for him at the unheated loft on the lower East Side where he, Anneke and baby Lorina resided. Abby Weitman, a pianist who had performed with Pete Seeger and People's Songs, recalled one such get-together.

"Woody was down and out. Friends and people who were in the folk music world were getting together to collect money for him . . . there was literally a hat on the floor of the loft where people put money into it. He was a miserable looking figure. It was all so very sad. He was in terrible shape."

Guthrie had indeed hit bottom. Never one for bathing, it was so cold in the loft that he didn't even bother anymore, even when the odor from his body consumed the entire loft. Occasionally, when he felt good, he'd visit Martha Ledbetter, widow of his old folk singing friend, Lead Belly, who lived a few blocks away. She could see that Guthrie was not only wasting away physically, but also mentally and emotionally. He had fallen far in the past, but not this far: a bum arm, no money, mouths to feed, and a disease that took hold of him and shook him, literally, made him want to run again.

And he did. Leaving Anneke and little Lorina in New York after an alcohol-fueled violent argument, Guthrie and young friend Jack Elliott, an aspiring folksinger who adored everything about Guthrie, hit the road for California. Guthrie couldn't stay still. To remain in one place would suggest a certain peace, of which Guthrie had none. Leaving Elliott behind in California, Guthrie embarked on a zigzag, hitchhiking escapade up to the Pacific Northwest and into Canada, then down to Texas and finally, back to New York. He had been arrested for vagrancy more than once during this time and looked worse than a bum on a bad night—torn, dirty clothes hanging on an emaciated body run by a brain that, though once filled with genius, was now almost always foggy and disturbed.

In September 1954 Woody Guthrie stopped running. He came back to New York, signed himself into Brooklyn State Hospital, and became a ward of the state. Except for weekend visits to see friends and family, he would spend the rest of his life in hospitals. Woody had no choice but to capitulate to the demons that together made up Huntington's disease—the twitching, the mental confusion, the emotional distress. The life of America's troubadour, the dustiest balladeer of them all, had hung up his travelin' shoes for good. He was 42 years old.

Anneke Guthrie stayed in New York long enough to realize that her marriage to Woody was all but over. She had to work long hours to pay the bills, and when she came home, she had to care for baby Lorina, then visit Woody in the hospital with whatever time was left in her day. This was hardly a life for a young woman whose fate was tied to a man twice her age and who would never be right or healthy again. She endured until she could take the grind no more. In the summer of 1956, she divorced him and moved on.

Marjorie, the compassionate woman that she was, moved back into Woody's life. She filled the space vacated by Anneke, but as a friend, not a wife or lover. Despite the emotional trauma she experienced as Woody's wife, Marjorie still cared for him. She forgave many of his faults, chalking them up to Huntington's disease, including the crazy, often violent mood swings and the drinking that came from having to deal with the dreaded disease. Marjorie knew that Woody had no one else to care for him, and she wasn't going to leave him to die a slow death by himself. She became his guardian angel.

It's difficult to imagine how Woody would have survived in a changed America had he not been afflicted with Huntington's. For folksingers like him, America had become an inhospitable place in the 1950s. The FBI watched their every move; agents kept detailed files about the songs they sang and the places they performed. Though there were still some workers, union members and urban intellectuals who embraced their songs and socialist slant, their numbers grew small. For all intents and purposes, playing folk music in America in the early 1950s was a subversive activity. Since the end of World War II in 1945, America had fought communism to a standstill in Korea and was preparing to do the same in Vietnam. But what seemed to be even more threatening than the reds in Southeast Asia were the reds in America's backyard.

It had all begun in 1950 when Senator Joseph McCarthy from Wisconsin told a Women's Republican Club in Wheeling, West Virginia, "I have here in my hand a list of 205—a list of names that were made known to the Secretary of State as being members of the Communist Party and who nevertheless are still working and shaping policy in the State Department." It was a great piece of political theater, and it shook the country. Overnight McCarthy inspired a red witch hunt that would stomp on personal freedoms, unjustly accuse people of crimes they did not commit, destroy careers and lives, and generally create a Cold-War panic that sent America reeling.

The Weavers experienced the result of such fear, crashing from their pop-music high in 1952. That February, Harvey Matusow, a former friend of the group and at one time a volunteer member of People's Songs, testified before the House Un-American Activities Committee that the Weavers were Communists. That was all it took to dry up concert tours, television appearances, and recording opportunities. Decca dropped the Weavers from its recording roster the following year, despite the fact that the group was still scoring hits. The Weavers' version of yet another Lead Belly song, "Sylvie (Bring Me Li'l' Water, Sylvie)," had made it to number twenty-seven on the charts in the spring of 1953. It didn't matter to Decca. The record company even stopped supplying distributors with back catalogue of the Weavers, in essence, completely severing ties with the group that had been one of the label's top acts just a few months earlier.

The attack on the Weavers was not a surprise to its members. Though the group experienced more chart success than any other folk group or solo folk artist ever had up until that time, the American Legion and other right-wing civic organizations had sought to bring down the Weavers even before Matusow lobbed his bomb. Some vigilant members of these organizations recalled that before the group signed to Decca, Seeger and Hays created musical havoc for mining and steel companies as well as the government in the Almanac Singers.

Senator McCarthy's cronies considered the Weavers dangerous artists after Matusow had told HUAC that the Weavers were using "their appeal to the young people as a means of getting the young people down to the meetings of the Communist fronts and indoctrinating them with the party line and later recruiting them." Despite being an outright lie, that was all it took to place the names of Ronnie Gilbert, Fred Hellerman, Lee Hays, and Pete Seeger on a blacklist that no one in the government admitted to but most every left-leaning artist knew firsthand was real.

Bookings began to fall off the group's ledger like leaves off a tree in autumn. The group sang contemporary and traditional folk songs, often with syrupy strings and mushy arrangements—no songs of political protest—and still its members were hounded by red hunters. Seeger could only imagine if the group's repertoire resembled that of the Almanac Singers. One song Seeger and Lee Hays wrote in 1949 called "The Hammer Song" (later retitled "If I Had a Hammer") was about political struggle and the zeal for justice. Though Seeger wanted to include it in the Weavers' live set, Pete Kameron, the Weavers' manager, thought it too risky to do so. All this made Seeger chuckle. The Almanac Singers wouldn't have lasted a day in America in the early 1950s.

Seeger had mixed emotions about the group's demise. He loved American folk music as much as he loved the activist path he felt he was destined to follow. Playing with the Weavers opened up the ears of many Americans who would not have had the opportunity to be introduced to folk music. But Seeger never felt comfortable with the commercial success of the group. With the group disbanded, he was now free to sing where and what he wanted. Gone were the glitzy nightclub gigs that the Weavers played to people in tuxedos, and the fancy food and nice hotels. But Seeger really wasn't interested in playing to that crowd any more, anyway. In place of these dates came opportunities to play to more appreciative audiences: kids.

Pete Seeger loved kids. To him they were pure souls, soon to enter a cruel world where injustice and oppression would surely kill the bright-eyed innocence he saw in every single one of them. They were the future, the hope and promise of America, and he would play songs for them, teach them how to sing, and show them how a nation's rich musical heritage embraced its democratic ideals and diverse cultural history. Years later Seeger wrote, "In my own experience, many of the most important gains for the human race have been accompanied by song." He never let himself forget that, even back in the '50s when the mere mention of a folk song could generate a sneer, or worse, in the wrong political circles.

Seeger figured that if he could arm kids with song—the more folk tunes he could teach them, the better—then these young people of America would have a song for every challenge to their freedom and stand a fighting chance of making their country a better place than they found it. Even the silliest song had value, Seeger reckoned, especially if it had a melody that could be carried or a beat that made your foot move or your hands clap.

So Seeger started singing in schools and summer camps in New York state and Massachusetts and other parts of the Northeast. He'd arrive with his banjo and a soft smile and in no time not only were the kids listening, but they were also singing. Seeger made the most of his sing-alongs. Even the shy kids at camp were encouraged to lend their voices to the group. Seeger was a natural at this sort of thing. His wife, Toshi, could see it and so could the liberal and progressive parents that were thrilled their children were learning about America through song, with Pete Seeger as their ever-faithful teacher.

One of the songs Seeger would later sing at summer camps and schools was "This Land Is My Land." Though written by Guthrie whom he had known for years, Seeger had always claimed that he had learned the song, not from Guthrie himself, but from the recording of the song Guthrie made for Moe Asch and was included in the *Songs To Grown On* collection. "I heard it as a kids' song at first," recalled Seeger. "I had simply never heard Woody sing the song live or even knew of it until the Folkways record came out."

For being so close to Guthrie, Seeger was oddly late in being introduced to "This Land Is My Land." As we know, Guthrie did perform the song on occasion before entering Brooklyn State Hospital in the summer of 1952 as evidenced by Guthrie set lists from the period. He even considered it one of his favorite songs, writing in a letter in 1955 to a young fan, calling "This Land" a song "which I've always been awful partial to in my deepest heart and soul."

As early as 1950, the New York-based Jewish Young People's Chorus, directed by Bob De Cormier, included "This Land Is My Land" in its repertoire. And around the same time, Guthrie used "This Land Is My Land" to accompany a production of *Folksay*, the dance routine that Martha Graham created years earlier with music by Guthrie and that had been recently revived by Sophie Maslow, Marjorie's old dancing mate. Malsow had hired Guthrie to once again supply the music for *Folksay*. The production occurred at Connecticut College and was attended by Abby Weitman, the former Brooklyn pianist for a People's Songs performance at the Brooklyn Academy of Music in 1949, who had earlier attended a rent party in Guthrie's New York loft.

Somehow Weitman wound up with the typewritten lyrics that Guthrie used in what could only be described as a new version of "This Land Is My Land." The verses had been completely rewritten, Guthrie keeping only the clinching line in each verse, "This land was made for you and me" as well as the two politicized verses about "private property" and the "relief office."

The first verse of the revised lyrics didn't significantly alter the song's original intention. They merely reflected it with new words and imagery. But the new second verse hinted at Guthrie's support of postwar union struggles in America:

I walked your low hills, and I walked your cliff rims,
Your marble canyons, and sunny bright waters,
I could see all around me,
And feel inside me,
This land was made for you and me.
I saw my people and heard them singing,
I heard them crying and saw them dancing,
I saw them marching into their union,
This land was made for you and me.

Those new verses were followed by Guthrie's original lyrics about "private property" and the "relief office." These recently discovered new verses inspire two observations:

One, Guthrie saw the song's lyrics as flexible and changeable, apparently depending on why, where, and for whom the song was being sung. Guthrie sometimes changed the lyrics to other songs of his, but rarely, if ever, to this degree. And this, of course, hadn't been the first time that he altered the lyrics to "This Land Is My Land." When he originally wrote the song in 1940, which then, of course, was called "God Blessed America," it contained the "private property" and "relief office" verses. When Guthrie first recorded the song four years later, he did so with all of the original lyrics intact.

But then in 1945, in a self-published mimeographed songbook called *Ten of Woody Guthrie's Songs*, he included a new verse for "This Land": "Nobody living can ever stop me/As I go walking my freedom highway/Nobody living can make me turn back/This land was made for you and me."

It was a fine verse, easily able to stand with the original verses to "This Land." But apparently Guthrie was still not satisfied, so he changed the song again, this time for the *Songs to Grow On* set titled, *This Land Is My Land*. For that recording, the date of which is unknown, he eliminated the 1945 verse. Because of its availability, it was this version of "This Land" that most of America would come to know. But then a couple of years or so later, as evidenced here, he apparently rewrote the verses yet again.

Second, later songwriters and performers were inspired by the license Guthrie took with the lyrics to "This Land Is My Land," to do their own rewrite of the song to meet particular political demands or social protest needs. In the '60s Seeger himself altered the lyrics and encouraged others to do so, creating a hodgepodge of verses, some good, some bad, but at least the chorus was retained most of the time. In his book, *Where Have All the Flowers Gone (A Sing-Along Memoir)*, Seeger wrote that "for many of the songs in this book I found new words to fit an old melody, or found a new melody for some old words. For some songs I was just a matchmaker, bringing an old melody together with someone else's words. Sometimes I made up new words and melody but used old chord patterns." In other words, whatever lyrics worked, use, which was Guthrie's music-making mantra too.

Howie Richmond entered the music business in the late 1930s, at the height of the big-band era in America. A song plugger, Richmond pushed songs to bandleaders and later represented them as their press agent. He worked with Glenn Miller, Gene Krupa, Woody Herman and singers such as Frank Sinatra and the Andrews Sisters before entering the service during World War II. When the war was over, Richmond began a new career in music, that of a music publisher. He called his fledgling company Cromwell Music, later changing it to The Richmond Organization, or TRO, when friend and fellow song plugger Al Brackman came on board.

Richmond and Brackman looked for an opening in the music publishing world and found it in novelty songs. One of their earliest successes, "Hop Scotch Polka" was given to bandleader Guy Lombardo who recorded it for Decca Records, giving TRO its first real taste of success. Another song, "Music! Music! Music!" got them their first number one hit. Written by Stephan Weiss and Bernie Baum, the song was recorded by Teresa Brewer on the London label and was a million-seller in 1950.

It wasn't the only million-seller for TRO that year. Howie Richmond had met Pete Seeger and the Weavers through Pete Kameron, the Weavers manager, who was also a former song plugger. Kameron suggested that Richmond work with the Weavers and the family of recently deceased Lead Belly, who wrote the song. "Goodnight, Irene." The sons not only went to number one on the pop charts in 1950, but took up residence there, ultimately staying the top-selling single in America for thirteen weeks. TRO went on to have a lot more success with the Weavers in the early 1950s. Richmond had only wished he could have done the same for Woody Guthrie.

Richmond met Guthrie through Kameron and Alan Lomax. In the late 1940s

Guthrie had sought a publisher for his hundreds of songs, but either because of his unconventional ways or his political stance, he was turned down wherever he went. One day in 1950 or '51 Guthrie showed up in Richmond's tiny New York office and offered to play some songs for him. Richmond, who knew of Guthrie from his radio shows, was only too happy to hear Woody's songs. To Richmond, Guthrie was a classic American folksinger and he was shocked that he didn't already have a publisher.

"My father knew that there was something unique about Woody Guthrie," recalled son Larry Richmond. "Woody would come to the office, play his music, sleep on the couch. That was who Woody was and my father didn't see anything but a great songwriter across from his desk."

Howie Richmond was impressed with Guthrie's knowledge of music publishing and the critical analysis he offered up when talking about his songs. "Woody was much more organized than you think, and he knew what a copyright was," added Larry Richmond. "When people talked about Woody and labeled him a hillbilly or someone from the Dust Bowl, they weren't referring to his knowledge of the music business. Woody wanted a taste of commercial success, just like the Weavers, and he wanted my father to help him get it."

When Woody came to Richmond's office, two things often happened: Woody would ask for some "advance" money on his songs, which Richmond usually gave him, despite only the promise of ever seeing it back, and two, Woody would play the latest batch of songs he wrote. There were so many of them that Howie Richmond couldn't keep up with their publishing details. Finally, he came up with a solution. He bought Guthrie a portable reel-to-reel tape recorder that Guthrie could use at home to record his new songs as well as many old ones that he had forgotten about or else were safely tucked away in one of his many notebooks.

Richmond's kindness and belief in Guthrie paid him back in spades when the Weavers turned his song, "So Long, It's Been Good to Know You," into a pop hit.

Being Guthrie's publisher, Richmond collected the license fee on Woody's behalf, delivering a bigger check—$10,000—than Guthrie had ever earned before. Both Richmond and Guthrie, along with their mutual friend, Alan Lomax, believed there could be more checks like that for Guthrie and his family now that the Weavers proved folk music could be a commercial entity.

But it wasn't meant to be. The blacklisting and break-up of the Weavers and the lack of any other folk group in the early 1950s able to step into their shoes made their commercial success something of a fluke. Burl Ives and other folksingers had a few small hits and some pop singers turned folk songs into pop songs with some success. But without the Weavers on the scene, folk music on the pop charts was more a novelty than a musical movement, at least until later in the decade when a group inspired by the Weavers, the Kingston Trio, took its version of the song "Tom Dooley" to the top of the pop charts, thus setting the stage for the folk music revival of the early 1960s.

Even If the Weavers did not disband, American folk music in the early 1950s did not stand much of a chance competing with a new pop sound in American music. In 1954 American music underwent a major transformation, the most radical and significant of the twentieth century. That year, in July, in Memphis, Tennessee, a young good-looking truck driver named Elvis Presley walked into the Sun Recording Studio and changed the course of American music and cultural history.

Not exactly knowing what he was doing, Presley proved that a powerful blend of blues, country, and gospel music, called rock and roll, could ignite such cultural fires that first one generation, then another, could take the heat from the music and burn its initials onto the American cultural landscape. Rock and roll became the soundtrack of young America in the 1950s and '60s, influencing everything from fashion and dance to technology, politics, sexual mores, and racial integration. Fortunately for folk music, a decade after the rock and roll explosion, the music first brought forth by Elvis Presley opened up to new influences and sounds. Some of them came from folk.

In the early 1950s Guthrie saw little more commercial success other than what Richmond and the Weavers had delivered him with "So Long, It's Been Good to Know You." But in another way, his stature in American music grew and solidified. The reason was "This Land Is My Land" and Richmond's TRO company was responsible for it.

Alan Lomax wasn't satisfied that he and his father, John, had preserved a treasure trove of American roots music during their years of song-collecting in the South. Lomax followed the musicological field work he did with his father by going out on his own and adding to their collection in the 1940s, discovering in the process bluesmen like McKinley Morganfield, also known as Muddy Waters, and of course, Woody Guthrie.

The vast collection was housed in the Library of Congress. Lomax wondered, for what purpose? For preservation's sake, yes, and for scholarly analysis, certainly. But he believed the songs were also living social and cultural documents that deserved a new life in modern America. He also hoped to capitalize financially on the collection, in order to at least finance further collecting trips and other folk music projects.

According to Howie Richmond, Lomax spoke to him about getting such songs published in American textbooks where they could become part of public school music curricula and be taught to a new generation of Americans. Richmond agreed with Lomax and set out to convince textbook publishers to include Lomax-collected folk songs in their texts. To further entice them, Richmond offered easy terms and low license fees—and added Guthrie's "This Land" as a special discounted bonus. To publish "This Land" in an American textbook cost simply a dollar.

"I really believed that 'This Land'—a truly great song about America, its natural wealth and beauty—was something that kids sitting in classrooms ought to know and learn to sing," reflected Howie Richmond many years later. "Plus, it was a great song for entire classes to sing. It had a great melody, great chorus, and those lyrics, well, they were so beautiful. I didn't mind practically giving it away."

Publishers took Richmond's deal and "This Land Is My Land" began appearing in songbooks and school textbooks. The lyrics to the song were from the edited version of "This Land," the ones heard on Folkways' *Songs to Grow On: This Land Is My Land*. As already noted, in this 1951 version of the song there was no mention of families on relief or how signs proclaiming "private property" had limited the average American's right to his country's vast natural resources. Few even knew who Woody Guthrie was, let alone the original lyrics to his song. But knowledge of "This Land" slowly grew, as did its popularity, and not just with school kids and summer campers.

In 1954, *Sing Out!*, the folk music magazine that evolved from the *People's Song Bulletin*, the publication put out by People's Songs in the late 1940s, published the words and music to "This Land Is My Land." Even at this late date, the song was still being referred to as "This Land Is My Land." Two years later, TRO issued the song as sheet music and copyrighted as well. Both *Sing Out!* and TRO published only the verses to "This Land" heard on the version of the song that appeared on *Songs to Grow On: This Land Is My Land*, which, of course, did not include the original lyrics.

Countless young songwriters who learned "This Land" from its publication in *Sing Out!* never knew the difference. Neither did the magazine's editors. Had they known of the original Depression-era lyrics, they probably would have published them, given their liberal editorial stance. It's highly doubtful, though, that TRO would have given "This Land's" early lyrics to textbook publishers, since Richmond was pushing it as a patriotic sing-along song. The only thing left to make permanent was the title, "This Land Is Your Land." By the late 1950s, that, too, would finally be done, though it happened organically, without any official change by Guthrie or TRO.

While American kids were learning to sing "This Land Is Your Land," Woody Guthrie was sitting home or in the hospital, mostly oblivious to the transformation of his song into an increasingly popular patriotic chant. For some teachers in American schools, "This Land Is Your Land" was the perfect musical counterpoint to the evil Communist empire that by 1957, with Sputnik successfully sent into space by the

Russians, seriously threatened American supremacy in things like science and math. "This Land Is Your Land" became a musical testament to the natural virtues of The Promised Land, this place where the wheat fields waved and the redwood forests stood strong and mighty, just like America. Young students liked to sing the song, not just because of what it stood for, but because it was also just plain fun to sing.

Three of those students just so happened to be Woody's kids, Arlo, Joady, and Nora. They had been attending a public school in Queens—in late 1952 the Guthrie family had moved out of their Brooklyn apartment and into a small Cape Cod house in the Howard Beach section of Queens—but switched to a small, progressive private school, the Woodward School, when Nora, the youngest, was in third grade, Joady in fourth, and Arlo in fifth. The music teacher there, Margot Mayo, had been friends with Woody, Lead Belly, Pete Seeger, Alan Lomax and other musicians in the New York folk scene. Marjorie thought her kids would receive a better education and better treatment from the liberal-minded faculty at Woodward, even if it meant a commute back to Brooklyn to get the kids there everyday.

Mayo was born in Texas and raised in Kentucky before making her way to New York, where in the 1940s she founded the American Square Dance Group and became a staunch advocate for folk dance. Mayo played piano but appreciated stringed folk instruments and loved folk music. In addition to being a teacher, she was also an amateur folklorist and song-collector.

"For years, she had been involved in folk music," recalled Nora Guthrie. "She was one of the first people in New York that saw the connection of dance to folk music. She had open dance sessions that featured square dancing and such, and Pete Seeger's wife, Toshi, would often go to them. So, in New York, what Woody was to folk music and Lead Belly to blues, Margot Mayo was to folk dance."

Mayo taught her students how to square dance and do Virginia reels and Irish jigs along with learning to sing American folk songs. Yet Mayo was no traditionalist.

Arlo, Joady, and Nora had learned the "Star Spangled Banner" at their old elementary school; Mayo taught her students the Negro national anthem, "Lift Every Voice and Sing." From Mayo, they also learned "This Land Is Your Land," which, recalled Nora, became an alternative national anthem at the school. "Whenever we stood up at the start of school to salute the American flag, we sang 'This Land Is Your Land,' not 'The Star Spangled Banner.' Every kid who went through the Woodward School in Brooklyn thought 'This Land' was the country's real national anthem."

Arlo vividly recalled his first day at the Woodward School. "My mom drops me off and I'm wonderin' what's gonna happen when I'm told to go to the auditorium. In the auditorium were all of these kids and the teacher, Miss Mayo, was getting them ready to sing a song. I'm wonderin' what song they're gonna sing, and all of a sudden they all break into 'This Land Is Your Land.' I was the only kid in that whole auditorium that morning who didn't know the words to the song. I knew it was my father's song, but I didn't know that anyone else knew it. It's one thing to hear a song of your dad's on a record, but it's another thing altogether to hear a whole auditorium full of kids sing it. It kind of blew my mind."

Arlo went home that day and told Woody what had happened. Woody smiled and told his son to get from his bedroom the Gibson guitar he had given him as a gift on his fifth birthday. As Arlo recalled, "'This Land Is Your Land' was the only song that Woody had actually taught me to play. We went over the chords and then the words so that I could memorize them and wouldn't look foolish in school the next day. But then he taught me three extra verses that weren't in the published version of the song. I didn't write them down, I just memorized them. Those, of course, were the original ones about the Depression, the ones that made 'This Land' a protest song."

In the summer of 1955, Pete Seeger was called to appear before the House Un-American Activities Committee in the Federal Building at Foley Square in New York City. It didn't take long for Frank Tavenner, the committee's counsel, to get right to the point, which was to get Seeger to admit that he was a member of the Communist Party. Tavenner held up an issue of a 1947 *Daily Worker* that had a listing that announced a Seeger and Allerton Section musical get-together in the Bronx.

Seeger was respectful, but firm. "Sir, I refuse to answer that question, whether it was a quote from the *New York Times* or the *Vegetarian Journal*." The committee tried again to have Seeger answer the question. Seeger's reply was classic: "I am not going to answer any questions as to my association, my philosophical or my religious beliefs or my political beliefs, or how I voted in any election, or any of these private affairs. I think these are very improper questions for any American to be asked, especially under such compulsion as this. I would be very glad to tell you my life story if you want to hear it."

Tavenner tried again, this time pulling out an April 1948 issue of the *Daily Worker* that announced Seeger's performance at a May Day Rally in Newark, N.J. Again, Seeger launched into a monologue: "I feel that in my whole life I have never done anything of any conspiratorial nature, and I resent very much and very deeply the implication of being called before this Committee that in some way because my opinions may be different from yours . . . that I am any less of an American than anybody else. I love my country very deeply, sir."

More give and take dialogue and Seeger yielded not an inch. Tavenner showed Seeger a May 1949 issue of the *Daily Worker* about another May Day program in which Seeger participated. More word gymnastics by Seeger, who, by now, had raised the heat in the room to a breaking point of frustration. Eventually Chairman of the House Un-American Activities Committee demanded that Seeger answer the questions put forth to him. "I feel these questions are improper, sir, and I feel they

Actor Will Geer, one of Woody's greatest supporters, appears before the House Un-American Activities Committee, 1951.

are immoral to ask any American this kind of question."

Unlike Lee Hays, who, when he was called to testify, invoked the Fifth Amendment, Seeger courageously opted to deal with the questions asked him by dancing around them, bobbing and weaving like an old boxer, and throwing vocal jabs whenever he could. More direct questions asking if Seeger was a member of the Communist Party and more verbal dancing by Seeger occurred.

Finally came the contempt threat. Still, Seeger refused to answer the questions put to him. A full reading of the proceedings reminds one of Abbott and Costello's famous baseball wordplay, "Who's on First." The Committee questioned and Seeger answered—but then again, he didn't, really. "My answer is the same as before, sir," Seeger would say. Tavenner or another Committee member would ask what the answer was before, and Seeger would take them round and round until they grew so frustrated that another question was asked in which Seeger answered the same way. Finally came the statement from Chairman Walter that Seeger wanted to hear: "The witness is excused."

In the folk music world, Pete Seeger was a primary target of the House Un-American Activities Committee. Bringing him down would make it easier to bring down others in the radical arena of folk music. Woody Guthrie would certainly have been called had he not been in the hospital. He had an FBI file that went all the way back to 1941. Matusow had implicated him too, claiming falsely that Guthrie "was a member of the cultural division of the Communist Party." What an interesting scene that would have made—Guthrie testifying in front of the House Un-American Activities Committee. One can only imagine Guthrie, with his smart sense of humor, turning on his hillbilly drawl and folksy charm, while stiff-lipped, sharp-suited Congressmen and lawyers tried to grill him about his support for the Communist Party and the words and music he wrote for socialist causes.

Pete Seeger never went to jail for his affiliation with the Communist Party as some on the Committee threatened. He remained a blacklisted performer, but Seeger was beyond that now. He played schools and churches and camps, and generally made enough money to keep his family warm in the winter and to put food on the table. And there was the reuniting of the Weavers to think about. But first he wanted to do something for his friend Woody and for his kids. In 1956, he and Harold Leventhal, organized the first Woody Guthrie tribute concert, which would act as a benefit concert for the newly created Woody Guthrie Children's Trust Fund.

The concert took place at Pythian Hall on the upper West Side of Manhattan in March. It was a small venue, barely holding twelve hundred, but its ornate façade, which resembled a Pharoah's temple straight out of Egypt, made it seem that things besides social events, meetings of the Knights of Pythia, and the occasional boxing match occurred there. That Woody Guthrie would be in attendance with his family made the concert even more special. Seeger didn't want to produce just any concert; rather, he asked Mill Lampell from the old Almanac Singers to create a script that tied some of Guthrie's best known songs together in a sort of musical narrative. Lee Hays from the Weavers was a narrator; he read from Lampell's script, with that big, bold voice of his, and from Guthrie's own writing.

Most everyone who had ever performed with Woody in the past, including Seeger and members of the Almanac Singers and People's Songs, along with the Weavers, played that night. The evening's encore was a spirited version of "This Land Is Your Land" led by Seeger. Woody sat in a theater box just above the stage with his children, Leventhal, Marjorie and her new husband, Al Addeo. Dressed in a sports jacket, white shirt but no tie, Guthrie politely sat through the show. Thankfully, the muscle spasms were minimal that night, but the glazed faraway look in his eyes suggested that something certainly ailed him.

After the final notes of "This Land" had been sung, Seeger pointed to Guthrie in his box and smiled. Most members of the audience turned to look at Guthrie, too, and got up out of their seats to give Guthrie a prolonged standing ovation. Guthrie stood, too, to acknowledge their love and respect. For many in the audience that night it would be the last time they'd ever see Woody Guthrie.

Seeger thought the concert was a terrific success. It had earned more than $1,500 for the trust, which was to pay for college and other educational expenses for the Guthrie kids. Musically, he thought it went well, too. What he liked most was how "This Land Is Your Land" brought the house down at the end. He had always believed it was one of the best American sing-along songs he knew. The Guthrie tribute concert only confirmed it. People in the audience who knew the words sang along and when Seeger called out the final line, "This land was made for you and me" tears welled up in the eyes of most everyone in Pythian Hall.

Seeger wouldn't forget the power of "This Land Is Your Land" as a concert clincher. A couple of months before the Guthrie tribute, in December 1955, the Weavers reunited and performed at Carnegie Hall to a sold-out house. They played their hits, with the audience clapping and cheering as much for the songs as for the fact that the Weavers had endured the pain and humiliation that went with being blacklisted a few years earlier. And now, here they were on the stage of one of New York's most prestigious venues.

To cap off the evening, Seeger led the Weavers and the audience in a spirited version of "This Land Is Your Land." The rousing success of the concert encouraged Vanguard Records to offer the group a new recording contract. One of the first things the Weavers did was cut a studio version of "This Land Is Your Land."

But it was live, in front of an audience, where "This Land Is Your Land" would serve Seeger best. He would use the song for his closing number again and again for a half century more, each time raising the audience to new heights as they sang the lyrics and celebrated the concept that "This Land Is Your Land" was a national music landmark.

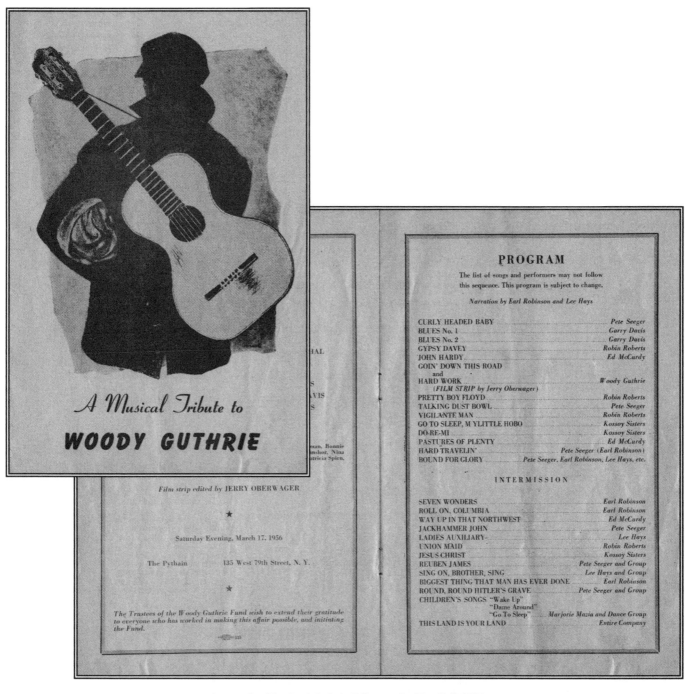

A Musical Tribute to

WOODY GUTHRIE

...nan, Bonnie
...nshor, Nina
...atricia Spirn,

Film strip edited by JERRY OBERWAGER

★

Saturday Evening, March 17, 1956

The Pythain   135 West 79th Street, N. Y.

★

The Trustees of the Woody Guthrie Fund wish to extend their gratitude
to everyone who has worked in making this affair possible, and initiating
the Fund.

PROGRAM

The list of songs and performers may not follow
this sequence. This program is subject to change.

Narration by Earl Robinson and Lee Hays

CURLY HEADED BABY	*Pete Seeger*
BLUES No. 1	*Garry Davis*
BLUES No. 2	*Garry Davis*
GYPSY DAVEY	*Robin Roberts*
JOHN HARDY	*Ed McCurdy*
GOIN' DOWN THIS ROAD and	
HARD WORK	*Woody Guthrie*
(FILM STRIP by Jerry Oberwager)	
PRETTY BOY FLOYD	*Robin Roberts*
TALKING DUST BOWL	*Pete Seeger*
VIGILANTE MAN	*Robin Roberts*
GO TO SLEEP, M YLITTLE HOBO	*Kossoy Sisters*
DO-RE-MI	*Kossoy Sisters*
PASTURES OF PLENTY	*Ed McCurdy*
HARD TRAVELIN'	*Pete Seeger (Earl Robinson)*
BOUND FOR GLORY	*Pete Seeger, Earl Robinson, Lee Hays, etc.*

INTERMISSION

SEVEN WONDERS	*Earl Robinson*
ROLL ON, COLUMBIA	*Earl Robinson*
WAY UP IN THAT NORTHWEST	*Ed McCurdy*
JACKHAMMER JOHN	*Pete Seeger*
LADIES AUXILIARY	*Lee Hays*
UNION MAID	*Robin Roberts*
JESUS CHRIST	*Kossoy Sisters*
REUBEN JAMES	*Pete Seeger and Group*
SING ON, BROTHER, SING	*Lee Hays and Group*
BIGGEST THING THAT MAN HAS EVER DONE	*Earl Robinson*
ROUND, ROUND HITLER'S GRAVE	*Pete Seeger and Group*
CHILDREN'S SONGS "Wake Up"	
"Dame Around"	
"Go To Sleep"	*Marjorie Mazia and Dance Group*
THIS LAND IS YOUR LAND	*Entire Company*

Concert booklet for *A Guthrie Tribute at Pythian Hall*, 1956.

9

As a high school kid growing up in mid-fifties Minnesota, Bob Zimmerman never wanted anything more from life than to be a rock and roll star. Under his name in his Hibbing High School yearbook was the audacious announcement that he intended to "join Little Richard," that great black pounder of the piano keys with the wild hair and make-up, the man who made musical sex with songs like "Good Golly, Miss Molly," "Long Tall Sally," "Tutti Frutti," and other tales of young lust in segregated America. In 1959, a lot of teenagers—black and white—harbored similar aspirations, though such fantasies faded and finally disappeared altogether when jobs and marriage entered the picture. Zimmerman would never entirely abandon his rock and roll dream. But later that year he'd find another musical path that would lead him in a different direction, and, in the process, change most everything we knew about American music.

Born in Duluth in 1941, Bob Zimmerman came from a middle-class Midwestern Jewish family whose roots extended back to the Ukraine. His father owned a furniture business in Hibbing, where the family moved when young Bob was six. His mother, pleasant and personable and liked by her neighbors, gave her son everything he needed to be happy. By all accounts his was as normal a childhood as could be expected in a town like Hibbing, with its small Jewish population and its location in northern Minnesota on the Mesabi Iron Range. Hibbing was hardly a tourist attraction, but it did have something no other American town had: the largest open-pit iron ore mine in the world.

Zimmerman graduated from Hibbing High School that spring and enrolled at the University of Minnesota in Minneapolis that fall, not knowing what he wanted to study or why, even, he was in college. About the only thing Zimmerman was passionate about was music, and it wasn't just music itself, but also the culture from which the music originated and the lives of the people who made it. He learned everything he could about Little Richard and other music heroes like Elvis Presley, Hank Williams and Buddy Holly. But none of them did to Bob Zimmerman what Woody Guthrie would do to him, namely, affect every cell in his body and stir his passion to *be* Woody in every way possible.

Zimmerman, who in early 1960 had begun calling himself Bob Dylan, thinking the name more compelling than the too-Jewish-sounding Zimmerman, was floored by his introduction to Guthrie. In volume one of *Chronicles*, his acclaimed 2004 memoir, Dylan wrote, "My life had never been the same since I'd first heard Woody on a record player in Minneapolis. . . . When I first heard him it was like a million megaton bomb had dropped."

Dylan had been drifting into folk music before he came to Minneapolis on a Greyhound bus in the summer of '59. He wound up in that part of the city called Dinkytown where record shops, bookstores and art galleries abounded and where clubs and coffeehouses featured live folk, jazz, and blues. Dylan decided to learn as many folk songs as he could, gobbling up albums and songbooks he borrowed from friends and meeting musicians like John Koerner and Tony Glover who broadened his musical horizons even more. His days became one long musical journey as he set

Alan Lomax (center) with Pete Seeger (right) and three unnamed musicians
practicing for the Folksong '59 concert at Carnegie Hall in 1959.

about unraveling the mysteries of American roots music and figuring how he could find a place for himself in it.

Dylan's introduction to Guthrie came from his discovery of the old Folkways albums Moe Asch had released ten years earlier. In *Chronicles*, Dylan recalled the moment when he first heard the Guthrie sides. "I put one on the turntable and when the needle dropped, I was stunned—didn't know if I was stoned or straight. . . . All these songs, one after another made my head spin. It was like the land parted." Dylan spent many Minneapolis afternoons that fall and the following year listening and relistening to Guthrie's songs, learning the chords and memorizing the words. "Woody Guthrie tore everything in his path to pieces," Dylan continued. "For me it was an epiphany, like some heavy anchor had just plunged into the waters of a harbor. . . . I decided then and there to sing nothing but Guthrie songs. It's almost like I didn't have any choice."

He probably didn't. Guthrie's tug was strong and unrelenting; his songs found a warm spot in the young folksinger's heart and lodged themselves there. Dylan marveled at their simple honesty and thought them a portal to a part of America that he never saw growing up in Hibbing, one filled with hoboes and misfits, men and women for whom the American Dream was nothing but a mirage. Yet, the way Guthrie described them, the land—from one coast to the next—and the possibilities that came from it were all somehow beautiful, too. In Guthrie's best songs, hope outweighed heartbreak even in the farthest corners of the country's dark side.

One of the songs Dylan heard from Guthrie and that he immediately included in his growing repertoire was "This Land Is Your Land." Unlike most young kids from New York, whose progressive-minded parents had sent them to upstate summer camps or who had attended schools where they sang "This Land Is Your Land" as a sing-along exercise about the natural grandeur and promise of America, Dylan had come upon the song straight up, from Guthrie himself. By spring of 1960 he was performing it in the occasional Dinkytown club and at friends' houses and parties.

In the spring of 1961 a friend of Dylan's did an amateur recording of some two dozen songs performed by Dylan, including "This Land Is Your Land." It was obvious that Dylan had carefully studied the nuances of Guthrie's vocal style and made pains to sing the song as if he had been born in a box car and raised on skid row somewhere rather than the comfortable confines of a Jewish home with loving parents. Dylan phrased the lyrics to "This Land" like Guthrie had on the Asch recording and his voice sounded grizzled and older than it really was. But somehow Dylan's version of the song was believable—he had made it his own, just like other young folksingers were doing across America as they too sought Guthrie's spirit and recast his songs for a new America and a new decade.

Guthrie's impact on Dylan deepened after a Minneapolis friend, Dave Whittaker, gave him a copy of Guthrie's autobiographical novel, *Bound for Glory*. "I went through it from cover to cover like a hurricane, totally focused on every word, and the book sang out to me like the radio," Dylan remembered in *Chronicles*. So absorbed was he by not just Guthrie's music, but also his life and his stories, that Dylan realized he had to do something more than read about Woody Guthrie, imagine him in his mind and mimic him in every way he possibly could. It had become clear to Dylan that he had to meet his mentor, see for himself the weathered face and wooly hair and the hands from which came the greatest folk songs in the American songbook. So Dylan did the only thing he could do: leave school and travel to New York because he wouldn't be satisfied, wouldn't feel complete or at peace with himself, until he shook the hand of the man who meant so much to him.

He arrived in New York in January 1961 in the middle of a bitter winter, winding up in Greenwich Village, that section of lower Manhattan where young, struggling folksingers could play some songs, pass the hat, and earn enough money to get by until the next night. He wasn't yet twenty years old. Aside from eagerly wanting to meet Guthrie, Dylan had come to New York to attempt his own career as a folksinger, following always in Guthrie's footsteps. He told his parents such before he left, along with anyone else in Minneapolis who cared to listen.

Greenwich Village was the spiritual and musical home of the old folk music scene of Guthrie, Lead Belly, Pete Seeger, the Almanac Singers, and the Weavers. It had the clubs, the cheap rents and lofts, the coffeehouses and Irish bars. It had New York University and Washington Square, and it was a short subway ride to radio stations, record companies and concert halls. In the early '60s, the Village had also become the hub of the nascent folk revival. Guthrie was in the hospital battling Huntington's disease and Seeger was living in Beacon, New York on a hill above the Hudson River. But there was a new generation of folksingers now—Dave Van Ronk, Carolyn Hester, Tom Paxton, David Blue, Fred Neil, Odetta, Len Chandler, Mark Spoelstra, Richie Havens, Phil Ochs, the New Lost City Ramblers, and a new folk group inspired by the Weavers called Peter, Paul and Mary. They were the ones now carrying on the folk tradition and reigniting interest in the music for new, younger audiences. Dylan's timing couldn't have been better.

His first New York performance occurred in late January at the Greenwich Village club Café Wha? on MacDougal Street. It was open-mic night, so Dylan was free to sing and pass the hat like the rest of the performers. According to people in the audience Dylan introduced himself by telling them that "I been travelin' around the country followin' in Woody Guthrie's footsteps." That wasn't true, but it made the people nursing their drinks more attentive. Dylan's romanticized vision of himself was only a lie if it was told with ill intention, and it wasn't. He probably half-believed that he'd been doing just that, given his Guthrie obsession. He certainly looked like he'd been traveling and he most certainly had copied Guthrie's working man uniform of boots, jeans, and a flannel shirt. No one really remembers what Guthrie songs Dylan performed that night, but a good guess was that "This Land Is Your Land" was one of them and he probably sang it just like he imagined Woody would.

How Dylan had found the whereabouts of the Guthrie family is also unknown, but a little while later, he showed up in the Howard Beach section of Queens where Marjorie and her kids—Arlo, Nora, and Joady—lived. Marjorie was at work when Dylan arrived on a cold grey late afternoon that January. Arlo answered the knock on the door. "It was some guy with work boots on looking for my dad," recalled Arlo. "There had been others like him, people who came wanting to see Woody, so I was kind of used to this sort of thing."

Arlo told Dylan that his father was in the hospital. Dylan wanted to know more, so Arlo invited him in the house. A teenage girl from the neighborhood, just a couple of years older than Arlo, who watched over the younger kids when Marjorie was away, grew nervous when Dylan sat down and planned on staying. "She knew we weren't supposed to have strangers in the house," Arlo continued, "but when he pulled a harmonica out of his pocket and started playing it, I got mine and we played a few tunes together. Then, after forty-five minutes or so, he said he had to be going, and left."

Dylan met Woody Guthrie a week or so later in New Jersey at the home of Bob and Sid Gleason, friends of the Guthrie family. Woody had moved to Greystone Hospital, in the suburban New Jersey town of Morris Plains, in 1956. The Gleasons lived in East Orange, not far from Morris Plains, and on many Sundays in the early '60s they'd drive to Greystone, pick up Woody, and give him a break from the drudgery of hospital life and hospital food. Marjorie and the kids made the trek from Queens to Jersey, as did friends such as Pete Seeger, Ramblin' Jack Elliott, and Harold Leventhal—and young aspiring folksingers like Bob Dylan.

Woody didn't do much except eat and listen to the conversation. That was all he could do. When Dylan arrived at the Gleason's home, he introduced himself to Marjorie, who approved of his visit with her former husband, and allowed Dylan to

Joady, Woody, Marjorie, Nora, and Arlo Guthrie. Café Society, New York City, 1957. Photo by Dave Gahr.

serenade him. It was difficult for Dylan to see his hero in such a sorry state. Guthrie, arms flailing uncontrollably, searching for words that didn't come without extreme effort, and walking like a drunken sailor on leave, nonetheless enjoyed the company. Once Dylan got used to Guthrie's condition, he gave Guthrie a sampling of Guthrie's own songs, played by Dylan with great attention to detail. He sounded so eerily close to Guthrie that someone remarked he was like a "Woody Guthrie jukebox."

It didn't take long for Dylan to accomplish his main goal in coming East. He could now boast that he and Woody Guthrie were friends. Next up was getting established as a New York folksinger who could earn his keep by singing and playing songs in the local clubs and coffeehouses. That didn't take long, either. In addition to learning still more Guthrie songs, Dylan grew even more obsessed with Guthrie, the legend. "Woody's songs were having that big an effect on me, an influence on every move I made, what I ate and how I dressed, who I wanted to know, who I didn't," said Dylan in *Chronicles.*

Harold Leventhal recalled that once or twice at Greenwich Village parties, he'd see Dylan excitedly telling a Guthrie story and then suddenly, with no apparent reason, Dylan would go spastic for a moment, imitating Guthrie playing out his battle with Huntington's; Leventhal couldn't say for sure. "The first time I saw him do it, I was shocked," remembered Leventhal. "Was he making fun of Woody? I didn't think so. It was just that Dylan had, in his mind, become Woody Guthrie, sickness and all. It was funny to see, but it was also touching in a strange sort of way."

Dylan showed his love and admiration for Woody Guthrie in a more memorable and respectful way when he penned "Song to Woody," shortly after a visit with his mentor. Dylan wrote it "in New York City in the drug store on 8ᵗʰ Street," he recalled in one of his earliest interviews, that with Gil Turner from *Sing Out!* "It was one of them freezing days that I came back from Sid and Bob Gleason's in East Orange, New Jersey. . . . And I just thought about Woody, I wondered about him, thought harder and wondered harder."

Dylan told Turner that he had written "Song to Woody" in "five minutes." It was Dylan's first original song of consequence, and for it, he used the Woody Guthrie style of folk song composition. Rather than write a melody, Dylan used the one from Guthrie's "1913 Massacre." Guthrie, in turn, had borrowed the melody from an old folk standard, "One Morning in May," which in some circles is known as "The Soldier and the Lady." And so the folk cycle continued.

Later that year, after Dylan met Columbia Records talent scout John Hammond and had signed a recording contract with him, Dylan recorded "Song to Woody" as one of two original songs on his 1962 self-titled debut. The other, "Talkin' New York," also had a connection to Guthrie. Dylan had studied Guthrie's talking blues songs, imitating his style and using New York as a song topic, much like Guthrie had back in 1940 when he first arrived in the city. Guthrie had written a batch of New York songs based on his earliest experiences there and employed the talking blues style in at least a couple of them.

Dylan had been playing "Song to Woody" in Village clubs like the Gaslight before he entered the recording studio with Hammond to cut the tracks that would comprise his first album. He was also playing a version of "1913 Massacre," as well as other Guthrie songs. And he wasn't the only one. It seemed as if every young folksinger working the Village clubs and "basket-houses"—places where they passed a basket instead of a hat for tips—had at least a couple of Guthrie songs in their repertoire. Many of them had "This Land Is Your Land."

Few of these young folksingers, if any, had ever seen Guthrie play live. They knew him only by reputation and his recordings. On rare occasion, Marjorie or Ramblin' Jack Elliott along with Arlo, would take Woody to Washington Square Park, where on warm spring weekends the place resembled a large folksinger's showcase mart. Guthrie didn't stay long and couldn't play any songs, and many people didn't even recognize him with his beard and the distant gaze in his eyes. Yet, for those Washington Square folksingers who did realize that the small twitching man was indeed Woody Guthrie, just being near him was enough for them to believe that they had been in the presence of a folk-music god.

Seeger, more than anyone else, was the Guthrie torchbearer. Despite being black-listed, Seeger carried on, nearly always spicing his set with Guthrie songs and often finishing it with "This Land Is Your Land," so that "people wouldn't forget that song or the man who wrote it." Years later, Seeger confessed that "when I first heard 'This Land Is Your Land,' I didn't perceive how great it was. I thought to myself, 'That song is just too simple.' I actually believed it was one of Woody's lesser efforts. Shows you how wrong you can be."

In October 1961, Seeger penned an Introduction to *The Nearly Complete Collection of Woody Guthrie Folk Songs* in which he described Guthrie's songs better than anyone had previously. "Yes, the words show a fine sense of poetry," wrote Seeger, "of reaching out for exactly the right word at exactly the right place. He used some fine time-tested tunes. The songs are honest; they say things that need to be said. . . . Some of his greatest songs are so deceptively simple that your eye will pass right over them, and you will comment to yourself, 'Well, I guess this was one of his lesser efforts.' Years later, you will find the song has grown on you and become part of your life."

Certainly that was the case for "This Land Is Your Land." Seeger loved the lyrics to "This Land" as well as the song's easy sway, but he especially loved how it got people singing along. Seeger was a sing-along addict. To him, the folk process wasn't complete unless it was communal and participatory. It wasn't the same when people passively sat in their seats and just listened to a performer play songs. Far better was when the audience sang too. Seeger thought the world could be healed with song and every time he strapped on his banjo, he strove for a cure.

Bob Dylan, circa 1961.

After the break-up of the Weavers in 1953, and despite a successful reunion concert that the group staged two years later at New York's Carnegie Hall, folk music all but fell off the American music map in the mid-fifties. It rarely appeared on the pop charts as blacklisting stifled or destroyed careers and rock and roll invaded American radio and youth culture. There were a couple of notable exceptions. Harry Belafonte, a strikingly handsome New York singer with Jamaican roots, had huge success with his album, *Calypso*, in 1956, which remained number one on the *Billboard* pop charts for an astonishing thirty-one weeks. The signature track from the album, "Day-O" (or "The Banana Boat Song," as it was often known), was a traditional Jamaican mento (folk) song that Belafonte gave new to life to; as a single, the song experienced similarly successful numbers, having made it into the Top Ten in 1957.

Belafonte wasn't the first to introduce the "The Banana Boat Song" to American audiences. After Seeger protégé Bob Gibson returned from a trip to Jamaica, he taught "The Banana Boat Song" to the folk group, the Tarriers, who recorded it and had a hit with it just prior to the American release of Belafonte's version. Because the Tarriers, which included future actor Alan Arkin, embellished the song's melody with chords from another Jamaican folk song "Hill and Gully Rider," the group is sometimes cited as the creator of "The Banana Boat Song," though its origins are clearly Jamaican. Later, Shirley Bassey and other singers recorded "The Banana Boat Song," capitalizing on its seemingly never-ending popularity.

Much of Belafonte's success could be contributed to his good looks, great voice and smart selection of songs to sing. "The Banana Boat Song" owns an irresistible melody and the mildly exotic "Day-O" call-and-response chorus got the attention of the American record-buying public. Belafonte also recorded and had hits with "Jamaica Farewell" and "Jump in the Line," further adding to his popularity. However, another part of his success stemmed from interest at the time in Caribbean music. Jazz trumpeter Dizzy Gillespie had introduced to American audiences the hot, saucy rhythms of the region, especially those of Afro-Cuban jazz. Belafonte did the same with his folk-pop and diluted calypso sounds. What he sang was mostly mento with only calypso overtones, but Belafonte was often dubbed "King of Calypso." He repudiated the title because he knew it wasn't true. Other Caribbean artists such as Lord Kitchener and the Mighty Sparrow were far more deserving of such royalty status, but most American record buyers had never heard of them.

Later, in the 1960s, Belafonte would get deeply involved in the civil rights movement, becoming a major spokesperson for it and a trusted friend of Dr. Martin Luther King Jr. He understood well how music could be an agent for social and political change. But in the mid-1950s, when his career was just taking off, Belafonte steered clear of politics, preferring to make music and movies and to establish himself in American pop culture, which he did convincingly.

Where folk music did hold its ground was on progressive college campuses, particularly in the Northeast, and in coffeehouses that featured singers and groups playing for small audiences. As already mentioned, Greenwich Village catered to a folk crowd, which often mixed with jazz and blues audiences, as did clubs in Boston, Chicago, San Francisco, Los Angeles, and other major cities. Thus was formed a small circuit where folk musicians played and folk music fans gathered, but it was largely a scene that operated under the radar of radio and record companies. That all changed in 1958.

The Kingston Trio was an unlikely group to jumpstart what Pete Seeger and the Weavers began a decade earlier. Clean-cut and clean-shaven, nicely dressed in striped shirts and pressed khakis, these were good boys with squeaky clean All-American looks and a sound to match. The trio's members—Bob Shane, Nick Reynolds and Dave Guard—might have been influenced by Woody Guthrie, which they later claimed. But they were a far cry from his rugged individualism and old dust-bowl scruffiness. Nothing about them was smirched by even the hint of socialism, or worse, the evils of Communism. "We weren't much for trying to put messages into our songs," recalled Shane. "Politics weren't what we sang about. We were just interested in playing and seeing where it would get us."

The Kingston Trio played spit-polish folk songs with pop overtones. When Capitol Records signed the group to a contract, one of the songs the Kingston Trio recorded was an old-time murder ballad from the mountains of Appalachia called "Tom Dooley," hardly the kind of song you'd expect from such a group, whose members hailed from Honolulu and were now based in California.

"Tom Dooley" was already known in folk circles, but most pop listeners hadn't a clue as to its origins. Alan Lomax knew the song; he included it in his book *Folk Song U.S.A.* The Folksay Trio recorded it in 1951, as did Frank Warner a year later. The Kingston Trio happened to hear "Tom Dooley" in 1957 during an audition at the San Francisco club, the Purple Onion, by an aspiring folksinger whose name has been lost to history.

The Trio recorded "Tom Dooley," sprucing it up with a narrated prelude, a pop arrangement and a lonely banjo. America loved it, sending the song straight to number one in late 1958 and landing the Kingston Trio on magazine covers, on television, and in the hearts of music fans across the U.S. Capitol Records recognized that something big was brewing; it shoved the Kingston Trio back into the recording studio, recording enough tracks to release three new studio albums in 1959 and one live album, all big sellers. Folk music was back on the pop charts and something that would eventually be labeled the "folk revival" had begun.

Those folk musicians who followed Pete Seeger in the 1950s and early '60s, playing folk music to small clusters of college students in coffeehouses, to kids at summer camps, and to adults at church socials, never believed that folk music needed reviving. It was always there, they argued, just forced underground by the blacklist and the conservative civic leaders and congressmen who believed that anyone with a banjo or guitar was up to no good. Like Seeger, they pressed on, insisting that folk music was such a vital expression of American culture that it was only a matter of time before the music was again accepted as legitimate and necessary. Had Woody Guthrie been healthy, he undoubtedly would have been on folk's front line, singing in the face of the Establishment, refusing to be silenced. But his active part in the struggle was over.

It wasn't just Seeger who was keeping Woody Guthrie's songs, especially "This Land Is Your Land," from being forgotten. In 1961 the Kingston Trio finally got around to paying tribute to Guthrie. Three Kingston Trio albums released that year contained Guthrie classics. *Make Way* contained "Hard Travelin'," *Close Up* had "The Sinking of the Reuben James," now called simply "Reuben James," and *Goin' Places* featured "Pastures of Plenty" and "This Land Is Your Land."

The success of the Kingston Trio encouraged a wash of other folk groups, each eager to capitalize on the new folk music craze and to follow the pop path cut by the Kingston Trio. The Chad Mitchell Trio, the Limeliters, the Brothers Four and the New Christy Minstrels all got recording contracts and hit the concert trail in the early 1960s. Many of them included Guthrie songs in their set, especially "This Land Is Your Land." "People felt good when they heard it and sang along with it," recalled the Kingston Trio's Shane. "Most everyone in the audience already knew the song and loved it, so it was an easy decision to include it in your set and even close with it."

The most popular of the new folk revival groups was a trio from the East Coast called Peter, Paul and Mary. Peter Yarrow, Noel "Paul" Stookey and Mary Travers came together in 1961 at the suggestion of Albert Grossman, a bear of a man and a manager who hoped to gain the kind of success with his new folk threesome that was enjoyed by the Kingston Trio. Yarrow had been part of the New York folk scene and performed on a 1960 television special called *Folk Sound U.S.A.* Stookey was a stand-up comic from the Midwest and a devout fan of rhythm & blues. Travers, a tall, beautiful blonde-haired singer and sometime actress, had made the rounds in New York before teaming up with Stookey as a duo. Grossman introduced Yarrow to Stookey and Travers. "Gradually, we all began to believe we might have something to say together," wrote Yarrow in one of the group's early concert programs. The result was Peter, Paul and Mary.

One of the first songs the trio learned was "This Land Is Your Land." "Peter and Mary had this wealth of folk music knowledge that I didn't have," remembered Stookey years later. "They knew the song, as did everyone else playing Greenwich Village clubs in the early '60s—you heard it all over—and they knew all about Woody Guthrie. They cherished his songs, as would I as I came to learn the immensity of his contributions to American folk music. But 'This Land' was our Woody Guthrie staple. We sang it at the end of our concerts for nearly fifty years."

The trio, with Peter and Paul wearing matching suits and ties and sporting sharp goatees, and Mary in a dress, looking every bit the folk music princess she'd quickly become, suggested an urban sophistication and a serious commitment to the music they sang. Their voices were seamless, and their songs, rich in spirit, made the group top concert draws and popular recording artists. With Grossman's guidance, Peter, Paul and Mary mostly avoided the saccharine stylings and folk-lite sound of the other folk pop groups, yet still managed to make wildly successful recordings. Their self-titled debut album remained in *Billboard's* Top Ten for nearly two years.

Grossman had an uncanny sense of pop timing. He realized that rock and roll had lost its steam and was foundering. Most of the music's pioneers had been taken out of the picture. Elvis was in the army. Buddy Holly and Ritchie Valens had died in a plane crash. Automobile accidents had stolen the careers of Carl Perkins and Gene Vincent and the life of Eddie Cochran. Bad judgment ruined Jerry Lee Lewis, who married his 13-year-old first cousin and bragged about it. Chuck Berry had gone to jail for transporting an underage girl across state lines. Johnny Cash had turned to country and Little Richard to God. Folk music, reasoned Grossman, would be the next big thing, and he was right. Along with the sound of soul music, mostly in the form of Motown; the girl groups; and the surf songs of the Beach Boys, folk music became pop music in the early '60s.

Peter, Paul and Mary didn't write many original songs. Their two most important early hits were interpretations of songs that came to them from their mentors—Pete Seeger and Lee Hays ("If I Had a Hammer") and Bob Dylan ("Blowin' in the Wind"), a colleague of theirs on the Grossman management roster. Together these two songs gave the group the chart success that Grossman craved and the credibility in that part of the folk community that was anxious to see songs of social and political protest in the set lists of the big acts.

With both Peter, Paul and Mary and Bob Dylan under management contracts, Grossman controlled the careers of two of the biggest acts in early '60s folk music. Despite his success, Grossman was generally disliked, despised even. Many folk purists saw him as a bully whose only aim was to make money on the backs of the best artists of the folk revival movement and push aside everyone else. His size—he stood well over six feet and weighed well over two hundred pounds—helped him intimidate people, and his aggressive approach with agents and club owners often made him an outsider in the tightly knit folk scene he helped create. Yet Peter, Paul and Mary and Dylan gained immeasurably from his antics, as did other artists who Grossman signed, making him folk's biggest and baddest dealmaker.

One major folk artist Grossman did not control was Joan Baez, not officially any-way. At the start of her career, when she began singing in Cambridge, Massachusetts coffeehouses like Club 47, Grossman booked Baez into Chicago's premier folk club, Gate of Horn, which he owned, thus expanding the excitement that was growing around her. Baez first performed publicly in 1958. In 1959 she appeared at the Newport Folk Festival, a guest of Bob Gibson, and secured a contract with Vanguard Records shortly thereafter. Her self-titled debut album came out in 1960; two years later the young singer with the angelic soprano voice and the innocent, homespun looks was on the cover of *Time* magazine and crowned Queen of Folk Music. She and Dylan would soon fall for each other, thus bringing Grossman into the picture, since Grossman deeply protected his relationship with his most valuable client, and no woman, he promised, would come between them.

Baez was floored with Dylan's talent the first time she heard him and advocated for him every chance she got. She saw the genius and at times seemed blinded by it. But it wasn't a fault only she experienced. Many others would encounter the same condition after the release of such critically acclaimed albums as *The Freewheelin' Bob Dylan* (1963) and *The Times They Are A-Changin'* (1964) which contained some of the most important and profound songs of political protest since the glory days of Woody Guthrie. The glowing reviews poured in. The requests for Dylan to sing at this rally and at that one kept the phone lines busy. Dylan went to Mississippi—a civil rights battleground—with Pete Seeger and did concerts in which the songs that received the most applause were those of a political nature. The media began calling him a spokesman of his generation. He hated it.

Not surprisingly, all five singers—Dylan, Baez, and Peter, Paul and Mary—were on the mall in the nation's capital in August 1963 for the famous March on Washington with Dr. Martin Luther King Jr., the heart, soul and undeniable leader of the civil rights movement. Standing on the stage in front of the Lincoln Memorial with King, who would deliver that day his "I Have a Dream" speech—one of the most eloquent and inspiring declarations in American history—Dylan, Baez and Peter, Paul and Mary entertained the mass of people that had come to advocate for justice and equality for African-Americans. It was a watershed moment for folk music and its renewed commitment to political and social causes. Listening in on the radio, Woody Guthrie celebrated privately, inside himself, where the cruel spasms of Huntington's disease could not reach.

Dylan had indeed become the new Woody Guthrie, the poster child of the folk revival and the revered songwriter who brought the fight for justice and peace back into the music where it had lived in the '30s and '40s when Woody, Will Geer, the Almanac Singers and others played at rallies and union meetings, urging workers to stand up for their rights and giving them the confidence to do it through song. *The Freewheelin' Bob Dylan*, with three political protest masterpieces on it—"Blowin' in the Wind," "A Hard Rain's A-Gonna Fall," and "Masters of War"—had set him apart from all the other young singer-songwriters influenced by Guthrie.

Where there was promise on *Bob Dylan* there was proof on *The Freewheelin' Bob Dylan*. In less than a year, Dylan had elevated himself to new songwriting heights that no one in the folk community could touch or saw coming. In a way, his story was not unlike that of bluesman Robert Johnson, who in the early 1930s sought to become a proficient blues guitarist and then suddenly had achieved brilliance beyond comparison. Where had it come from? Word had it that Johnson sold his soul to devil. How else could a young Mississippi man with no formal guitar training go from a struggling player to a blues guitar master seemingly overnight?

No one claimed that Dylan did the same. The evidence of his amazing progress as a songwriter was evident if one was fortunate enough to have heard him in Greenwich Village clubs like the Gaslight and Gerde's Folk City in 1962 and 1963, and then on stages of small concert halls. In them, one would have heard the song list grow and the compositional maturity increase. Dylan kept his Guthrie connection; he still performed "This Land Is Your Land" and one or two other Guthrie tunes.

But it was becoming increasingly clear that the student had grown into a master himself. The head of the clan that would eventually be called "Woody's Children" was about to leave the roost and start his own flock.

Another of "Woody's children" was Phil Ochs. Raised in rural New York state, young Ochs went to military school in Virginia and actually enjoyed it. However, it wasn't long after enrolling at Ohio State that Ochs found his calling. One of his first musical experiences was as a member of the Singing Socialists, which is proof enough of Ochs' political conversion. By 1961, he had moved to New York, gone solo and begun writing political songs with a razor's edge.

Ochs became one of the most passionate players in the political protest song arena in the '60s. It seemed as if every idea—the more radical, the better—became a song, and every song a salvo in the war against the War (as in the war in Vietnam), against poverty, against racism, against political oppression, etc. With black hair combed back, dark eyes, and a leather jacket, Ochs seemed more suited to play alongside Marlon Brando in a teen rebel movie, than to follow in the footsteps of Woody Guthrie. Some saw Ochs as arrogant; he saw himself as supremely talented and a necessary part of a new America.

Ochs never recorded any of Guthrie's songs but according to Michael Ochs, his brother, Phil was deeply influenced by him. "Phil knew all of Guthrie's songs, but he chose not to record them because he was writing so many songs himself. You couldn't be interested in protest music in the 1960s and not be influenced by Guthrie. Phil definitely saw music as a means to an end, which meant that everyday he expected from himself the inspiration and the idea to write the next great song of political protest."

Like Dylan, Ochs had made the pilgrimage to Greystone Hospital in New Jersey where he visited with Guthrie. However, according to Ochs biographer Michael Schumacher, "Guthrie's health had deteriorated to such an extent that Phil was unable to converse with him or play music for him, as Dylan had done during his earlier visit." Not to be outdone by Dylan, with whom Ochs ferociously competed, and who had written "Song to Woody," as a tribute to his mentor, Ochs penned the song "Bound for Glory," taking the title from Guthrie's book by the same name.

"Bound for Glory" was less personal but more sweeping in its admiration for Guthrie than Dylan's "Song for Woody." Ochs' song celebrated Guthrie the man as much as Guthrie the author of seemingly countless songs of conscience. Ochs urged listeners not to let Guthrie's now-legendary status push aside why he wrote the songs in the first place. The lines "Oh why sing the songs and forget about the aim/He wrote them for a reason, why not sing them for the same" perfectly summed up "Bound for Glory's" intent.

It was a fine song, spot on with its theme. Had Guthrie been able to process the song and hear it played by Ochs, he likely would have approved of it. "Bound for Glory" was what Guthrie often called "a hard-hitting song," one that pulled no punches or was soft on its message. Many music historians credit Ochs as having written the best of the many Guthrie tribute songs that came out of the 1960s. Yet, because Guthrie's name does not appear in the title, like Dylan's "Song to Woody," many Guthrie admirers remain unaware of "Bound for Glory's" lyrical riches and the Guthrie connection.

Ochs certainly knew "This Land Is Your Land," but instead of jumping on the song's bandwagon in the early '60s, Ochs sought to match the song—or better it—with one of his. "His song 'The Power and the Glory' was a direct attempt at doing just that," added Michael Ochs. "If you listen to the song and pay attention to its lyrics, you'll hear the connection. It would be pretty difficult to top 'This Land,' but that wouldn't have stopped Phil. In his mind, he was definitely capable of writing an equally important song about America."

"The Power and the Glory" is indeed a fine song. Inspired by Guthrie's poetic description of the American landscape, Ochs developed a scene of national majesty and beauty of his own. He invites the listener to "take a walk with me through this green and growing land/walk through the meadows and the mountains and the sand." Shades of Guthrie, for sure. There are other visions of an idyllic America in "The Power and the Glory" with "beauty that words cannot recall." Despite the deep misgivings Ochs had about the American government and the white-collar Establishment, he loved the natural treasures of the country and the way Guthrie memorialized them in song.

The folk revival of the early '60s gave rise to folk festivals around the country. The idea of a folk festival wasn't new. There had been folk music festivals and fiddlers conventions, mostly down South in the Carolinas and Virginia, Tennessee and Kentucky for years before the folk revival took hold in America. The White Top Mountain Festival in Virginia began in 1932 and attracted First Lady Eleanor Roosevelt the following year. The festival endured the toughest years of the Depression only to fold in 1940. The National Folk Festival began in Tennessee in 1936 and continues on today. None of them, however, was as nationally known or as prestigious as the one that occurred in Newport, Rhode Island beginning in 1959.

George Wein, a concert promoter and jazz pianist, first put Newport on the American music map when he established the Newport Jazz Festival in 1954. With support from jazz historian Marshall Stearns, maestro Leonard Bernstein, and Columbia Records talent scout John Hammond, Wein made certain to build the festival on firm footing. At first, a high society jazz crowd frequented the festival, but by the late 1950s, more and more college kids came to Newport, sending city fathers in a tizzy with the late-night drinking and carousing. But hotels and restaurants filled up and anyone with a business in Newport made a bundle that weekend in August, so the festival was allowed to continue.

Wein wanted a second festival in Newport, this one a folk festival. Smartly sensing that if college kids would come to hear jazz, they'd certainly come to hear folk music, given the folk scenes surfacing on college campuses across the Northeast in the late '50s. So Wein, along with Pete Seeger, fellow folksingers Theodore Bikel, Oscar Brand, and Albert Grossman began the Newport Folk Festival in 1959, and it promptly became the most prestigious of all folk fests and the spiritual hub of the folk revival.

The first Newport Folk Festival is most memorable for the debut of Joan Baez, who at the time was little known, shy and unsure of what such an appearance at the festival would mean. Here was a young woman, marveled the promoters and the crowd, who could take folk music to a higher plane. The Kingston Trio, who was the first day's headliner, had to agree. Joan Baez brought new meaning to folk music. With a voice that could hit the highest register and a sincerity that flew in the face of the folk pop on the radio, Joan Baez made her mark. That night in Newport the folk revival had found its young queen.

The 1960 Newport Folk Festival featured Pete Seeger, a pair of powerful blues singers who had recently come on the East Coast blues scene—Robert Pete Williams and John Lee Hooker—and the New Lost City Ramblers, a group made up of Mike Seeger (Pete's step-brother) on fiddle and other stringed instruments, Tom Daley on banjo, and John Cohen on guitar. Of all the folk groups sprouting from the folk revival, the New Lost City Ramblers was the one most committed to folk authenticity and preservation. Instead of folk-pop, the Ramblers played old-timey music from the 1920s and '30s that they learned by listening to old 78 rpm records. The group's music would never be found on pop radio, but Seeger, Bob Dylan and folk purists respected them like no other folk group of the period.

At the 1963 Newport Folk Festival Joan Baez did for Bob Dylan what Bob Gibson had done for her in 1959. She brought Dylan onstage during her set and introduced him to the Newport crowd, some of whom had already known him from his first two albums, but had never seen him perform before. It was a watershed moment for

Dylan. He wowed the Newport audience with his performance, and his emotional connection to Baez made their duets glow. That weekend, folk fans left Newport thinking the music had its first royal couple. Dylan played Newport again in 1964. But this time he was the festival's headliner, a certified folk music star.

Then came Newport, 1965. Once again Dylan was the big draw, but rather than conform to Newport standards—that is, acoustic instruments onstage honoring the tradition of folk music—Dylan, whose revolutionary rock single "Like a Rolling Stone" had just been released, appeared onstage with an electric guitar and a plugged-in band. Half the Newport audience was horrified, the other half confused.

Dylan played his short electric set and followed it with a brief acoustic one. They both were busts, the former because of the shock of it all and the bad sound, the latter because most people in the audience still hadn't come to grips with the electric set they just heard. Dylan, shaken by the boos that came from some in the audience, struggled to regain his composure. Yet, history was made that night, too. With one bold move, Dylan turned the folk revival world upside down and then blew it up.

How could he? railed the traditionalists. He, the Promised Son, the savior of folk music, the anointed successor of Woody Guthrie, spokesman of his generation and guardian of America's folk legacy. How could he abandon the music when he was at the very top of it? Observers swore they saw Pete Seeger with an ax, trying to cut the electric cables and thus stop the madness. Seeger hated the set, but not because it was electric. "I couldn't stand the sound of it," Seeger later explained. "The screeching and the volume were just too much. My actions had nothing to do with the music. I just wanted to hear what Dylan was playing without blowing out my ears."

But the damage was done and the deed changed everything. Dylan was done with folk music, at least in the conventional sense. When he finished his Newport set in 1965, the folk revival was done, too.

In the midst of it all, Woody Guthrie grew weak and his health worsened. Already wiry and thin, he had lost much weight, mostly because he no longer could chew food. Rather than take him to the Gleasons, Marjorie now brought him home on weekends where she hoped he would feel closer to his family and where Arlo could play records with Woody's songs on them by artists he had never heard of and languages he didn't know.

Before he had lost his full ability to speak, Woody had recited the original lyrics of "This Land Is Your Land" to Arlo so they wouldn't be forgotten. Guthrie was pleased that so many artists were covering "This Land" on record, but disturbed that none of them recorded the song with its original lyrics. "In the best way he could, he told me the lyrics and made me put them down on paper so that when I sang the song, I could sing it in the way he meant it to be sung," recalled Arlo. "At the time, I wasn't much interested in singing 'This Land,' not when everyone else was already doing it. But that would eventually change."

Arlo had begun a career of his own. In the early '60s, in part because he was "Woody's son," under-aged Arlo was allowed into folk clubs where he would watch with studious eyes the early performances of Dylan, Phil Ochs and other rising folk stars. After a while, Arlo started to sit in with his new friends, eventually doing his own sets that included his father's songs and a few of his own, too. The weight of being the son of Woody Guthrie was heavy, but Arlo didn't mind. He had plans of becoming a folk artist in his own right, which was exactly what his father would have expected of him.

In September 1967, eighteen-year-old Arlo brought to Creedmoor State Hospital in Flushing, Queens—where Marjorie had moved Woody the previous year—an early copy of a recording that he made after signing a contract with Warner Bros./Reprise. The album was called *Alice's Restaurant* and there was no doubt the songs on it were written and sung by Woody's son. The record was due out in November, just in time for the Thanksgiving holiday that it parodied, along with poking fun at the police and draft board and just about anything else in the song that got in his way. It had Woody's fingerprints all over it.

It wasn't just Dylan that had once picked up Woody's way with words and vocal mannerisms. Arlo had done the same, but he had received his father's influence organically. The title track, a genuinely clever and humorous talking blues song about a Thanksgiving dinner gone awry, was an instant classic. Those who knew Woody's talking blues style could easily hear his influence in the song. Pete Seeger and other longtime friends of Woody heard the song and the rest of the album, and tears filled their eyes.

Woody never saw or heard the final product, nor knew just how far Arlo had come as a performer. Early in the morning on October 3, 1967, Woodrow Wilson Guthrie, America's dustiest folk balladeer and most travelingist troubadour, had breathed his last breath.

CH. 10

There was no public memorial service to mourn the passing of Woody Guthrie, no line of fans and folksingers waiting patiently to pay their respects and say farewell to one of America's greatest songwriters. Guthrie had instructed Marjorie and the rest of his family to keep anything they did as a way of saying their final good-bye, both private and simple. Woody was cremated shortly after his death. Then the family gathered on the beach in Coney Island to scatter his ashes in the ocean. When Marjorie and then Arlo had problems prying open the canister that contained Woody's remains, Arlo heaved it into the water and everyone watched as it bobbed in the surf for a few minutes then slowly sank. It was a hobo's funeral, the proper send-off for Woody Guthrie, who was now bound for glory in a new place.

Guthrie's passing provoked sorrow, but also relief. His had been a slow death that long ago sucked away any deep grief his family and close friends might have felt when the twitching and the spasms finally ended. Visiting Guthrie in his last months was difficult to do, even for Marjorie and the children. Physically, there was little left of him; he was skin and bones, nothing more. His arms and legs seemed like sticks and his head seemed unusually large for such an emaciated frame. Swallowing even a small drink of water took a large effort.

In the end he was barely able to communicate. Marjorie had made "yes" and "no" cards that she used in order to get the most elementary response from him. To look at Woody in such a state robbed his friends and family of visions of better times, when Woody was, well, Woody. He had been sick for so long that pretty much everyone close to him had given up on a cure and had become accustomed to the idea that it was only a matter of time before Huntington's disease took him. And when it did, they saw his departure as a final act of freedom.

Beyond Woody's inner circle, his death stoked a very different response. The major television and radio news networks picked up the story of his passing and lauded Guthrie's life as a folksinger and great American songwriter. Almost all of the reports cited him as the author of "This Land Is Your Land." Newspapers such as the *New York Times* called Guthrie "a rambler and balladeer" and referenced fellow folksinger Odetta's belief that "This Land Is Your Land" ought to be America's new national anthem. In Guthrie's home state of Oklahoma, the *Tulsa World* described him as "America's folk poet of the downtrodden, their singing, guitar-playing apostle of self-esteem" and highlighted the fact that "he wrote more than a 1,000 of them [songs], the best known being 'This Land Is Your Land.' "

In the late 1960s most Americans recognized Guthrie as the author of "This Land Is Your Land," but knew little else about him. He had been out of the public eye for so long—unable to perform, record, or make appearances on television or radio—that with the exception of older, longtime admirers of his music, along with a small but passionate group of young music fans and musicians, few other Americans could recall his life story and some of the other great songs he had given to the American folk music treasury. "This Land Is Your Land" had become Guthrie's true calling card. It was his main connection to American pop culture and music.

If rock hadn't so overwhelmed American music in the late '60s, forcing the folk revival to desperately hold onto its gains, maybe Guthrie's legacy at the time of his death might have been more well known. But in 1967—the year of the Beatles' *Sergeant Pepper's Lonely Hearts Club Band*, the Summer of Love in San Francisco, and the Monterrey Pop Festival—many folk and roots musicians struggled to get the attention of young people and of new audiences.

They had the most success at folk festivals, which by the end of the decade had sprouted all over the country, or when rock artists referenced their music or better, interpreted it. This happened on occasion in the 1960s, especially in the blues and in traditional country music. Artists in these genres who were still alive and musically active took advantage of the small surge of renewed popularity. But dead ones or incapacitated ones like Guthrie had no way of feeling the spotlight, and thus it was left for other artists to keep their music and legacies alive.

In Guthrie's case, no one did it better than Pete Seeger. Guthrie's longtime personal champion, Seeger had been friends with Guthrie the longest and understood him the best, both as a person and songwriter. Seeger not only believed deeply in the poetry and power of Guthrie's songs, but also revered him as the spiritual head of American folk music. Nearly every time Seeger performed, he witnessed how much the country had come to embrace "This Land Is Your Land" as a unique national gift, for it was a rare Pete Seeger concert that didn't include in the clinching role, "This Land Is Your Land."

In 1963 Seeger had written a letter to Guthrie in which he addressed him as "my friend and teacher." In it, he described the growing popularity of "This Land Is Your Land." "Woody, it would do your heart good to hear the young people joining in your songs," wrote Seeger. "They know them so well by now, especially some of them like 'This Land Is Your Land,' that I need only to start the first two words and right away they are joining in and singing all the way through with that nice, relaxed quality that comes when you know a song by heart and can swing right along with it without any straining."

The lyrics to "This Land Is Your Land" that they were singing were not the original ones Guthrie wrote in 1940 that brought attention to the plight of the Depression-era poor. Though such lyrics would have seemed less relevant to many fans of the song a quarter century later, Seeger, along with Arlo Guthrie and a few other artists, began in the late '60s to sing "This Land" with the protest verses intact. In 1966 Secretary of the Interior Stewart Udall honored Guthrie for "the fine work you had done to make our people aware of their heritage and land." He was referring to the songs Guthrie wrote in 1941 for the Bonneville Power Administration, but Udall also acknowledged, if indirectly, Guthrie's celebration of America in "This Land Is Your Land"—unaware that there were also lyrics in the song that denounced the country's care of its poor people.

Pete Seeger had published the original lyrics to "This Land Is Your Land" in 1961 in his book *America's Favorite Ballads: Tunes and Songs as Sung by Pete Seeger*, even though back then he usually didn't sing them. Then in the fall of 1968 John Cohen, the guitar player from the New Lost City Ramblers, did the same in *Sing Out!*. Cohen, a longtime member of the New York folk scene and a fine photographer, first met Guthrie in 1950. He had been to Greystone Hospital to visit Guthrie and had discussed Guthrie as a literary figure with poet Allen Ginsberg and novelist Jack Kerouac. He knew about the original lyrics to "This Land Is Your Land" by going through Guthrie's song notebooks during a visit to the Gleason's home one Sunday afternoon. Cohen believed every interpreter of the song should sing the original lyrics. "I just thought that was the right thing to do," recalled Cohen. "In the late 1960s, it was a great protest song to sing if it was sung with the original lyrics, but people just weren't doing that."

Over the years "This Land Is Your Land" had lost much of its original protest fervor; instead, it had become the great American feel-good folk song. In June 1963, Seeger performed to a sold-out Carnegie Hall audience. The concert was recorded by Columbia Records and released later that year as *We Shall Overcome*. This original version of the album included only selections from the now famous show, which acted as a "bon voyage" for Seeger and his family, who were set to travel around the world to "learn more about some of the other three billion human beings who share this earth, learn about their past and present, and their hopes for the future." During the show Seeger sang "This Land Is Your Land" and got everyone in the house to sing along.

Earlier in the year he had done a children's concert at Town Hall in New York and released a live album called *Pete Seeger, Children's Concert at Town Hall,* which opened with "This Land Is Your Land"—the abridged version. And in 1958, with the Weavers, Seeger and the group opened the recording, *The Weavers at Home,* with a rendition of "This Land Is Your Land."

But by the late 1960s, Seeger was having second thoughts about "This Land Is Your Land." In June 1968 in Washington, D.C. during a Poor People's Campaign rally, Seeger was leading a "This Land Is Your Land" sing-along with another singer, Jimmy Collier, when Henry Crow Dog, a Native American, voiced his resentment of the performance. "This land isn't your land, it belongs to me," said Crow Dog. Seeger was visibly shaken and didn't know how to react. Crow Dog had made a valid point. America was originally the land of Henry Crow Dog's fathers. White people had stolen it. And what about the black people in the crowd, struggling to achieve some semblance of civil rights and human dignity in a land that had long denied them the most basic equalities. What could "This Land Is Your Land" possibly mean to them?

Seeger actually considered dropping the song from his repertoire altogether. But in December of that year he wrote, "The song 'This Land Is Your Land' really needs some new verses to add to the old ones. Images should include red men talking to brown and black—and white." That's exactly what happened. Topical songwriters, eager to use the familiarity of "This Land Is Your Land" as a means of getting an idea across to a receptive audience, began making up new verses to replace Guthrie's original ones, or to add to them.

"This Land Is Your Land" soon became an anti-pollution song ("the sun was shining, but the hazes hid it . . ."), a pro-American Indian song ("This Land is your land, but it once was my land . . ."), a pro-education song ("These schools are your schools, these schools are my schools . . ."), an anti-logging and mining song ("We've logged the forests, we've mined the mountains . . .") and so forth. "This Land Is Your Land" was being pulled and tugged and tossed and turned, rewritten and reborn with new lyrics and new ideas. It was difficult to keep up with all the new verses and uses of the song. One couldn't help but think that Woody Guthrie was somewhere smiling at the ruckus his most famous song was making.

Pete Seeger had been on tour in Japan when news of Guthrie's death reached him. "I remember singing to myself his song 'So Long, It's Been Good to Know Ya,' and trying to picture the man he once was," Seeger recalled in an interview years later. *Life* magazine contacted Seeger shortly after Guthrie's death and asked him to write a remembrance. Seeger penned a poignant piece in which he praised his long-time folk-singing friend as the author of dozens of great songs, "and one of them has become loved by tens of millions of Americans." Seeger, of course, was referring to "This Land Is Your Land," which he quoted in the eulogy. "Woody will never die," reflected Seeger, "as long as there are people who like to sing his songs."

Upon Seeger's return to America, he and Woody's son, Arlo, along with manager

Harold Leventhal, began formulating plans for a Guthrie tribute concert. Leventhal, who had also managed Arlo and represented the Guthrie family in music matters, became the driving force behind the concert, much like he had in April 1965 when he staged "The Woody Guthrie Hootenanny" at Town Hall in Manhattan. Guthrie himself was too sick to attend that concert, which raised funds to finish his kids' education, but the event made him feel loved and respected despite his now total absence from the New York folk scene.

When Dylan heard the news of Guthrie's death, he immediately called Leventhal's office. "He told me that if there should be any kind of memorial, to count him in," Leventhal wrote in a later essay called "Remembering Woody." With Dylan agreeing to perform, Leventhal knew their Woody Guthrie tribute concert would be a major music event.

The concert would take place at Carnegie Hall in Manhattan, just a few blocks from where Woody lived when he first arrived in New York. But because of numerous bookings at the hall, the approaching holidays, and the complexities of creating the event, it was decided to wait until January to do the tribute, which would raise money to find a cure for Huntington's disease. Leventhal, Arlo, and Seeger put together an artist invite list. Starting with Dylan, there were so many artists who had expressed deep interest in performing. The problem wasn't who would play, but who to leave off the bill.

The sold-out concerts—there was a matinee and evening show—took place on January 20, 1968. Tickets to the concert sold out in a dash, not so much because the event would honor Guthrie, but because Dylan's appearance onstage at Carnegie Hall would mark his first public performance since his 1966 motorcycle accident and exile from public life and the concert stage. The rock press scrambled to secure passes. It was the biggest music news story in some time. Plans were made to record the shows, and Columbia agreed to release a live album with the net proceeds going

Bob Dylan (center) performs with The Band's Levon Helm (on drums), Rick Danko (left), and Robbie Robertson (right) at the benefit tribute to Woody Guthrie at Carnegie Hall, January 20, 1968.

to Huntington's disease research.

Leventhal and Seeger knew that the audience would demand more than a cursory appearance by Dylan, who had just released *John Wesley Harding* to widespread critical acclaim. The much-anticipated album marked a striking departure from his previous works. Made in Nashville with country musicians, *John Wesley Harding* was sparse, organic and thick with allegory. Despite the change in style and looks—gone was the wild-haired urban hipster and in its place was a new Jewish-cowboy persona—Dylan had been playing with his old backup band, the Hawks, upstate in Woodstock, casually laying down tracks that would one day see the light of day as *The Basement Tapes*. Because of all the jamming they did, Dylan brought the group with him to the tribute to back him up there as well. Robbie Robertson, Levon Helm and the rest of the group called themselves the Crackers that night but would be known as simply The Band upon release of its debut album later that year called *Music from Big Pink*.

A roar tore through Carnegie Hall when Dylan took the stage. Strapping on his guitar, he came out smoking, ignoring his acoustic, Guthrie-inspired folk roots sound, and instead blasted out rock versions of two Guthrie standards, "I Ain't Got No Home" and "Grand Coulee Dam," along with a more obscure Guthrie tune, "Dear Mrs. Roosevelt." Dylan didn't say much, and he didn't sing "Song for Woody." Some in the audience felt it wasn't appropriate for Dylan to turn Guthrie folk songs into rock numbers. Not only was Dylan electrified but he sang Guthrie's songs with a certain angst and a charged tempo that was a far cry from what everyone else on the bill delivered.

The Band's Robbie Robertson later recalled his impression of the set to Dylan biographer Clinton Heylin. "Everybody else was taking a different plan musically, you know, it was a very folk-oriented show. But we just played what we were doing at the time. I can't help but think Woody Guthrie would have approved. I mean, if a song is going to live, it must live in its contemporary surrounding."

The concert was so successful that Leventhal decided to do a second one in California in 1970. Staged at the Hollywood Bowl on September 12, the West Coast concert did not include Dylan and the hysteria that went with his performance at the New York shows. But a number of performers who had been onstage in New York, including Judy Collins, Tom Paxton, Richie Havens and Odetta, made the trip west to sing Guthrie songs for a Los Angeles-area audience. Also on the bill was Country Joe McDonald, Joan Baez, and Ramblin' Jack Elliott. McDonald had recently released an album of Guthrie songs called *Thinking of Woody Guthrie*. Baez, a longtime admirer of Guthrie, had occasionally sung a song or two of his in concert. Ramblin' Jack Elliott was the original "Woody Guthrie jukebox," long before Dylan had been tagged with the title. His presence at the concert was a natural.

Both the New York and Hollywood shows ended with spirited versions of "This Land Is Your Land," drawing tears and recalling tender moments. Guthrie might have been America's most talented topical songwriter, having penned such gems as "Deportee," "1913 Massacre," "Do Re Mi," "I Ain't Got No Home," and "Pretty Boy Floyd," but "This Land Is Your Land" was the one song that continued to rise above all the others. And when it came time to culminate the celebration of his legacy, only one song could do it justice. Arlo Guthrie, Odetta and the others onstage sang "This Land Is Your Land" on both coasts, choosing to include the Depression-era lyrics, which resulted in spirited applause from the audience. For a while, anyway, "This Land Is Your Land" had come full circle.

Guthrie's idea as to how music could be used to change America was employed more in the 1960s than at any other time since the Great Depression. The decade had witnessed the rise of the civil rights movement, which was fueled by music, principally gospel songs set with new words that inspired civil disobedience and activism. The movement's theme song, "We Shall Overcome," gave people hope when there was no place else to find it. It helped activists fight off fear when faced with snarling police dogs, helmeted police with billy clubs, and the very real threat of death.

Dylan and Phil Ochs, along with Peter, Paul and Mary, Joan Baez and, of course, Pete Seeger, used song as a weapon in the '60s, not just against Jim Crow and racial bigotry, but also to demonstrate opposition against nuclear weapons, poverty, and the growing war in Vietnam. By the late '60s, rock had begun to use its awesome power to sway listeners and inspire action. In 1965 P.F. Sloan's "Eve of Destruction," a potent warning and diatribe about the end of the world, was sung by Barry McGuire and made it to number one on the pop charts. Buffalo Springfield, which included at the time Neil Young and Stephen Stills, recorded the latter's "For What It's Worth," about rioting on the Sunset Strip and police brutality. The song made it to number seven on the pop charts in early 1967. The following year the Rolling Stones included "Street Fighting Man" on its acclaimed album, *Beggar's Banquet*, and released it as a single. Although Mick Jagger was vague as to his intentions with the song, young people around the world saw it as a call to take to the streets and, if necessary, fight the Establishment with any means necessary, including violence.

In 1969, the Jefferson Airplane presented its interpretation of the power of song. In "Volunteers," Marty Balin and Grace Slick urged listeners to "Look what's happenin' in the streets/got to revolution, got to revolution." The band sang "Volunteers" at Woodstock that summer, the rock festival in upstate New York that quickly came to mark the apex of '60s youth and rock culture. To close the festival, Jimi Hendrix, arguably the era's most innovative guitarist and most electrifying performer, reimagined "The Star Spangled Banner," complete with feedback and wild distortion, as the ultimate song of political protest.

Even black performers, who were not generally known for expressing straightforward political discontent in popular music, had gotten into the act by the late 1960s. In 1939, a year before Guthrie wrote "This Land Is Your Land," the great jazz singer Billie Holiday penned "Strange Fruit," one of the most haunting accounts of lynching ever recorded. For years it remained the pinnacle of black protest music in popular music. By the late '60s, however, another powerful black artist, Nina Simone, demonstrated that the rage over racism could still be effectively put into a song the same way Holiday did thirty years earlier. Simone's social protest masterpiece, "Mississippi Goddam," flowed with lyrical fury as she shone a light on the murder of Medgar Evers, the black civil rights activist in Mississippi in 1963. Gil Scott-Heron, whom many consider a pioneer of rap, turned heads with his 1970 song, "The Revolution Will Not Be Televised," a razor-sharp condemnation of America and its failure to live up to the promise of the civil rights movement.

Less angry but more impactful, Marvin Gaye's 1971 landmark album, *What's Goin' On*, remains the greatest of all soul-driven protest works. With a voice that illustrated the highest power of soul, Gaye pleaded with his listeners to take action, but in a less militant way than many of his black contemporaries. Gaye probably didn't realize it at the time, but the spirit of Guthrie lived in him and all other songwriters—black and white—as they sought to use song to change America. If this land, this America, was really their land, too, then black songwriters and performers, along with Latino and Native American artists, had to stand up and claim it in song.

In February 1970, from his home high above the Hudson River in Beacon, New York, Pete Seeger set about to document the origins of "This Land Is Your Land." It had been thirty years since Woody Guthrie penned the words to a song he originally called "God Blessed America" in Hanover House, a fleabag hotel smack in the middle of Manhattan. Seeger wanted to commemorate the occasion by writing a brief history of the song and to make some predictions as to its future in American music.

"What will happen to the song now?" Seeger asked. "My guess is, it depends on who sings it, and how, and for what purpose." Clearly the song had gone far beyond Guthrie's original intentions—whatever they were. Did he write the song to poke fun at Irving Berlin's "God Bless America," or to angrily repudiate it, as many have surmised? Did he write it to describe what he had seen of America's sweeping natural landscape on the endless highway he traveled? Or did he jot down the song's now famous lines to merely entertain himself on a cold February afternoon in his sparsely furnished hotel room, while outside his window New York hummed a tune of honking car horns and bustling feet on the frozen snow? Guthrie never supplied an answer to one of American folk music's biggest head-scratchers. Seeger didn't speculate; instead he pointed out that if the song's recent history was any indication, "This Land Is Your Land" would remain a go-to song for just about anyone and for any reason for as long as Americans found value in song.

By the late '60s Pan American Airlines was using it in a television commercial while United Airlines would use it for inspiration in its 1972 television marketing campaign, "The Friendly Skies of Your Land" with lyrics such as "Your land is our land." That same year Senator George McGovern, the Democratic presidential candidate, claimed "This Land Is Your Land" as his theme song. He accepted the presidential nomination by quoting the song's lyrics.

In his essay Seeger attacked the idea of making "This Land Is Your Land" the new national anthem, as some still hoped, arguing that to give the song such responsibility would "rob it of its poetic career, and doom it to a political straight jacket, no matter how well fitting that jacket might seem to be at the time."

Seeger also explained in the essay how over the years original Guthrie verses had been altered and that new ones had been added. He admitted to adding a few of his own, including: "Maybe you been working/As hard as you're able/And you just got crumbs/From the rich man's table/Maybe you been wondering/Is it truth or fable/ This land was made for you and me."

Seeger saw the song as a living, breathing musical document. To add new verses and new ideas to the song was in keeping with the folk process as Woody knew it and practiced it, believed Seeger. After all, hadn't Guthrie himself borrowed melodies and musical ideas and used them to create new songs, relevant to the times? And hadn't Guthrie himself changed the lyrics and title to "This Land" again and again? Seeger was of the same mind. A song such as "This Land Is Your Land" was meant to be used, manipulated even, for good causes, just causes. If changing the lyrics would bring greater relevancy to the song and help achieve a worthwhile objective, so be it. "The best thing that could happen to the song is that it would end up with hundreds of different versions being sung by millions of people who do understand the basic message," Seeger wrote. He then went on to add a bit of instruction: "If a song leader has time to talk a little bit, he or she might consider starting with the following verse which was made up a few years ago and which has been widely picked up around the country:

"This land is your land, but it once was my land
Before we sold you Manhattan Island
You pushed my nations to the reservations,
This land was stole by you from me."

Seeger didn't know who wrote it, but its meaning was clear. Native American activists, who had begun a campaign to secure their fair share of the American Dream and what was legally owed them—land and money long promised by the government but never acted upon—did not see the song in the same light that white

Americans did. Seeger understood that and accepted it. For him the true value of a folk song was how well it served the folks, and for the past thirty years, "This Land Is Your Land" had done a mighty fine job of serving Americans of all color and creed. Seeger's hope was that it would continue to do just that.

Bob Dylan still saw value in a song he performed in his first official concert in 1961, some ten years earlier. Only a handful of people showed up for that show, which occurred at the Carnegie Chapter Hall, a relatively small performance chamber adjacent to the larger and more famous Carnegie Hall on 57th Street in Manhattan. Dylan played to just fifty-three people that evening, and according to Woody's daughter, Nora, he borrowed a jacket from Guthrie's closet to do so. Dylan's official debut wasn't exactly a smash. "His voice quavered and broke," wrote David Hajdu, in his book *Positively 4th Street*, and he sounded "distracted." Dylan did play "This Land Is Your Land," laying his claim to the song, even though it would not be his best performance of it.

That came in 1975 when Dylan resurrected the song to be used as the closer for his crazy, traveling, musical medicine show. Titled the Rolling Thunder Revue, Dylan created the concept with improvisation, unpredictability, and old-style vaudeville in mind, and it wound up one of the wildest tours Dylan ever led. It was a mélange of musicians, shapeless and loose, influenced by a poet (Allen Ginsberg) and a painter (Larry Poons), and saw musicians acting out strange road scenes for not one, but two film crews, and a playwright, Sam Shepard. It was Shepard who was supposed to write a script for the film but instead wrote a wonderful book called *Rolling Thunder Logbook* that detailed the travails of this motley collection of very talented players and sought to make sense of it all.

For the Rolling Thunder Revue Dylan drafted longtime associate Bobby Neuwirth, guitarists Mick Ronson and T-Bone Burnett, fiddle player Scarlet Rivera, the former Byrd Roger McGuinn, former flame Joan Baez, bass player Rob Stoner, drummer Howie Wyeth, and others. Drugs were prevalent. A carnival atmosphere prevailed. For some performances, Dylan painted his face white. Other performances featured guest stars like Joni Mitchell and The Band's Rick Danko. It was all so whacky and wild, and somehow, it worked, at least part of the time.

That Dylan ended many Rolling Thunder shows with a spirited version of "This Land Is Your Land" was odd. By the mid-'70s Dylan had moved so far away from his Guthrie roots as to be hardly recognizable. Dylan had become the master of rock and roll reinvention after his Guthrie infatuation. First he fashioned himself an urban hipster, then a country crooner, followed by a rocker, a mocker, and now a minister of burlesque and the bizarre on the Rolling Thunder tour. About the only thing that reminded fans of Dylan's old connection to Guthrie was the presence of Ramblin' Jack Elliott on the tour. Elliott had known Guthrie since the late '40s and had never lost his love of the Guthrie lifestyle or the songs he wrote. Elliott and "This Land Is Your Land" were only two things that now linked two of the greatest songwriters America had produced in the twentieth century.

In 1972 America was still at war with itself. The '60s had seen much progress: The civil rights movement, despite despicably violent moments of resistance by Southern white racists, had moved into the mainstream, thanks to the genius of Dr. Martin Luther King Jr. and others who held steadfast to his "Dream." Women had begun their quest for broader respect and equal pay. The Environmental Movement was born. Native Americans began clamoring for their rights. Nuclear holocaust had been avoided and the Cold War never turned hot. A man walked on the moon.

Americans recognized that within her borders existed millions that were impoverished and illiterate, and something was now being done to diminish that number.

But there were still mountains to climb and setbacks to be overcome. Political assassinations, drug abuse, a military industrial complex that was out of control, and a still-raging war in Southeast Asia kept America tense and tried its patience. The Kent State massacre was an American horror. Police officers killed Black Panthers and the Black Panthers killed police officers. Republican President Richard Nixon had promised to end the war—"peace with honor" he called it—but for many Americans, the daily reports of casualties and the scene of body bags with dead American soldiers in them was impossible to ignore while he negotiated a U.S. exit from Vietnam.

In August 1972 George McGovern secured the Democratic nomination to run against Nixon in November. McGovern, a liberal from South Dakota, lacked certain qualities—an embraceable charisma and a gift of persuasion being just two of them—but he earnestly wanted to end the war. In steamy Miami, McGovern accepted his party's nomination well past midnight. During his "Come Home, America" speech, McGovern quoted the lyrics to "This Land Is Your Land," and then smiled broadly as the convention—teary-eyed, tired, and emotionally drained—all sang Guthrie's song together.

It wasn't the first time that a Democratic presidential hopeful referenced Guthrie and used "This Land Is Your Land" as the campaign's theme song. Four years earlier, Senator Robert Kennedy had embraced Guthrie and his song to rally supporters before his tragic assassination in Los Angeles in June 1968. Kennedy's team had actually changed the song a bit, referring to it as "This Man Is Your Man" as sung by Bobby Darin and other Kennedy supporters. And when he campaigned, crowds often broke into "This Land," linking Guthrie's vision of America with Kennedy's and, once again, proving liberal America's continuous love affair with the song.

Taking a page from Bobby Kennedy's political playbook and claiming "This Land Is Your Land" as his own did little for McGovern's campaign. That November he was soundly trounced by Nixon and the Republican machine, winning only one state—his home state of South Dakota. Nixon returned America back to its more conservative element until the Watergate cover-up two years later forced Nixon to resign to avoid certain impeachment.

"This Land Is Your Land" stayed out of presidential politics for the remainder of the 1970s, but wound up in Hollywood, of all places. For years, Harold Leventhal believed that Guthrie's book, *Bound for Glory* would make a great film. Others in the movie business thought so, too, but the project never seemed to garner enough momentum to get off the ground. Finally director Hal Ashby picked up on the idea. Fresh from such critical smashes as *The Last Detail* that starred Jack Nicholson and *Shampoo* with Warren Beatty, Ashby began the all-important task of finding someone to play Woody Guthrie in the biopic.

The offer went first to Richard Dreyfuss, but financially he and Ashby were worlds apart. Ashby was then set to ask the folksinger Tim Buckley to play Guthrie—an odd choice since Buckley had never really acted and didn't claim Guthrie as a major influence—but a tragic heroin overdose not only prevented Ashby of filling the lead actor role, but also robbed popular music one of its most innovative voices. The one proven actor who desperately wanted the role was David Carradine. Known as a difficult, unpredictable talent, Carradine was taller than Guthrie and older than him, at least during the time of Guthrie's life that the film would deal with.

Ashby turned him down, but Carradine refused to take no for an answer. Finally, with friend Warren Beatty's endorsement, Carradine got the part. During the filming of *Bound for Glory*, Leventhal, Marjorie Guthrie and her kids, and even Woody's first wife, Mary, visited the set regularly, all agreeing that Carradine had indeed captured Woody's spirit and style.

The film was released in 1976 in the midst of America's bi-centennial celebration; the movie's posters contained some of the lyrics to "This Land Is Your Land" and celebrated Guthrie as the author of one of America's most beloved folk songs. In the film Carradine sang "This Land" and other Guthrie tunes and brought Guthrie to life for millions of Americans who hadn't known much of his story. Leventhal made certain that the artistic license that Ashby employed was limited and that Guthrie's legacy had not been sold out or stained with celluloid sap.

The strategy paid off. In addition to mostly good reviews, *Bound for Glory* was nominated for six Academy Awards, including Best Picture. It won two—Best Cinematography and Best Music, Original Score. Nearly ten years after his death, Woody Guthrie's story and his music—including "This Land Is Your Land"—was on the big screen. It played in Pampa, Texas and Okemah, Oklahoma; Los Angeles and New York; and nearly every place in between that Woody Guthrie roamed and rambled. His story was now an American story. Hollywood made it so.

11

In 1977, Joe Klein, a frequent contributor to *Rolling Stone*, wrote a feature story about Arlo Guthrie for the magazine. After the success of "Alice's Restaurant," a performance at the 1969 Woodstock festival, and widespread popularity in dope-smoking hippie circles, Arlo recorded Chicago songwriter Steve Goodman's tune, "City of New Orleans," in 1972. The catchy song was as much about America as it was about an Illinois Central train called the "City of New Orleans" and its journey through the country's heartland. Not only did Arlo make the song his own by giving "City of New Orleans" a subtle warmth and easy flow from verse to verse, but the lyrics about a train rolling through America recalled the best hobo days of his father.

Arlo's interpretation of the song became a big pop hit, and though he was still a folkie at heart, the success of "City of New Orleans" brought him renewed attention from the rock media and a wider audience and fan base. The album that contained the song, *Hobo's Lullaby*, Arlo's fifth since his 1967 debut, was considered to be his best. Many critics began including Arlo's name in what was then being called the Singer-Songwriter movement in rock that featured artists like James Taylor, John

Prine, Jackson Browne, Carole King, and Carly Simon.

Klein mostly wrote about politics, but had become intrigued with folk music and where it fit onto a mid-'70s pop music plate that had disco at one end and punk at the other. At the time, Klein's knowledge of the legacy of Arlo's father, Woody, was minimal. "When I began work on the story about Arlo, I didn't know all that much about Woody Guthrie," wrote Klein. "I knew that he had written some famous songs like 'This Land Is Your Land,' and that he'd died from a rare disease, and that he was supposed to have been a major influence on Bob Dylan and other folksingers in the 1960s."

During the research for his Arlo Guthrie story, Klein ran into Woody's name more than a couple of times, which led Klein to read Guthrie's book, *Bound for Glory*, and to see the recent movie by the same name. Around this time he also met Harold Leventhal who recognized Klein's increasing fascination with Woody's story. Leventhal told Klein that an in-depth biography of Woody had never been done. "It couldn't really be done before," Leventhal said, "because many of Woody's friends would have found it difficult to speak candidly about their past associations, but I think the political climate has changed enough so that they can now."

Leventhal suggested that Klein write the book. Klein was flattered with the invitation and said that he'd think it over. In order to make the decision as to whether or not to spend the next few years researching obscure details about Guthrie's life and putting his story to paper, he and a friend drove to Oklahoma and Texas, getting a feel for Guthrie's roots. Klein could sense the Guthrie saga in the open, arid plains and hills where Guthrie grew up and cut his musical teeth, and he grew increasingly excited about the prospect of telling the folksinger's story. He spoke to people who had known Woody, and they told him stories of a man unlike most others from those parts. Klein's interest in Guthrie broadened and deepened. Upon his return from the Southwest, Klein called Leventhal and Marjorie Guthrie, whom he had met earlier, and told them that he'd accept their offer to write Woody's biography.

Marjorie Guthrie gave Klein complete access to her husband's letters, journals, lyrics, and other personal possessions. She allowed herself to be interviewed at length, reliving both the best and worst times she spent with Woody. Harold Leventhal filled in details where he could and provided important introductions to the likes of Pete Seeger, Ramblin' Jack Elliott, and others who knew Guthrie well. The deeper Klein got into the Guthrie story, the more tangled it seemed to get. Klein discovered an American artist tortured yet ultimately triumphant, simple on the surface, yet incredibly complex underneath, and a man for whom movement in every which way was both a source of inspiration and a means of escape.

Woody Guthrie: A Life was published in 1980. Critically acclaimed, Klein's biography of Guthrie set his story in a new context, one that went far deeper than *Bound for Glory*, the movie, and revealed Guthrie not as just a carefree hobo with a penchant for writing catchy folk songs, but also as a frequently flawed husband and father and a man whose remarkably layered character was often at odds with his homespun Okie persona.

One of the people who read *Woody Guthrie: A Life* was Bruce Springsteen, who had been given a copy of the book in November 1980, just after the election of Ronald Reagan. Like Klein early on, Springsteen had known of Guthrie primarily because of the influence he had on Bob Dylan, one of Springsteen's musical heroes. As a child Springsteen had heard "This Land Is Your Land" like so many other baby boomers. He had also performed at a couple of New Jersey-based George McGovern rallies during the presidential campaign in 1972 where "This Land Is Your Land" was most likely played, given its connection to the McGovern camp. But Springsteen knew little more than that about the song or the man who wrote it, until finishing Klein's book.

Woody Guthrie: A Life profoundly affected Springsteen, who, in the early 1980s, was on the cusp of becoming an international rock star. (That would happen in 1984 with the release of the album *Born in the U.S.A.* and the sold-out world tour that followed.) Springsteen strongly connected to Guthrie's story and how his songs seemed to sprout out of an American experience where dreams and hope were rarely realized. He marveled at Guthrie's up-and-down life and the way he created captivating stories with full-blown characters, plots and settings—in essence, small novels set to song. He especially loved the tragic element in many of Guthrie's songs, namely, how common, hard-working people fought the odds, not always winning, but somehow keeping their dignity and principles in place.

At the time, Springsteen, who hadn't really gone to college—he barely spent a semester at a community college on the Jersey Shore—had been self-educating himself about American history and culture. His manager Jon Landau, a former music critic with *Rolling Stone* and other music magazines, was quite familiar with *The Grapes of Wrath* and other John Steinbeck novels, along with the writings of progressive historians Henry Steele Commager and Allan Nevins. Landau turned Springsteen onto these writers and encouraged him to delve deeper into America's soul by reading more of the American literary giants of the twentieth century. Springsteen made the connection to their works with the music of Jimmie Rodgers, Hank Williams, Robert Johnson, and other major American musicians he was exploring for the first time. But it was Guthrie who appealed to him the most.

Springsteen was particularly taken by the story of how and why Guthrie wrote "This Land Is Your Land." According to Springsteen biographer Dave Marsh, "Springsteen's interpretation of what the song was about was smack dab in the middle between Woody Guthrie, who wrote as a Marxist disillusioned with the America of fable, and Irving Berlin, who wrote as a man who had seen his every dream fulfilled and in one lifetime moved from the hellish pits of New York's Lower East Side to Beekman Place, the shortest, most exclusive street uptown."

Springsteen was having plenty of his dreams fulfilled, too. He had been born into a working-class family in Freehold, N.J., and early on came to see rock and roll as both his identity and salvation. After numerous successful bands on the Jersey Shore—but none so big that they led him to a recording contract—Springsteen began playing as a solo artist in New York City in the early 1970s. It was there that he got the chance to audition for Columbia Records' John Hammond, who, a decade earlier, had given Dylan his first recording contract. Hammond was stunned by Springsteen's rare songwriting gift and signed him to Columbia in 1972, thinking he had found the "new Dylan."

From the start, Springsteen was a keen student of rock and roll. He embraced Dylan, Van Morrison, the Rolling Stones and other British Invasion bands. Later on in the '60s, he digested the sounds of Cream, the Allman Brothers Band, and Led Zeppelin. But he also had a deep understanding of rhythm & blues and soul, thanks, in part, to performing and living in shore cities such as Asbury Park and Long Branch that had black communities in them and bars and clubs where these music forms were played nightly.

Springsteen's first two albums—*Greetings from Asbury Park, N.J.* and *The Wild, the Innocent and the E Street Shuffle* were critically acclaimed but commercial busts. Columbia Records considered dropping him from their artist roster. Then in the fall of 1975, with the release of *Born to Run*, Springsteen suddenly found himself on the covers of *Time* and *Newsweek*—the same week—proclaimed as the latest savior of rock and the music's best chance at remaining the driving cultural force it had become in the '60s. Neither accolade did him much good. Pressure mounted and legal problems with his first manager, Mike Appel, kept Springsteen and his E Street Band struggling emotionally and financially. Springsteen had split with Appel and had hired Jon Landau to be his manager and co-producer, but after the success of *Born to Run*, a court injunction kept them out of the studio and prevented them from recording the all-important follow-up album.

The inability to record forced Springsteen and his band to let their creative urge explode onstage. For nearly two years, Springsteen and the E Street Band delivered some of the most musically intense and riveting rock shows ever. Slow songs, fast ones, soaring sax solos and wild guitar riffs coupled with onstage melodrama that brought each and every song Springsteen sang to life, made his concerts quasi-religious experiences. Fans walked away from the three-hour-plus concerts exhausted, emotionally drained and soaked with sweat. There were times when Springsteen himself needed help getting offstage, so fatigued and dehydrated was he after the marathon rock extravaganzas he delivered in his unique no-holds-barred style. It wasn't surprising that critics began calling Springsteen and the E Street Band the greatest live act in the history of rock and roll.

Since his debut in 1973, Springsteen had become so associated with his home state of New Jersey that it was next to impossible for him to be seen as anything other than a Jersey rocker. It was true that Springsteen wrote magnificently about the Jersey Shore's boardwalk sub-culture, the back roads and mean streets. Some of his best songs were about the youth-fueled drive to escape a dull and meaningless existence that sunk people who didn't strive to make their dreams real into a hole they couldn't climb out of. Other Springsteen song-stories, not unlike Guthrie's, often had characters that were given a bad hand and spent most of their life struggling to find a place in a cold world. New Jersey rock fans embraced Springsteen's music as if it were scripture. He told great stories and now the rest of the country was listening. He was their William Faulkner and their John Steinbeck, and they loved every minute he spent onstage playing *their* songs.

In the 1970s, it had been assumed by some sociologists that New Jersey was a microcosm of America, with its broad ethnic diversity, frequent cultural rifts between cities and suburbs, and strong working-class roots. Thus, when Springsteen began broadening his songwriting palette to include all of America, it seemed a natural transition from his earlier, mostly Jersey-inspired material. Now his songs began exploring ideas, myths, and symbols with a national identity. And when that happened, Bruce Springsteen joined the ranks of the other great musicians and songwriters, including Woody Guthrie, who helped the rest of us understand the meaning and uniqueness of being an American.

Springsteen and the E Street Band had been on tour in the fall of 1980, playing incredibly engrossing shows that only elevated their reputation as demonstrators of the sheer energy and redemptive power of rock music. For the New Year's holiday, they were to perform at Nassau Coliseum on Long Island, long a place where Springsteen, or simply, "Bruce," was a rock hero. Having just finished Klein's biography of Guthrie, it was there that Springsteen decided to include his version of "This Land Is Your Land" into the set.

With the E Street Band taking a much needed break, Springsteen came out to the center of the stage, a harmonica in a rack around his neck, and an acoustic guitar across his sweaty body, and began blowing the harp against a backdrop of guitar chords from the opening of "This Land Is Your Land." Most in the audience hadn't a clue as to what song was coming up and hushed enough to seek clues as to its identity. Without an introduction, Springsteen began singing the song like he would sing a hymn, slow and deliberate, careful to get the point across in unmistakable fashion. Some in the audience recognized the lyrics, but when Springsteen sang the line, "from California to the New York island," Nassau Coliseum suddenly erupted in a celebration of place. When Springsteen finished the song, a connection to Guthrie was made and that bond would last for years.

The following spring Springsteen and the E Street Band played Europe, and he continued to include "This Land Is Your Land" in the set. But now, the need to explain the song to non-Americans was imperative and Springsteen didn't fail. "This is an old song about an old dream," said Springsteen in Paris. "It's hard to think what to say about this song, because it's sung a whole lot in the States, and it's been misinterpreted a whole lot. It was written as a fighting song and it was written, I feel, as a question everybody has to ask themselves about the land they live in, every day."

Springsteen loved playing "This Land Is Your Land" live and he seemed to gain some kind of inspiration from it every time he sang it. Fans of his began to see American music lineage unfold in front of their eyes each time Springsteen sang the song's lyrics, making the connection to Guthrie and becoming educated in how certain songs could affect change or at least point the way to change. When he sang "This Land Is Your Land" Springsteen became part of the ongoing story of American music and its role in enriching American culture. Springsteen's audience was more than willing to listen and take in each and every word.

As the '80s unfolded, Bruce Springsteen began to share the responsibility of maintaining and celebrating the legacy of Woody Guthrie and "This Land Is Your Land" with Pete Seeger and Arlo Guthrie. In 1982, Springsteen released his first solo album, *Nebraska*, a stark and haunting collection of songs recorded on a portable tape recorder in his New Jersey bedroom. Critics raved about its raw honesty and powerful imagery of an America where dreams often fall by the wayside and tragedy more times than not prevailed over triumph.

Nebraska was soaked with Guthrie influences, along with those of Robert Johnson, Dylan, Hank Williams, and other American music icons who didn't fear making music that spoke truths instead of reveling in fantasies. *Nebraska* was originally intended to be an E Street Band album, but Springsteen believed the songs' compelling emotionalism was diluted when they became electrified and drawn out in an ensemble. *Nebraska's* tracks were meant to be open and simple, direct and devoid of anything that might hinder the songs' sensibilities.

"If there's a theme that runs through the record," recalled Springsteen in his book *Songs*, "it's the thin line between stability and that moment when time stops and everything goes to black, when the things that connect you to your world—your job, your family, friends, your faith, the love and grace in your heart—fail you. I wanted the music to feel like a waking dream and the record to move like poetry. I wanted the blood on it to feel destined and fateful."

The Guthrie references were more direct on what might be seen as *Nebraska*'s sister album, 1995's *The Ghost of Tom Joad*, which included a title song that referenced the character in *The Grapes of Wrath* and Guthrie's "Tom Joad." According to Springsteen, the song, which began as a rock song, was originally meant to be included on his *Greatest Hits* album. "As with *Nebraska*, on 'Tom Joad' and the songs that followed, the music was minimal," explained Springsteen. "The melodies were uncomplicated, yet played an important role in the storytelling process. The simplicity and plainness, the austere rhythms defined who these characters were and how they expressed themselves."

By now, Springsteen was America's biggest rock superstar, quoted by presidents and looked upon as the quintessential modern-day chronicler of the American experience. He'd been playing arenas and stadiums around the world; during the heralded *Born in the U.S.A.* tour, the stage set had come complete with a gigantic American flag as the band's backdrop. Now, because he was being seen as a sharp observer of America, much like Walt Whitman, Carl Sandberg, Ralph Waldo Emerson, and Woody Guthrie had done earlier, Bruce Springsteen *was* America in the eyes of his fans and most of the rest of the world.

From such a high perch it would be difficult for Springsteen to match the success he enjoyed with his rock albums with the American stories he told in the songs of *The Ghost of Tom Joad*. "I knew that *The Ghost of Tom Joad* wouldn't attract my largest audience," recalled Springsteen. "But I was sure the songs on it added up to a reaffirmation of the best of what I do." *The Ghost of Tom Joad* wasn't a chart buster; there were no anthems on it or pop hits. But Springsteen was right; as an American songwriter, he was entering rare space and centering on issues like immigration reform and poverty that didn't translate into great radio songs, but needed to be written and recorded nonetheless.

All the while Springsteen kept "This Land Is Your Land" close by, pulling it out and inserting it into his set list whenever it seemed appropriate to do so. Over time, he began calling "This Land Is Your Land" the "greatest song that's ever been written about America," and the way he sang it depended on the situation or setting.

Sometimes he presented it slow and dirge-like, and a sense of disappointment crept in under the lyrics as if the basic beauty of the words had somehow been violated, or lost. He'd often preface the performance of the song by stating that it was written by Woody Guthrie and that "it gets right to the heart of the promise of what our country was supposed to be about. And, as we sit here tonight, that's a promise that is eroding for many of our fellow citizens every day, with thirty-three million livin' at or below the poverty line."

Other times he sang the song with jubilation and optimism, as if America could and would live up to the high expectations it set for itself. Like Pete Seeger before him, Springsteen created a communal spirit of patriotism with his rendition of "This Land Is Your Land," as if the song was a reaffirmation of the promise of America. But almost always, no matter what manner he sang it, Springsteen made certain his rendition of the song included a warning. "I guess I'd like to do this for you tonight," Springsteen would tell his audience, "asking you to be vigilant, because with countries, just like with people, it's easy to let the best of yourself slip away."

Woody Guthrie was inducted into the Rock and Roll Hall of Fame in 1988 in the

Early Influence category. Also honored that year was Bob Dylan, who was inducted by Bruce Springsteen, an irony not lost on a lot of people who paid good money to attend the prestigious event at the Waldorf Astoria Hotel in New York that March. Neil Young inducted Guthrie, an interesting choice given that Young wasn't an artist usually considered to be one of "Woody's children." As events like this go, with record executives and music industry bigwigs that owned million-dollar salaries, with lots of tuxedos and other formal wear, with flowing fancy wine and champagne, it was hardly an event that Guthrie would have felt comfortable at. But the honor was appreciated by the Guthrie family and well deserved. If nothing else, Woody Guthrie gave rock and roll a conscience.

That was much in evidence in 1996 in Cleveland when Woody Guthrie was chosen to be the first honoree in the newly opened Rock and Roll Hall of Fame and Museum's American Music Masters series. Called "Hard Travelin': The Life and Legacy of Woody Guthrie," the event, which stretched over an autumn week at the Rock Hall and at nearby Case Western Reserve University, consisted of a photo exhibit and educational programs, an academic conference, a couple of hootenannies, and a formal concert in Cleveland's Severance Hall, the home of the renown Cleveland Orchestra.

The concert featured a wide slate of artists, all of whom came to honor Guthrie and to raise money for the Rock Hall's education department and the New York City-based Woody Guthrie Archives, which had opened in 1995. The headlining artist was Bruce Springsteen, but the concert also included Pete Seeger, Arlo Guthrie, Ramblin' Jack Elliott, the Indigo Girls, Billy Bragg, David Primer from the group Soul Asylum, Ani DiFranco, actor/singer Tim Robbins and others, making it the biggest and most prestigious Guthrie event produced since his passing nearly thirty years earlier.

The concert sold out quickly, in part because of Springsteen's presence. But the star of the show was Guthrie and his songs. Springsteen insisted that he not be listed as the headliner and, in fact, did not close the show. Seeger insisted on purchasing a ticket—it was a benefit after all—and sat in the audience with his banjo by his side until it was his time to perform. He even brought with him a brown-bag sandwich so organizers of the concert didn't need to spend money on any backstage spread.

There were precious moments at Severance Hall that Sunday night in late September: Ramblin' Jack's stirring version of Guthrie's "1913 Massacre," a song he had mastered long ago, but that evening gave even more depth and emotional detail; Ani DiFranco's spellbinding version of "Do Re Mi" that opened the show; Springsteen's humorous prelude to Guthrie's children's song, "Ridin' in My Car," during which he staked his claim to "car songs"; and Arlo's equally funny tale of "'Til we outnumber 'em," that he learned from his father and which morphed into "This Land Is Your Land" with the entire concert cast onstage, sharing microphones and singing space. And, of course there was Pete Seeger out front—leading everyone, including the audience, in full sing-along form.

Those who knew the lyrics to "This Land Is Your Land" sang the loudest, with Seeger cheerleadering them all the way. Those who didn't know all the lyrics, mainly the young people in the audience, learned them quickly so as not to be left behind, something Seeger would have no part of. Everyone knew the moment was special and wanted to be a part of it. When Seeger called for the final run of "This Land's" chorus, many in Severance Hall were sad for the song to end. One woman sitting a few rows from the stage shook her head and annouced to anyone listening, "I feel like that song has magical powers," she said, wiping her eyes. "Every time I hear it and then especially when I sing it, I feel America inside me."

It was as cold as it was supposed to be in the nation's capital on the morning of Tuesday, January 20, 2009. Thermometers registered twenty-eight degrees—cold, but not so cold as to freeze the enthusiasm or the excitement for what was to occur at noon in front of the U.S. Capitol. That was the time mandated by the 20th Amendment to the U.S. Constitution that Barack Obama would become the 44th President of the United States. In front of him stood more than a half-million Americans, all of them eager to see history happen as the Democratic junior senator from Illinois became the first-ever African–American to lead his country.

In schools and malls, in living rooms and waiting rooms, in coffee shops and in corporate offices, millions more Americans watched the monumental event on television and computer screens, or listened on radio to Supreme Court Chief Justice John Roberts administer the oath of office to Obama. With his wife Michelle and their two children at his side, Obama raised his right hand and swore to uphold the principles of the Constitution and to assume the responsibilities that go with being President of the United States of America.

Around the world, still millions more watched the grand spectacle: in Europe, Asia, Africa, the Mideast, literally, on every continent and in every country. Collectively, they marveled at the scene they were witnessing. For many of the world's citizens, the historic event restored the hope they once had, but had lost, for the United States. With the tragic events of September 11, 2001, the ensuing wars in Iraq and Afghanistan, and the economic collapse all still standing in the way of world peace and prosperity, Obama's inauguration was a welcome sight.

It was a joyous, emotionally deep moment as America proved to itself and everyone else that a black man could occupy the White House. How incredible it was that just two generations removed from the civil rights movement of the 1960s, when African-Americans fought and won essential rights and freedoms denied to them by more than two centuries of racism and oppression, an African-American born in 1961 just as the movement was gaining momentum, would become President.

A couple of days earlier, on the evening of Saturday, January 17, Pete Seeger shivered in the darkness on the steps of the Lincoln Memorial. He was there with his grandson Tao Rodriquez-Seeger and Bruce Springsteen to rehearse their role in the "We Are One" concert scheduled for the following day. The concert, a main part of Obama's inauguration celebration, was set to be broadcast to the nation on HBO. In addition to Springsteen and Seeger, the concert also featured James Taylor, U2, John Mellencamp, Stevie Wonder, Beyoncé, Garth Brooks, Jon Bon Jovi, Mary J. Blige and many other great American pop stars. Seeger was, by far, the most senior of the bunch. Just shy of ninety years old, Seeger nonetheless looked spry, jogging to and fro his spot on the stage during rehearsals and despite the cold, smiling throughout his performance like a kid who was visiting Washington, D.C. for the first time.

That wasn't the case, of course. He could remember all the way back to the late 1930s when he worked in the city with Alan Lomax at the Library of Congress, collecting and securing for the nation its great catalogue of folk and roots music. He could also recall the times during the 1960s when he protested the war in Vietnam here, or sang to support the civil rights struggle for black people in this country. He couldn't help but feel a notion of triumph on this cold night. America had come a long way, he thought. Then he caught himself: yes, but it still had a long way to go. Not surprisingly, in Seeger's mind, the struggle would continue. With Obama's victory, a battle had been won, but the fight for human rights, economic equality, a cleaner environment, and a world without war carried on.

Seeger wore a coat and knitted wool cap for rehearsals, but the following day opted to wear only a flannel shirt, jeans, and hat when the performance was for real. It had remained equally cold on Sunday, but Seeger nevertheless dressed lightly. He looked as if he was about ready to chop firewood to warm the huge crowd in front of him rather than to celebrate the inauguration of the nation's first African–American president. He claimed he couldn't remember when he last wore anything formal, like a suit, or clothes other than work clothes. "I wouldn't have felt right wearing something else," laughed Seeger later, "especially given the song we were singing."

That song was "This Land Is Your Land."

A few weeks earlier at his home in upstate New York, Seeger took a phone call from Springsteen, asking him if he'd perform "This Land Is Your Land" in Washington, D. C. at the Obama Inauguration. Springsteen would also sing "The Rising," his epic piece about 9/11, but for the show's conclusion he planned to sing "This Land Is Your Land" and wanted Pete onstage with him.

"I told him I would, but only if he agreed to sing the song with its original lyrics," recalled Seeger. "All these years I sang 'This Land Is Your Land' but never with so many people watching and listening. Washington, D.C was filled with people. Television cameras were everywhere. I wasn't going to let the opportunity pass by. I wanted to make absolutely certain that the world knew the lyrics that Woody originally wrote."

Pete Seeger (center), Bruce Springsteen (right), and Seeger's grandson, Tao (left), perform "This Land Is Your Land" at President Barack Obama's inauguration during the "We Are One: Opening Inaugural Celebration at the Lincoln Memorial" on January 18, 2009.

Springsteen was familiar with Guthrie's early lyrics to "This Land Is Your Land." He'd been singing them, or a version of them, since he first added "This Land Is Your Land" to his live set in the early 1980s. More recently, Springsteen, who had campaigned for Obama, had been using "This Land Is Your Land" on campaign stops in cities like Cleveland where both he and the song received hearty applause. For Springsteen, singing Guthrie's original lyrics to "This Land Is Your Land" was an easy call.

At the end of the two-hour concert, Seeger and Springsteen took the stage, Seeger with his trademark banjo and Springsteen with an acoustic guitar. Standing to the side of Seeger was Tao, also with a guitar. Behind the three of them was a large background chorus dressed in red, white and blue. "We'd like you to join us in perhaps the greatest song ever written about our home with the father of American folk music and his grandson, Tao," Springsteen told the huge audience. "Lead us, Pete."

Suddenly the shivering stopped and adrenaline rushed into every fiber of Pete Seeger's old, rail-thin body. He stepped up to the microphone and shouted like he had done countless times over past sixty years: "You sing it with us! We'll give you the words!" Suddenly, the largest audience ever to sing "This Land Is Your Land," which included the president-elect and his family, fell in on cue, adding their voices to Seeger's and Springsteen's and making "This Land Is Your Land" on this important day in American history, a national song of celebration.

People in the crowd swayed and held hands. Most sang. Some had tears running down their cheeks and felt a warm rush of blood in their arms and legs. President-elect Obama smiled with approval and encouraged his two daughters, Malia and Sasha, to sing along, too. For a brief instance, America was one.

And with that, the soul of Woody Guthrie floated from the stage, into the audience, then across the mall, out into the heart of Washington, D.C. and then finally over the rest of country, from California to the New York island. At that very moment, this land was Woody's land, and your land, and my land. Just like the song said.

THIS LAND IS YOUR LAND

ORIGINAL LYRICS

THIS LAND IS YOUR LAND

WORDS AND MUSIC BY WOODY GUTHRIE

Chorus:
This land is your land, this land is my land
From California, to the New York Island
From the redwood forest, to the gulf stream waters
This land was made for you and me

As I was walking a ribbon of highway
I saw above me an endless skyway
I saw below me a golden valley
This land was made for you and me

Chorus

I've roamed and rambled and I've followed my footsteps
To the sparkling sands of her diamond deserts
And all around me a voice was sounding
This land was made for you and me

Chorus

The sun comes shining as I was strolling
The wheat fields waving and the dust clouds rolling
The fog was lifting a voice come chanting
This land was made for you and me

Chorus

As I was walkin' - I saw a sign there
And that sign said - no trespassin'
But on the other side . . . it didn't say nothin!
Now that side was made for you and me!

Chorus

In the squares of the city - In the shadow of the steeple
Near the relief office - I see my people
And some are grumblin' and some are wonderin'
If this land's still made for you and me.

Chorus (2x)

COMMON LYRICS

THIS LAND IS YOUR LAND

WORDS AND MUSIC BY WOODY GUTHRIE

Chorus:
This land is your land, this land is my land
From California, to the New York Island
From the redwood forest, to the gulf stream waters
This land was made for you and me

As I was walking a ribbon of highway
I saw above me an endless skyway
I saw below me a golden valley
This land was made for you and me

Chorus

I've roamed and rambled and I've followed my footsteps
To the sparkling sands of her diamond deserts
And all around me a voice was sounding
This land was made for you and me

Chorus

The sun comes shining as I was strolling
The wheat fields waving and the dust clouds rolling
The fog was lifting a voice come chanting
This land was made for you and me

Chorus

BIBLIOGRAPHY

Allen, Ray. *Gone to the Country: The New Lost City Ramblers & the Folk Music Revival*. Urbana: U. of Illinois Press, 2010.

Bindas, Kenneth J. *America's Musical Pulse: Popular Music in Twentieth-Century Society*. Westport, Connecticut: Praeger, 1992.

Brand, Oscar. *The Ballad Mongers (Rise of the Modern Folk Song)*. New York: Funk & Wagnalls, 1962.

Brend, Mark. *American Troubadours: Groundbreaking Singer Songwriters of the '60s*. San Francisco: Backbeat Books, 2001.

Cantor, Norman. *The American Century: Varieties of Culture in Modern Times*. New York: HarperCollins, 1997.

Carlin, Richard. *Worlds of Sound: The Story of Smithsonian-Folkways*. New York: Smithsonian Books, 2008.

Carmen, Bryan K. *Race of Singers: Whitman's Working-Class Hero from Guthrie to Springsteen*. Chapel Hill: U. of North Carolina Press, 2000.

Carney, George, O., ed. *The Sounds of People & Places (A Georgraphy of American Folk and Popular Music)*. Lanham, Maryland, Rowmand & Littlefield, 1994.

Cohen, Ronald D., ed. *Alan Lomax: Selected Writings, 1934-1997*. New York: Routledge, 2003.

————. *Rainbow Quest: The Folk Music Revival & American Society*, 1940-1970. Amherst: University of Massachusetts Press, 2002.

————. *Work and Sing: A History of Occupational and Labor Union Songs in the United States*. Crockett, Ca.: Carquinez Press, 2010.

Collins, Ace. *Songs Sung, Red, White, and Blue (The Stories Behind America's Best-Loved Patriotic Songs)*. New York: Harper Collins, 2003.

Cray, Ed. *Ramblin' Man (The Life and Times of Woody Guthrie)*. New York: W.W. Norton & Co., 2004.

Dunaway, David. *How Can I Keep from Singing: Pete Seeger*. New York: DaCapo, 1981.

Dunaway, David and Beer, Molly. *Singing Out: An Oral History of America's Folk Revivals*. New York: Oxford University Press, 2010.

Dylan, Bob. *Chronicles, Vol. One*. New York: Simon & Schuster, 2004.

Egan, Timothy. *The Worst Hard Time*. Boston: Houghton Mifflin, 2006.

Epstein, Daniel Mark. *The Ballad of Bob Dylan: A Portrait*. New York: HarperCollins, 2011.

Filene, Benjamin. *Romancing the Folk: Public Memory & American Roots Music*. Chapel Hill: U. of North Carolina Press, 2000.

Goldsmith, Peter D. *Making People's Music: Moe Asch and Folkways Records*. Washington, D.C., Smithsonian Institution Press, 1998.

Guthrie, Woody (edited by Robert Shelton). *Born to Win*. New York: Collier, 1965.

Guthrie, Woody. *Seeds of Man*. New York, E.P. Dutonn, 1976.

Hajdu, David. *Positively 4th Street (The Lives and Times of Joan Baez, Bob Dylan, Mimi Baez Farina and Richard Farina)*. New York: North Point Press, 2001.

Harvey, Todd. *The Formative Dylan (Transmission and Stylistic Influence, 1961-1963)*. Lanham, Maryland, Scarecrow Press, 2001.

Hedin, Benjamin, ed. *Studio A (The Bob Dylan Reader)*. New York: W.W. Norton, 20004.

Heylin, Clinton. *Bob Dylan: Behind the Shades Revisited*. New York: William Morrow, 2001.

Kaufman, Will. *Woody Guthrie, American Radical*. Chicago: University of Illinois Press, 2011.

Kimball, Robert and Emmet, Linda, eds. *The Complete Lyrics of Irving Berlin*. New York: Alfred Knopf, 2000.

Klein, Joe. *Woody Guthrie: A Life*. New York: Alfred A. Knopf, 1980.

Kyvig, David. *Daily Life in the United States, 1920-1940*. Chicago: Ivan R. Dee, 2002.

Jackson, Mark Allan. *Prophet Singer: The Voice and Vision of Woody Guthrie*. Jackson: University Press of Mississippi, 2007.

La Chapelle, Peter. *Proud to be an Okie: Cultural Politics, Country Music, and Migration to Southern California*. Berkeley: University of California Press, 2007.

Lieberman, Robbie. *My Song Is My Weapon: People's Songs, American Communism, and the Politics of Culture, 1930-1950*. Urbana: U. of Illinois Press, 1989.

Lomax, Alan, ed. *Hard Hitting Songs for Hard-Hit People*. Lincoln, Neb., University of Nebraska Press, 1999.

Longi, Jim. *Woody, Cisco, & Me: Seamen Three in the Merchant Marine*. Urbana, Illinois: U. of Illinois Press, 1997.

Lynskey, Dorian. *33 Revolutions Per Minute (A History of Protest Songs, from Billie Holiday to Green Day)*. Harper Collins, New York, 2011.

Marsh, Dave. *Two Hearts (Bruce Springsteen: The Definitive Biography, 1972-2003)*. New York: Routledge, 2004.

Marsh, Dave and Leventhanl, Harold, eds. *Pastures of Plenty: A Self-Portrait (The Unpublished Writings of an American Folk Hero, Woody Guthrie)*. New York: Harper Collins, 1990.

McElvaine, Robert. *The Great Depression*. New York: Times Books, 1984.

Olmsted, Tony. *Folkways Records: Moses Asch and His Encyclopedia of Sound*. New York: Routledge, 2003.

Parrish, Michael. *Anxious Decades (America in Prosperity and Depression, 1920-1941)*. New York: W.W. Norton & Co., 1992.

Partington, John S., editor. *The Life, Music and Thought of Woody Guthrie*. Burlington, Vt.: Ashgate Publishing Co., 2011.

Partridge, Elizabeth. *This Land Was Made for You and Me: The Life and Songs of Woody Guthrie*. New York: Viking, 2002.

Rodnitzky, Jerome. *Minstrels of the Dawn (The Folk-Protest Singer as a Cultural Hero)*. Chicago: Nelson-Hall, 1976.

Robbin, Ed. *Woody Guthrie and Me*. Berkeley, California, Lancaster-Miller, 1979.

Santelli, Robert. *The Bob Dylan Scrapbook, 1956-1966*. New York: Simon & Schuster, 2005.

Santelli, Robert and Davidson, Emily, editors. *Hard Travelin' (The Life and Legacy of Woody Guthrie)*. Hanover, N.H.: Wesleyan University Press, 1999.

Scaduto, Anthony. *Bob Dylan*. London: Helter-Skelter, 1996.

Schumacher, Michael. *There But for Fortune (The Life of Phil Ochs)*. New York: Hyperion, 1996.

Seeger, Pete. *The Incompleat Folksinger*. Lincoln, Neb.: U. of Nebraska Press, 1972.

————. *Where Have All the Flowers Gone: A Singalong Memoir*. Bethlehem, Pa.: Sing Out!, 1993.

Shelton, Robert. *No Direction Home (The Life and Music of Bob Dylan)*. New York: William Morrow, 1986.

Shepard, Sam. *Rolling Thunder Logbook*. New York: Viking, 1977.

Smith, Kate. *Upon My Lips A Song*. New York: Funk & Wagnalls, 1960.

Sounes, Howard. *Down the Highway: The Life of Bob Dylan*. New York: Grove Press, 2001.

Szwed, John. *Alan Lomax: The Man Who Recorded the World*. New York: Viking, 2010.

Wein, George, with Chinen, Nate. *Myself Among Others: A Life in Music*. New York: DaCapo Books, 2003.

Weissman, Dick. *Talkin' 'Bout a Revolution: Music and Social Change in America*. New York: Backbeat Books, 2010.

————. *Which Side Are You on? An Inside History of the Folk Music Revival in America*. New York: Continuum, 2005.

Wilentz, Sean. *Bob Dylan in America*. New York: Doubleday, 2010.

Wilkinson, Alec. *The Protest Singer: An Intimate Portrait of Pete Seeger*. New York: Vintage Books, 2009.

Willens, Doris. *Lonesome Traveler: The Life of Lee Hays*. New York, W.W. Norton, 1988.

Woliver, Robbie. *Hoot! A 25-Year History of the Greenwich Village Music Scene*. New York: St. Martin's Press, 1986.

Worster, Donald. *Dust Bowl: The Southern Plains in the 1930s*. New York: Oxford University Press, 1979.

Yaffe, David. *Bob Dylan: Like a Complete Unknown*. New Haven: Yale University Press, 2011.

Yurchenco, Henrietta. *A Mighty Hard Road (The Woody Guthrie Story)*. New York: McGraw-Hill, 1970.

Zak, Albin J. III. *I Don't Sound Like Nobody: Remaking Music in 1950s America*. Ann Arbor: U. of Michigan Press, 2010.

Zinn, Howard. *The Twentieth Century*. New York: MJF Books, 1980.

ACKNOWLEDGMENTS

There are many people who helped me in my journey to tell the story of Woody Guthrie and his song, "This Land Is Your Land." A book on Woody is really not possible without broad and regular assistance from the Woody Guthrie Archives in New York, and that is exactly what I got during the research and writing of mine. I am indebted to Tiffany Colannino, its Archivist, and to Anna Canoni, the Publishing and Public Relations Manager for Woody Guthrie Publications, who is also Woody's granddaughter. I'm especially grateful for the sage advice and general encouragement that Nora Guthrie, Woody's daughter, gave me through the writing process. Not only was her support incredibly helpful, but her friendship warmed my soul. Arlo Guthrie, Nora's brother and Woody's son, let me interview him more than once, despite a hectic touring schedule, providing invaluable insight and information about his father.

Archivist Jeff Place from the Smithsonian's Ralph Rinzler Folklife Archives and Collections opened up his files and extended his friendship as he has always done for me. Jeff is the keeper of so much that has to do with American folk music; the thousands of songs, recordings, papers, and general ephemera that tell the story of American music and that are housed in the Archives couldn't be in better hands. Certainly Dan Sheehy, Director and Curator of the Center for Folklife and Cultural Heritage of Smithsonian Folkways Recordings, and Mary Monseur, Production Manager for Smithsonian Folkways, need to be thanked as well. They, along with Jeff, are making certain that Woody's music will be available in a whole new context in 2012, the centennial of Woody's birth. Smithsonian Folkways Records will release a boxed set called *Woody at 100 (The Woody Guthrie Centennial Collection)* that will surely act as the soundtrack for this book.

Pete and Toshi Seeger opened up their house and hearts to me on numerous trips to upstate New York where they live. Pete shared Woody stories and brought light to things about Woody that for years remained in the shadows of his work and life. The late Harold Leventhal took me under his wing years ago and just before his passing in 2005, allowed me a few final interviews for which I'm most grateful. Howie and Larry Richmond of TRO Music were particularly important in providing information on how and why "This Land Is Your Land" became the popular American folk song that it is. Dave Marsh and Bruce Springsteen certainly need to be acknowledged as well, Dave for his long friendship and support of my many Woody-related projects beyond this book, and Bruce for past interviews in which he described his love and admiration for Guthrie.

Noel Paul Stookey, John Mellencamp, John Hiatt, John Doe, Chuck D from Public Enemy, Judy Collins, John Legend and other artists provided interviews and anecdotes. Photographer, filmmaker and singer-guitarist John Cohen from the New Lost City Ramblers offered up recollections of his time spent with Woody in the 1950s and '60s, along with ideas about the book and its theme that I found essential. To all of you, a sincere thank-you.

I traveled to Pampa, Texas to research Woody's time there and met the indomitable Thelma Bray who took me around and then placed me in front of the local Chamber of Commerce podium where I gave an impromptu speech about Woody that was as surprising to me as it was to the group's members. The entire staff of the Pampa Public Library went out of its way to help me find Woody Guthrie tidbits nestled in the library's archives. While conducting research at the Library of Congress in Washington, D.C., Jan Lauridsen, Assistant Chief of the Library of Congress, Music Division, and Raymond A. White, Senior Music Specialist in the Music Division, helped me learn more about Irving Berlin and Kate Smith. Rene Reyes at the Paley Center for Media in Los Angeles, and my very dear friend, Jackie Davis, who heads the New York Public Library for the Performing Arts, were there for me when I needed them and graciously provided me with materials about Woody Guthrie I couldn't find anywhere else.

Over the years that I'd been researching this book I had done dozens of interviews, few of them more meaningful than the ones I did with Mary Boyle, Woody's first wife, and Mary Jo Guthrie-Edgmon, Woody's sister. Both wonderful women graciously gave me their time and memories. I treasured the afternoons I spent with them in California and Oklahoma, respectively. Woody's niece, Marie Nunley, also spoke with me, and Anne Jennings, Mary Boyle's daughter from a later marriage, was instrumental in setting up my interview with her mother. Other friends who supported me in my research and writing include the documentary filmmaker Jim Brown; Guthrie collector Barry Ollman, whose love for Guthrie and commitment to honoring him know no bounds; Bob Merlis and Marilyn Laverty, the top names in popular music public relations; and friend and neighbor Darryl Holter, a labor historian and Guthrie booster in downtown Los Angeles. Add to that list Leslie Reynolds, Bob Shane of the Kingston Trio, and Abby Karp (Weitman), all of whom shared with me their love and knowledge of Guthrie.

Sandy Choron, my friend and agent for over thirty years, and Greg Jones, my editor at Running Press, provided everything in the way of help, advice, and support that any author could ever ask for, and Josh McDonnell provided the artistic eye to give the book its wonderful design. And finally a heartfelt thanks goes to my family: my wife, Cindy; my three children, Jaron, Jenna, and Jake; and my son-in-law, James. All of them understood my need to work on the book at crazy hours of the day and on weekends and holidays, and gave their love and support unconditionally. You guys are the best.